"*The Black Antifascist Tradition* gives us the materials we need to face an uncertain future. The book gives us the possibility of hope based on histories and trajectories it maps and recovers. This remarkable book documents how those who began the struggle against anti-Black racism were always already 'pre-mature antifascists.'"

—**DAVID PALUMBO-LIU**, author of *Speaking Out of Place*

"As we confront, arguably, the greatest assault on our already severely limited form of liberal democracy, *The Black Antifascist Tradition* is essential reading for not only diagnosing the problems that we face, but rather for providing us with historical tools to fight ascendant fascism and right wing authoritarianism in the United States. Drawing inspiration from Octavia Butler to anti-lynching campaigns and the 'We Charge Genocide' movement, Hope and Mullen offer a powerful lens onto the Black Radical Tradition that moves the discussion of fascism from a narrow focus on interwar Europe to the transnational questions of racial apartheid, settler colonialism and anti-Black racism. Beautifully written and cogently argued, this book is a must read for this moment. I can't wait to assign it in my undergraduate and graduate classes." —**DONNA MURCH**, author, *Assata Taught Me: State Violence, Racial Capitalism, and the Movement for Black Lives*

"*The Black Antifascist Tradition* is a primer on the history and legacy of over a century of Black antifascist activism. This timely collection introduces readers to the political organizing, theoretical interventions and world-making of some of the leading change makers and theorists of our times. This book is the missing link between present and past that is so urgently needed as a new generation confronts a new manifestation of an old problem. A must read and infusion of hope." —**ROBYN C. SPENCER-ANTOINE**, author of *The Revolution has Come: Black Power, Gender and the Black Panther Party in Oakland*

"The Roman slave empire ruled by punishment and death, flogging, and beheading. The bundle of rods with a protruding axe blade—the fasces—were both means of execution and emblem of sovereign power. Ever since, incarceration and systematic premature death have remained the foundation of fascism. *The Black Antifascist Tradition* is an absolutely needed chronicle showing how Black people lead antifascism. It begins with Ida B. Wells-Barnett's *Red Record* against lynching in the early twentieth century and concludes with the new abolitionism against the carceral and death-dealing state in the twenty-first century. In between are the essential campaigns by the thinkers and actors of Pan-Africanism (1930s), Double Victory (1940s), We Charge Genocide (1950s), Black Power (1960s), and the anarchist antagonistic autonomy of our times, which have fought for life and for our commons." —**PETER LINEBAUGH**, author, *The Magna Carta Manifesto*

"*The Black Antifascist Tradition* offers an indispensable framing that places Black experience at the center to show how anti-Blackness is inseparable from the development of US fascism, past and present. Through a crisp synthesis of essential writings by Ida B. Wells-Barnett, W. E. B. Du Bois, Aimé Césaire, William Patterson, Huey P. Newton, Angela Y. Davis, Ruth Wilson Gilmore, and Mariame Kaba, Jeanelle K. Hope and Bill V. Mullen make a compelling argument for reconceptualizing a race-based history of Black life through the lens of racialized fascism. An important read for anyone interested in understanding how we arrived at today's US style of authoritarianism and state repression." —**DIANE FUJINO**, author, *Heartbeat of Struggle: The Revolutionary Life of Yuri Kochiyama*

"From the sophisticated understanding of law as an agent of fascism articulated in the anti-lynching activism of Ida B. Wells-Barnett, to the abolitionist theorization of fascism as both a theory of anti-Blackness and a structure of oppression by scholar-activists such as Ruth Wilson Gilmore and Angela Davis; and with explorations of anti-colonialism, antiwar movements, and Black Power along the way, *The Black Antifascist Tradition* offers a careful history of Black thought and art by way of a celebration of the exquisite threads of antifascism woven inextricably into the Black Radical Tradition. Hope and Mullen detail the ways the Black Radical Tradition has not simply always been antifascist but that it has been powerfully, effectively, originally responsible for formulating antifascist analysis and strategy."
    —**MICOL SEIGEL**, author, *Violence Work: State Power and the Limits of Police*

"*The Black Antifascist Tradition* is a handbook a century in the making. It is a historical synthesis of how the forerunners of anti-colonial struggle, Pan-Africanism, and Black revolutionary theory and practice identified and confronted fascist emergence and organization from a local to an international scale and across the formative epochs. Richly detailed and thoroughly researched, this highly accessible and readable text is also wide-angled and multi-layered in scope—adeptly interconnecting people, places, events, and actions with their resultant insights, observations, and

practical formulations. This book is the complete exposition of Black antifascist thought, and a necessary guide for the antifascist struggles of today."
—**JUSTIN AKERS CHACÓN**, author, *Radicals in the Barrio*

"Jeanelle K. Hope and Bill V. Mullen have written the definitive history for one of the most important, and least discussed, pieces of the antifascist movement. Weaving together historical analysis, trenchant critique, and future visioning, this is one of the most important books on antifascism ever written." —**SHANE BURLEY**, author, *Why We Fight: Essays on Fascism, Resistance, and Surviving the Apocalypse*

"*The Black Antifascist Tradition* is a dazzling work of reclamation and admonition that simultaneously reaches into the folds of past and future to make an urgent, formidable case that fascism, capitalism, and anti-Black violence are profoundly interconnected. Hope and Mullen give voice to activists and intellectuals of two centuries with compelling clarity. They have produced a volume providing an astute and knowledgeable guide to a complex legacy with which every partisan of 'freedom dreams' needs to critically engage." —**ALAN WALD**, author, *Trinity of Passion: The Literary Left and the Anti-Fascist Crusade*

"Through the dialectic of 'Anti-black Fascism' and the 'Black Antifascist Tradition,' Jeanelle Hope and Bill V. Mullen expertly convey how African descendant antifascists in the United States and beyond developed a unique interpretation of the fascist threat through their experience of, and fightback against, Jim Crow, Euro-American (settler) colonialism and imperialism, and policies and practices of white supremacy. A stunning work of historical recovery, political analysis, and critical interpretation, *The Black Antifascist Tradition* reads guerrilla intellectuals like Ida B. Wells-Barnett and Ruth Wilson Gilmore into the tradition of Black Antifascism, highlights prominent Black Antifascists like Aimé Césaire and George Jackson, and recovers lesser-known critics of Anti-Black Fascism like Thyra Edwards and Lorenzo Kom'boa Ervin. In doing so, it not only makes an invaluable contribution to scholarship on the Black radical tradition (or the Tradition of Radical Blackness), but also paves the way for deeper and more serious study of antifascisms emanating from Black realities. In our current moment of naked acts of genocide, intensified racialized police and military violence, and the bold resurgence of rightwing authoritarianism, Hope and Mullen, and the freedom fighters they examine, remind us of the long and rich praxis of resistance on which we can—and must—build. Everything is at stake." —**CHARISSE BURDEN-STELLY**, author of *Black Scare/Red Scare: Theorizing Capitalist Racism in the United States* and coeditor of *Organize, Fight, Win: Black Communist Women's Political Writing*

"In *The Black Antifascist Tradition*, Hope and Mullen unearth a distinct and underacknowledged lineage of Black antifascist organizing, from Ida B. Wells-Barnett and the anti-lynching movement to Black Lives Matter and the struggle for police abolition. Drawing on the contributions of past and present thinkers and activists, this book offers an essential overview of the ways that Black radicals have understood the relationship between fascism and white supremacy and organized to confront both. The book introduces readers to a history of Black internationalist and antifascist organizing, including lesser-known campaigns by Black soldiers during the Spanish Civil War and the Black Panther Party's United Front Against Fascism. In so doing, the authors raise provocative arguments about the existential violence Black people experience even under 'normal' conditions of capitalist exploitation, underscoring the role of anti-Black racism in anticipating the rise of fascism long before its formal ascent to power. Importantly, Hope and Mullen show how resisting the conditions that threaten Black life in particular has produced strategies that are equally relevant to struggles against violent, anti-democratic movements everywhere. By broadening our horizons around what counts as antifascist organizing, *The Black Antifascist Tradition* insists on the inseparability of antifascism from the struggle for Black liberation." —**HALEY PESSIN**, coeditor, *Voices of a People's History of the United States in the Twenty-First Century*

THE BLACK ANTIFASCIST TRADITION

★ FIGHTING BACK FROM ANTI-LYNCHING TO ABOLITION ★

JEANELLE K. HOPE AND BILL V. MULLEN

HAYMARKET BOOKS
CHICAGO, IL

© 2024 Jeanelle K. Hope and Bill V. Mullen

Published in 2023 by
Haymarket Books
P.O. Box 180165
Chicago, IL 60618
773-583-7884
www.haymarketbooks.org
info@haymarketbooks.org

ISBN: 979-8-88890-133-5

Distributed to the trade in the US through Consortium Book Sales
and Distribution (www.cbsd.com) and internationally through Ingram
Publisher Services International (www.ingramcontent.com).

This book was published with the generous support of Lannan Foundation, Wallace
Action Fund, and Marguerite Casey Foundation.

Special discounts are available for bulk purchases by organizations
and institutions. Please call 773-583-7884 or email
info@haymarketbooks.org for more information.

Cover and interior design by Eric Kerl.
Cover photos: Top: (Left) A police officer keeps a watch on 30 demonstrators as they
parade through a predominately Black section of the city during the second night
of racial unrest. There were scattered firebombing and rock throwing incidents but
no serious violence. (Photo by Bettmann Archive/Getty Images). (Center) Ida B.
Wells-Barnett. (Right) Young Black women high school students organized a sit-in
at Millennium Park on Monday afternoon to make #BlackLivesMatter. (Photo by
Sarah-Ji). Bottom: (Left) Elaine Brown and Huey Newton with other Black Panther
Party members. (Center) Claudia Jones, (Right) Clash between young African
Americans and Ku Klux Klan members in Miami after the murder of a 20-year-old.

Library of Congress Cataloging-in-Publication data is available.

CONTENTS

The Black Antifascist Tradition: An Introduction. 1

CHAPTER 1: Premature Black Antifascism:
Ida B. Wells-Barnett, "Lynch Law,"
and the Conspiracy of Anti-Black Fascism. . . . 31

CHAPTER 2: Anticolonial, Pan-Africanist
and Communist Antifascism 47

CHAPTER 3: Double V Antifascism and World War II. 73

CHAPTER 4: Legal Antifascism:
The "We Charge Genocide" Campaign 99

CHAPTER 5: Black Power Antifascism 125

CHAPTER 6: 4A Black Antifascism: On Anarchy,
Autonomy, Antagonism, and Abolition 153

CHAPTER 7: Abolitionist Antifascism. 181

EPILOGUE: The Modern Global Fascist Echo Chamber
and BLM-Antifa. 209

The Black Antifascist Tradition Syllabus. 217

Reading List 223

Notes 233

Index 267

Acknowledgments. 278

THE BLACK ANTIFASCIST TRADITION
— An Introduction —

Fascism was a monster born of capitalist parents. Fascism came as the end-product of centuries of capitalist bestiality, exploitation, domination and racism—mainly exercised outside of Europe.
>   —**Walter Rodney**, *How Europe Underdeveloped Africa*[1]

The only effective guarantee against the victory of fascism is an indivisible mass movement which refuses to conduct business as usual as long as repression rages on. It is only natural that Blacks and other Third World peoples must lead this movement, for we are the first and most deeply injured victims of fascism.
> —**Angela Davis**, "Political Prisoners, Prisons & Black Liberation"[2]

For certain people, America has been fascist all along, and it just depends on what side you are on.
>   —**Robin D. G. Kelley**, interview with Vinson Cunningham[3]

OCTAVIA BUTLER'S *Parable of the Sower* has long been a critically acclaimed, pioneering work of Black speculative fiction and a canonical text within Afrofuturism and the Black literary tradition. In 2020, the book gained renewed and widespread interest, topping various literary charts, most notably the *New York Times* bestseller list. First published in 1993, *Parable of the Sower* takes place in 2024. Butler casts a post-apocalyptic future for the United States animated by ravaging climate change; the collapse of government and rise of corporatism; the reintroduction of slavery; a major water and energy shortage; the omnipresence and proliferation of a drug that drives the masses to pillage, burn, and rape any remaining communities; an immigration/

border crisis; and a societal takeover led by religious fundamentalists. Reading/re-reading *Parable of the Sower* in 2020 proved to be a jarring and ominous experience, as much of what Butler predicted for 2024 had already come to fruition—or at least the seeds had been sowed. The convergence of a worldwide pandemic, the global rise of far-right politicians buoyed to power by religious fundamentalists (from Christian Evangelicalism to Hindutva), the catastrophic effects of climate change (stronger hurricanes, colder winters, dangerously hot summers and wildfires, historic droughts, and more), and the rise of corporatism under the Trump administration via massive deregulation and corporate tax breaks all echoed Butler's dystopian future. When one couples this already decaying landscape with 2020's mass uprisings and fleeting period of "racial reckoning" spurred by the deaths of far too many Black people, particularly George Floyd, Breonna Taylor, and Ahmaud Arbery, Butler's novel offers a frightening commentary on what's to come and acts as a cautionary tale, providing African Americans a parable loaded with hints as to how to prepare for the seemingly perilous, not too distant future.

In her world-building, Butler also lays out the framework for the rise of Fascism, intimately detailing the erasure of democracy, elimination of government safety nets and norms, and gratuitous violence. She specifically spells out the menace of American Fascism through the eyes of a Black teenage girl, Lauren Olamina. Lauren is determined to survive the onslaught of fascism by fleeing her ravaged Southern California community, freeing herself of existing religious doctrine, and working to create a wholly new future through Earthseed—a tight-knit community and new religion that believes "God is change," uses "God" as a synonym for "Earth," and invokes an Indigenous/pre-colonial reverence for land, while simultaneously recognizing that the future "is in the stars," as Earth has fallen into disrepair. It is through Lauren's character that Butler challenges readers to become Black Antifascists, Anarchists, Abolitionists, Socialists, and Afrofuturists if they are truly vested in surviving the twenty-first century. *The Black Antifascist Tradition* makes a similar call to its readers.

THE BLACK ANTIFASCIST TRADITION

This book will illuminate a distinctive history of theoretical analysis, political organizing, revolutionary praxis, and life-affirming world-making that we call the Black Antifascist Tradition. Grounded in the writing, agitation, and political thought of figures such as Aimé Césaire, Ida B. Wells-Barnett, Langston Hughes, Walter Rodney, Angela Davis, C. L. R. James, George Padmore, Cedric Robinson, Claudia Jones, Assata Shakur, George Jackson, W. E. B. Du Bois, Mariame Kaba, and Ruth Wilson Gilmore; and organizations such as the International African Friends of Ethiopia, the Black Panther Party, the Civil Rights Congress, the Black Liberation Army, prisoner rights groups, the We Charge Genocide movement, and modern-day battles to make Black life matter, this book argues that Black Antifascism is a vital stream in the wider freedom struggles of Africans in the diaspora and a theoretical cornerstone for what Cedric Robinson has called the "Black Radical Tradition." Indeed, the Black Antifascist Tradition intersects with and informs virtually every important Black political and social movement of the twentieth and twenty-first centuries. Black Antifascism is embedded with and in dialectical relationship to such transformative Afro-diasporic moments as the Campaign Against Lynching, the Pan-African Movement, Anticolonialism, Anti-imperialism, International Communism, the Civil Rights Movement, the Black Power Movement, Black Feminism, LGBTQIA+ struggles, Black Anarchism, and the contemporary Abolitionist movement.

Each of these moments helped give birth to a new consciousness for Black radicals, further illuminating the nature and potential of Fascism as a political ideology and political threat. Their analyses and understanding were generated by the objective conditions faced by people of African descent across the diaspora, many of which have contributed directly to the development of Fascism: slavery, Jim Crow, colonization, settler colonialism, apartheid, race laws, sexual policing, eugenics, war, imperialism, police brutality, the prison-industrial complex, and more. As Cedric Robinson has argued, the experience and memory of living under and resisting racial capitalism has often made Black radicals "prematurely" aware of the history of Fascism as a political ideology, its potential to take hold in the future, and the need to fight against it. As Angela Davis eloquently put it, Black people have often been "the first and most deeply injured victims of fascism," whether it be Italian Fascism colonizing North Africa, American Nazis and neo-Nazis attacking Black protesters for civil rights in the United States, or white supremacist street gangs attacking Black Lives Matter activists.[4]

Davis also points to the importance of anti-Black racism in the development of both Fascism as a political ideology and anti-Fascist consciousness among peoples of African descent. Throughout the book we illustrate how, at each stage in the development of racial capitalism, anti-Black racism has been a fixture of and has contributed to the development of Fascism as a political project. Thus, on a general level, the Black Antifascist Tradition can be described as the effort to anticipate, analyze, destroy, and replace global hierarchies of anti-Blackness that have contributed to Fascism as a political project. Anti-Black Fascism, in fact, embodies an ominous counter-history of modernity within Fascism itself. Descending from Aimé Césaire's contention that the root of European Fascism lay in the "daily barbarisms" practiced on Black life in the colonies, and Walter Rodney's argument that Fascism "came as the end-product of centuries of capitalist bestiality, exploitation, domination and racism," *The Black Antifascist Tradition* argues that Anti-Black Fascism both names and embodies Western modernity's historical drive to eliminate, remove, exploit, divide, and dispirit the lives of Black people; in short, to insist that Black Lives don't matter.[5]

At the same time, departing from many theories of anti-Blackness, we argue that the Black Antifascist Tradition insists on naming its enemy—anti-Blackness—as a permanent feature of Fascism, in order to challenge, destroy, and replace it. For thinkers and organizers in the Black Antifascist Tradition, Fascism as a political ideology and system of racial capitalism has made legible, articulable, and deeply felt the world-historical threat of anti-Blackness as well as urgent tools and strategies for overcoming it. Beginning with the antilynching movement of the early twentieth century, continuing through the mass drive to liberate African colonies from the threat of Fascism at mid-century, up to the fight to eliminate prisons in the twenty-first, Black Antifascism organizes itself around imaginative overturnings of racial capitalism's globalized efforts to make Black life a baseline for the immiseration of human beings everywhere.

The force of anti-Blackness in the development of Fascism also helps to explain the centrality of class struggle in the Black Antifascist Tradition. Fascism as a political movement has historically targeted the destruction of the working class. Black people have been specially attuned to this threat in part because, under racial capitalism, they have always comprised a disproportionately large share of the working class itself. For this reason, many key figures in the Black Antifascist Tradition consider themselves Socialists, Communists, and/or Abolitionists, dedicated to smashing hierarchies of both race and class. In their influential writing on Fascism in the late 1960s and early 1970s, for example, Angela Davis and Bettina Aptheker argued that "Fascism is the preventive counter-revolution to the socialist transformation of society. . . . the advent of fascism is not a single event—a sudden coup d'etat—but rather a protracted social process." In the United States, Davis argued, this "counter-revolution" relied primarily on state repression of the "most radical and politically conscious section of the working class—the Black, Puerto Rican and Chicano communities."[6] Fast-forwarding to the contemporary Abolitionist movement, activists and organizers like Ruth Wilson Gilmore and Robin D. G. Kelley have theorized neoliberal Fascism as the state's targeted effort to destroy labor unions, workers' movements, and the right to organize, while the prison-industrial complex has locked up countless hundreds of thousands of Black and Brown workers. Thus, notes Kelley, Abolitionism is a movement "dead set on ending fascism once and for all."[7]

Finally, challenging racial capitalism's anti-Blackness as a feeder for Fascism has animated the Black Antifascist Tradition toward a politics of resistance, revolution, and survival. Black Antifascism, we argue, is another name for the practice of life-making over and against Fascism's march to genocide. The tradition of Black Antifascism we illuminate organizes to dismantle racial capitalism as a necessary step toward salvaging social life for *all* of the global oppressed, those whom Frantz Fanon—a veteran of the Free French Forces that fought Nazi Germany—called the "wretched of the earth." Some of the most important texts, slogans, and practices within the Black Antifascist Tradition––"Hands Off Ethiopia!," "Double Victory," "We Charge Genocide," "Survival Pending Revolution," #blacklivesmatter—define anti-Black Fascism as not only a political death threat against the Black race but also as an alarm and bellwether for the future of the human. Black Antifascism thus describes an oppositional lived experience under racial capitalism that understands the conditions of Black life as a litmus test for the survival of the species and the planet. Black Antifascism seeks to build and sustain radical forms of solidarity—whatever forms they take—to midwife both the extinction of anti-Black Fascism and the potentiation of a new world beyond it. Leaning into history in order to leap over it, Black Antifascism is profoundly and boldly Afrofuturist.

American Fascism: Anti-Blackness, the Law, and the State
Like many scholars of Fascism, we understand its political ideology and social formation to be broadly defined by a set of fundamental characteristics, including but not limited to the following: dual application of the law, far-right nationalism, the appeal of a charismatic or cult-like leader, an undergirding belief in racial purity and superiority, the bolstering of racial capitalism, extreme militarism and authoritarian governance, suppression of democracy, state-sanctioned white terrorism and violence (ethnic cleansing and genocide, in other words), and resolute misogyny/misogynoir. These features of Fascism have been enumerated in recent years by a number of scholars attempting to describe what has been called the authoritarian, neofascist, and even post-Fascist global turn of the past twenty years.[8] Many of these writers have drawn directly on the robust tradition of writing on Fascism in the Marxist tradition, which has emphasized Fascism as a symptom of capitalist crisis, decline, and dissolution, intended to restore a failing order mainly by attacking internal state enemies like Communists, Socialists, trade unionists, immigrants, ethnic minorities, and the working class more

THE BLACK ANTIFASCIST TRADITION

broadly. This tradition of writing extends from Clara Zetkin, Leon Trotksy, and Antonio Gramsci in the early years of the twentieth century to more recent writings by the likes of the late Stuart Hall, Ugho Palheta, David Renton, Prabhat Patnaik, Jason Stanley, Gerald Horne, Jasson Perrez, Charisse Burden-Stelly, Alyosha Goldstein, and Simon Ventura Trujillo.[9]

Within this broader surge of what might be called the New Fascism Studies has come a recovery of writers and writings on Fascism generally overlooked by earlier generations. Many of these writers reside in what we are calling the Black Antifascist Tradition. Characteristic of their work has been a willingness to challenge the description and analysis of Fascism as a political project endemic only to early twentieth-century Europe. It has also challenged the historiography of Fascism by viewing its roots as less in Europe and more in the globalization of racial capitalism prior to and including the twentieth century. Cedric Robinson, for example, has argued:

> From the perspective of many non-Western peoples . . . the occurrence of fascism that is, militarism, imperialism, racialist authoritarianism, choreographed mob violence, millenarian Crypto-Christian mysticism, and a nostalgic nationalism—was no more an historical aberration than colonialism, the slave trade, and slavery. Fascism was and is a modern social discipline which much like its genetic predecessors, Christianity, imperialism, nationalism, sexism, and racism, provided the means for the ascent to and preservation of power for elitists. . . . It is, then, a mistake to posit fascism as an inherent national trait or to ascribe it to a particular culture or class.[10]

Robinson has helped to recover a host of writers within a "Black Radical Tradition" firmly rooted in a tradition of Antifascism. These writers would include not only those central to his book of that name—W. E. B. Du Bois, C. L. R. James, and Richard Wright, as examples—but a score of other writers and activists we take up in these pages. Drawing extensively on histories of slavery, colonialism, imperialism, and the experiences of people across the African diaspora under racial capitalism, these writers have examined Fascist tendencies, organizations and ideologies once considered outside the orbit of Fascism's history. They have foregrounded the role of race in the specific enumeration of national Fascist movements. They have also challenged perspectives positing that the United States and other Western capitalist states are at worst "bourgeois democracies"—a deceptive bastardization of democracy that largely bolsters the bourgeois class, with governance controlled by elites. But "bourgeois democracy" does not fully capture the Black experience under racial capitalism. Rather, Zoé Samudzi and William Anderson's "societal fascism," described as "the process and political logics of state formation wherein entire populations are excluded or ejected from the social contract . . . conditional inclusion at best," better encapsulates how anti-Black Fascism has functioned in the US.[11] Yet, even their work stops short of placing anti-Black Fascism in conversation with European fascism, as they argue that societal fascism "differs from the political fascism represented, for example, by the regimes of Benito Mussolini, Francisco Franco, Adolf Hitler, and others."[12] The point here isn't to pit American Fascism and European Fascism against each other but to underscore that our understanding of "traditional Fascism" (Nazism, in other words) has its roots in anti-Blackness vis a vis American settler colonialism, slave codes, Jim Crow laws, and a litany of policies and acts of state-sanctioned violence that have explicitly targeted Black people. Put another way, there is no Fascism anywhere that is not also anti-Black.

For example, the passage of the Nazi Nuremberg Race Laws in 1935 and the Italian Race Laws in Mussolini's Italy in 1938 ushered in a tiered citizenship system that categorized those people who were non-Aryan (largely Jews, but also those from the Roma and Sinti ethnic groups, as well as people of African descent) as biologically inferior, undeserving of citizenship and basic human rights. Influenced by the already existing Jim Crow laws in the US, European Fascist laws prohibited Jews from having interracial marriages, restricted Jews from using public facilities, legalized employment discrimination, and stripped Jews of their ability to vote. In reading across Holocaust archives, Jim Crow archives, and

Italian Fascist archives, it becomes unequivocally evident that European Fascism had its roots in American Anti-Black Fascism, as much of the language on racial purity and citizenship, as well as legalized segregation and marginalization, mirrored the legal subjugation of Black people in the US decades, and in some cases centuries, earlier. Yet, throughout the historiography on the rise of Hitler, Nazism, and fascism in Europe more broadly, seldom have historians drawn connections between the Nuremberg Laws, Italian Racial Laws, and the Jim Crow laws of the US. Furthermore, Nazism and the Holocaust are often portrayed as unprecedented and unrivaled acts of human terror, in part to stress the sheer atrocity (specifically because the events happened on European soil), but also as a means to ignore or perhaps erase the insidious role the US played in one of the darkest moments in global history, in the service of a redeeming liberal narrative of "Allies vs. the Axis."

In *Hitler's American Model: The United States and the Making of Nazi Race Law*, legal scholar James Whitman makes an important intervention in the history of Fascism by arguing that "Nazis found examples and precedents in American legal race order that they valued highly."[13] This argument is an essential one that our book builds upon. *The Black Antifascist Tradition* identifies the epicenter of modern racial Fascism as being in the United States, not Europe. Throughout the book, we trace how Anti-Black Fascism is enshrined within American law and related political forms and ideologies, and how, unlike with European Fascism, there is no need for a singular Fascist regime or dictator to ensure its existence. American Anti-Black Fascism's strength lies within the law itself, which commands law enforcement, legislators, and everyday citizens across the political spectrum to uphold and maintain anti-Black systems from generation to generation. In this respect, we include in our definition of anti-Blackness the ancestral line of racializations, racisms, and modes of racial oppression visited upon and sometimes transferred to non-white US subjects.

Slave codes, at the outset of colonial American history, were inherently anti-Black doctrines that codified an authoritarian relationship between Black people and the law. As slavery developed into a more formalized institution, additional laws were written to further protect white enslavers and ensure the enslaved had no legal means of gaining freedom or equal rights under the law. By 1740, it was illegal for the enslaved to grow their own food, learn to read, assemble, move freely, or earn money in South Carolina and most other states.[14] The four hundred years of American chattel slavery exercised on people of African descent was a period of brute authoritarian force enacted by plantation owners and justified through laws, with the ultimate goal of bolstering modern capitalism and cementing white domination. Slavery's founding role in the production of race law was to become one pillar of fascism globally. The passage of the Thirteenth Amendment, in 1865, effectively abolished slavery with the caveat that enslavement could persist as a form of criminal punishment. This loophole set the stage for the rise of Black "criminality" and mass incarceration. Moreover, Reconstruction was not the hopeful period that the formerly enslaved had imagined and longed for, as it devolved quickly into an era defined by white racial terrorism and lynchings, criminalization and incarceration of the formerly enslaved, and the emergence of sharecropping. For former white plantation owners, these systems of domination were essential to helping establish a new Southern economy and maintaining white domination. Near the turn of the century, states began introducing laws that sanctioned white supremacy and legalized racial segregation. Thus, as Jasson Perez has recently argued, "One can't help but think of the overthrow of Reconstruction as a form of fascism."[15]

During the 1890s and early 1900s, there was a major proliferation of pseudoscholarship in the US that tied criminality to Blackness. The publication of Frederick Hoffman's *Race Traits and the Tendencies of the American Negro* and the founding of the *Journal of Criminal Law and Criminology* were two milestones that helped advance the formal—albeit deeply biased—study of crime and the law. This work was largely made possible as states began keeping more detailed crime, death, and census records that allowed for deeper, and deeply flawed, statistical analysis. Early criminologists typically took one of two approaches to the field of study—determinism or positivism. Determinists believed that criminal behavior was a symptom caused by an individual's environment, and their work offered more structuralist critiques of crime. In contrast, the positivists believed criminality to be a "heritable trait," a sort of natural extension of social Darwinism, race science, and eugenics. Positivists were proponents of using incarceration to "defend society" from the "biologically inferior."[16] Hoffman, a German-educated statistician and positivist, deduced from his examination of mortality and birth rates and arrest records that Black people were prone to experiencing "excessive mortality" and criminality because of their "poor biological composition" and "childhood neglect."[17] Hoffman's self-proclaimed "irrefutable" study was used by the Prudential Insurance Company to legitimize racial discrimination in the insurance industry.[18] Hoffman's research failed to account for the extrajudicial killings, state-sanctioned violence, and overall racial terror to which many Black people were subjected. Furthermore, his work proclaimed, dubiously, that the law could not be racist; the Black race was inherently immoral and drawn toward criminal behavior.

The latter half of Hoffman's book firmly cemented his racial animus and positivist approach to interrogating crime and the law. Coupling his deeply biased analysis of specious crime and mortality data with the work of race scientists, Hoffman offered a tour de force of future white supremacist talking points: anti-miscegenation, the hypersexualization and vilification of Black women's bodies, a condemnation of the "mulatto" or mixed-race persons, a characterization of Native Americans' and Black people's social tendencies as being closely related to "pauperism and immorality," and, finally, a call for the formerly enslaved to be relegated to agricultural and manual labor, just short of a full proposition to reinstitute slavery. Hoffman vehemently believed that the abolition of slavery, Reconstruction campaigns spearheaded by the federal government, and the expansion of educational access to Black people had moved the race backward.[19] At his most insulting, Hoffman claimed that his data revealed that the Negro "committed fewer crimes than the white man" during enslavement and that the Negro race under slavery was "superior to the present generation."[20] Hoffman's work

THE BLACK ANTIFASCIST TRADTION

must be understood as canonical to the nineteenth-century American race science that proved essential to the shaping of Anti-Black Fascism. Hoffman's *Race Traits* was published in 1896, the same year as the landmark Supreme Court decision in *Plessy v. Ferguson*, which legalized segregation at the federal level.

In the four decades immediately following, states passed a myriad of laws aimed at racially segregating public life, from housing and employment to transportation and entertainment. Jim Crow segregation was the law of the land, effectively stymieing Black life throughout the first half of the twentieth century and beyond. Even more macabre, the extrajudicial killing, or lynching, of Black people, often by white mobs, became more commonplace.[21] In some cases, entire Black towns, such as the Tulsa Greenwood District, were burned and leveled to the ground by white vigilantes, while law enforcement aided, abetted, and/or failed to sanction these criminal acts. Moreover, legalized racial exclusion and segregation were not just targeted at Black people; incoming waves of Asian immigrants and Mexicans also drew the ire of white politicians and vigilantes. Lynchings, Jim Crow, and other discriminatory federal laws, such as the Chinese Exclusion Act of 1882 and the Geary Act, were crafted to move beyond the black-white binary of legalized segregation. This history of racism and legal exclusion was certainly unique to the US, eliciting contempt from some nations, while viewed as a source of inspiration by others.

In 1928, Adolf Hitler completed his follow-up to *Mein Kampf*, which had not gathered much attention at the time of its publication. *Zweites Buch*, better known as "Hitler's Second Book," detailed the Fascist leader's analysis of foreign affairs, with a sharpened gaze on what he viewed as America's swift economic and industrial rise, deeming the US a model living standard—yet weakened by its multiracial composition. He attributed America's global ascendance to its strict immigration laws, which disproportionately favored European immigrants. He surmised, "By making entry to American soil dependent on definite racial prerequisites on the one hand, as well as on the definite physical health of the individual as such, bleeding Europe of its best people has, indeed, perforce been legally regulated." Hitler was inspired by American immigration and racial exclusion laws and the US eugenics movement.[22] He preached that racial purity, anti-immigrant rhetoric, and new economic policies would provide Germany with better footing to compete with its global rivals. Hitler understood that the law could serve as the ultimate tool for control, declaring, "Nothing that is made of flesh and blood can escape the laws which determined its coming into being," thus outlining the primary mode in which Fascism would take form—the law, with explicit influence from American race laws.

During the 1920s, Henry Ford, founder of the Ford Motor Company, sponsored the publication of the *Dearborn Independent*, which gained notoriety for its publication of antisemitic propaganda, such as *The Protocols of the Elders of Zion*, and included a recurring section entitled, "The International Jew: The World's Problem." With a readership of almost one million at its height, the *Dearborn Independent* helped Ford effectively spread antisemitic views in the US. In Europe, the publication was also making its rounds among antisemites, including a leading writer of modern antisemitism, Theodor Fritsch, who translated and republished issues of the newspaper into an edited volume, *The International Jew*, for a German audience. Fritsch gained prominence in Germany, starting in the 1880s, as a radical antisemite who proliferated writings on scientific racism.[23] Prior to his publication of *Handbuch der Judenfrage* (*The Handbook of the Jewish Question*), a nearly five-hundred-page work positing the superiority of the Aryan race, Fritsch was especially fixated on American race laws and eugenics, specifically how the country leveraged the law to create a second-class status/contested citizenship for those who were non-white.

Fritsch was especially keen on the treatment and legalized marginalization of Native Americans and Puerto Ricans.[24] The former had been subjected to land dispossession and state-sanctioned genocide, actions that would be mirrored in Nazi Germany against Jews and other groups. Following the Spanish-American War, Puerto Ricans were granted a second-class citizenship status, systematically denying them full constitutional rights, while the US government maintained political and economic control over the island. This same limited citizenship was also extended to the Philippines, Guam, and Cuba. However, America's conception of a second-class citizenship status must be traced back further, to its anti-Black roots. Both the "Three-Fifths Compromise" in the US Constitution (declaring the enslaved three-fifths of a person for purposes of proportional voting) and the *Dred Scott v. Sandford* Supreme Court decision, which stated that enslaved persons were not citizens of the United States, laid the legal foundation for the creation of a tiered citizenship system. While the passage of the Fourteenth Amendment provided a pathway to citizenship for the formerly enslaved, the constitutional amendment only emboldened states, especially those in the South, to create laws and policies (such as grandfather clauses, literacy tests, racial covenants, and more) that would systematically limit Black people's constitutional rights and freedoms as citizens, most glaringly in the areas of voting, employment, education, and housing.

American Fascism: Racial Purity and White Supremacy

Reproductive rights have remained a contested legal and civil rights issue in the US, dating back to slavery and early American settler colonialism.[25] The passage of the landmark *Roe v. Wade* Supreme Court decision spurred generations of "pro-life" and pro-natalist activism from conservatives, evangelicals, and those on the far right. As neofascist movements swell, in part as a response to a long-held right-wing conspiracy and white supremacist belief—the Great Replacement Theory—population control and notions of racial purity have once again become major political organizing issues, with anti-immigrant and anti-abortion laws, as well as heinous acts of racial violence (such as racially motivated mass shootings) being undertaken in an attempt to detract from shifting racial and social demographics, and, ultimately, to buoy white supremacy.[26] The lingering white supremacist fear of being "replaced" by "third-world voters" or "somebody else's babies" has spawned a host of laws to regulate, surveil, and police birthing people's bodies for the sake of bolstering the white race and to maintain "racial purity"—a central tenet of Fascism.[27]

THE BLACK ANTIFASCIST TRADITION   15

By the time the regimes of Hitler and Mussolini began to theorize racial purity and Aryan identity politics, discussing race in this quasi-biological sense in the US was old news. The making (and evolution) of race has been an intrinsic feature of the multiracial and multi-ethnic United States. As Michael Omi and Howard Winant posit, the foundation of the nation rests on the "advent of a consolidated social structure of exploitation, appropriation, domination . . . first in religious terms, but soon enough in scientific and political ones, [which] initiated modern racial awareness."[28] Physical and cultural differences were used as a justification for the conquest of the Americas and for slavery. From the outset, race making in the US has been about the maintenance of white supremacy and racial capitalism. Thus, it became essential in the American colonial project to deem Native American people as "savage" and lower on the racial hierarchy to justify land dispossession and genocide. Moreover, many Native American, Black, and Puerto Rican women were forcibly and coercively sterilized through the 1970s via US government–funded programs.[29]

As the number of mixed-race persons swelled across the colonies and antebellum South, it became crucial to quantify race, in particular Blackness, with the introduction of terms like *mulatto*, *quadroon*, and *octoroon*, and the belief in the "one drop" rule. For example, during a 1938 antilynching debate, Mississippi senator Theodore G. Bilbo argued that "one drop of Negro blood placed in the veins of the purest Caucasian destroys the inventive genius of his mind and palsies his creative faculty."[30] Bilbo was a Southern racist who saw the rise of Hitler across the Atlantic as an opportunity to double down on Anti-Black Fascism. Bilbo went so far as to praise the Germans and their race laws, claiming that they "appreciate the importance of race values. They understand that racial improvement is the greatest asset that any country can have . . . They know, as few other nations have realized, that the impoverishment of race values contributes more to the impairment and destruction of a civilization than any other agency."[31] According to James Whitman, Bilbo even "was going further than the Nazis were willing to go."[32]

Similarly, *blood quantum* was widely used as a metric, following the Indian Reorganization Act of 1934, as a means to "formally" recognize one's tribal identity or "Indian blood" (a test of one's racial purity) and grant or deny an individual eligibility for federal benefits. These laws in particular were studied by the Nazis: Hitler praised the US government for killing its Indigenous population. At the core of American laws on race-mixing, segregation, and white identity politics, Blackness is understood as existing on the opposite end of the racial hierarchy, as an aberration and in unending juxtaposition to whiteness.

Discourse on American race-making and its concepts, metrics, and laws served as a blueprint for European Fascists. In both the Nuremberg and Italian race laws, the quantification of racial purity was essential to establishing a tiered citizenship system. For the Nazis, Aryan racial identity was predicated on having zero documented Jewish ancestry. However, understanding race within Italian Fascism is much more complex. The Italian race laws were an extension of an earlier philosophical work—the "Manifesto of Racial Scientists"—authored by Dr. Guido Landra, Italian anthropologist and the founding director of the Racial Office of the Ministry of Popular Culture.[33] Historian Michael Livingston argues that, early on, Italian Fascists largely associated Jewish identity with religious and cultural elements (that is, ethnicity). This was evidenced in their prioritization of implementing policies to stifle Jewish property ownership, ban books written by Jewish authors, and, overall, limit their cultural influence and mobility (segregation and marginalization), rather than "immediate elimination of the offending minority," as undertaken by their Nazi counterparts.[34] By the 1920s, Italian Fascists began to articulate a vision of racial purity, often conflating "Aryan" with Italian and even introducing the contradictory racial identities of "Nordic Aryan" and "New Italian." Mussolini's quest for racial purity involved eugenics, calls to bolster the birth rate of Aryans, and anti-miscegenation laws. In 1938, for example, the Italian magazine *La Difesa della Razza* codified Italian state raciology, insisting, "It is necessary to make a clear distinction between the Mediterranean races of Western Europe on the one side and the orientals and Africans on the other."[35] The magazine used Nazi criteria to assert that Italians were decidedly "Aryan," "Hebrews" were decidedly not, British were "degenerate," and Negroes, particularly US Negroes, "congenitally inferior."[36]

Under Nazi Germany, the notorious 1933 "Prussian Memorandum," which was to become the basis for the Nuremberg Race Laws two years later, did "away with the 'liberal' criminal law of the Weimar Republic in favor of the harsh new approach typical of Nazi politics."[37] To that end, the memorandum pointed to two examples to follow: the medieval expulsion of Jews in Europe, and modern-day American Jim Crow.[38] The paramount endeavor to avoid "race-mixing" and preserve Aryan blood depended on the criminalization of race-mixing itself. Here, the memorandum turned again to the US example of legal bans on intermarriage and the formal and legal segregation of the races, noting that "it is well known . . . that the southern states of North America maintain the most stringent separation between the white population and coloreds in both public and personal interactions."[39]

While European Fascists sought to define race and racial purity as something fixed, the more subversive American Anti-Black Fascism has thrived because of the shifting conception of race in the nation. Returning to Omi and Winant, racial formation, a "sociohistorical process by which racial categories are created, inhabited, transformed, and destroyed," encapsulates how race can never be objective or biological. Instead, race, especially whiteness, has been defined through various Supreme Court cases such as *Thind, Cartozian,* and *Ozawa.* Instead of focusing on defining those who were considered non-white, much of American law has sought to create clear lines of demarcation to define and safeguard whiteness—its privileges, identity, property, and legal entitlements.[40] Steve Martinot calls this fixation on whiteness and the law "white-identity fascism."[41] Furthermore, unlike European Fascism, American Anti-Black Fascism has thrived because of the malleability of whiteness, which has arbitrarily bent to include the many European immigrant groups and even select Asian ethnic groups such as Armenians, while being able to snap back to a more rigid state to deny whiteness to those deemed as too far removed from European (synonymous for white) culture and ancestry. In order to preserve a white racial, political, and cultural majority, whiteness in the US context has had to be adaptable and move beyond notions of racial purity. The malleability of whiteness allows Fascism to thrive beyond the political imagination and insidious violence of an "Aryan-identified" white nationalist. For example, an Armenian or white Jewish American, who also benefits from the privileges of whiteness, might align themselves with the state and its anti-Black violence even though their people both have traumatic histories of enduring state-sanctioned violence, ethnic genocide, and other elements of Fascism.

While Hitler derided immigration, maintaining deeply xenophobic sentiments and anti-immigrant policies throughout his rise to power, American Anti-Black Fascism has held an ostensibly contradictory position on immigration, mainly depending on the ascribed racial identity of the immigrant group. White-presenting European immigrants, no matter how marginalized they may have been in Europe, are largely seen as a net gain to American whiteness.[42] Non-white waves of immigration have spurred countless anti-immigrant laws and policies, inhumane practices at US borders, and mass deportations, all while those "strangers from a different shore" and just south of the US-Mexico border fill integral, low-paying service, agricultural, and manufacturing jobs that keep the US afloat. This duality is exemplified in contemporary geopolitical and immigration discourse. American politicians across both major political parties have supported European immigration in times of crisis, like the war in Ukraine, while simultaneously working overtime to restrict or criminalize the immigration of those from what former president Donald J. Trump blanketly referred to as "shithole countries" (in other words, the Global South), who are also fleeing war, poverty, and crimes against humanity but fail to meet the white racial preference of an American-style Anti-Black Fascism. In the same speech in which Trump condemned immigrants coming from the Global South, he also suggested, "We should have more people coming from Norway," a glaring use of dog-whistle politics to invoke Nazi and Italian Fascist rhetoric. He stopped just short of calling for more "Nordic Aryans."

In summary, pro-slavery, Jim Crow, anti-immigrant, and anti-miscegenation laws have served as both the foundation for American

THE BLACK ANTIFASCIST TRADITION   19

Anti-Black Fascism and a legal blueprint for twentieth-century Fascism in Europe. Understanding American law as inherently anti-Black and distinctly Fascist allows us to 1) trace a longer genealogy in documenting the rise of global Fascism; 2) illustrate how European Fascists drew on early American laws for their own Fascist regimes and gains, and; 3) place the US at the center of Fascist discourse, not on the periphery, as more liberal historiographies have concluded. Furthermore, this examination of the law details how central anti-Blackness was (and is) to the formation of American Fascism. While Fascism in Europe largely targeted Jews, ultimately leading to the death of an estimated six million Jewish people during the Holocaust, American Anti-Black Fascism has resulted in widespread loss of Black life in stages due to the prolonged, sophisticated, and at times covert nature of Anti-Black Fascism in the United States.

From Anti-Black Fascism to Black Antifascism: Roots and Routes

> I believe that the trade in human beings between Africa and America, which flourished between the Renaissance and the American Civil War, is the prime and effective cause of the contradictions in European civilization and the illogic in modern thought and the collapse of western culture.
> —**W. E. B. Du Bois**, *The World and Africa*[43]

The history of white supremacy, legal subordination, state-sanctioned violence, social brutality and genocidal creep particular to the experiences of Africans in the diaspora has historically made people of African descent among the first to rise against the threat of Fascism. Robin D. G. Kelley and Cedric Robinson have spoken of Black radicals as "premature antifascists," who have perceived well before others in the world the links between the threat of Fascism and other subcurrents of racial capitalism. As early as 1915, for example, Du Bois viewed the imperial torture, internment, and savage killings of Africans by German colonists in Southwest Africa as the white supremacist logic that had produced World War I. "In a very real sense," wrote Du Bois, "Africa is a prime cause of this terrible overturning of civilization which we have lived to see; and these words seek to show how in the Dark Continent are hidden the roots, not simply of war to-day but of the menace of wars to-morrow." For Du Bois, the "color line" of slavery and colonialism both predicted Fascism and provided its scaffolding. As he later wrote, "I knew that Hitler and Mussolini were fighting communism, and using race prejudice to make some white people rich and all colored peoples poor. But it was not until later that I realized that the colonialism of Great Britain and France had used exactly the same object and methods as the fascists and the Nazis were trying clearly to use."[44]

Thus, during the 1930s, well before most of the world was aware of the extent of the Fascist threat in Germany, Africans in the diaspora were already fighting it. Fascist Italy's invasion of Ethiopia in 1935, an event often left out of popular Western accounts of World War II, triggered what was arguably the first global Antifascist movement. From London to the Caribbean to New York, Black radicals and Black workers declared, "Hands off Ethiopia," and began raising material and financial support for victims of Italian aggression. More than one hundred African Americans, in turn, volunteered to travel to Spain to fight against Francisco Franco's Fascist regime in the worldwide Abraham Lincoln Brigade. In both cases, anti-Black racism established by European colonialism in Africa—Ethiopia was an Italian protectorate, and Spain enlisted Moors in its North African colonies to fight *for* Fascism—was a spur to battle. By the end of World War II, hundreds of thousands of African Americans would enlist in the "Double Victory" campaign launched by the Black press, declaring their fight against Jim Crow racism at home and against Fascism in Europe to be two fronts of the same fight. For many people of African descent, Hitler's attacks on Black people and Jews in the name of white supremacy represented the history of the Western world coming home to roost. As Du Bois declared in 1940, "The democracy which the white world seeks to defend does not exist."[45]

Several years later, the brilliant Martinican Marxist Aimé Césaire, in his 1950 masterwork *Discourse on Colonialism*, would describe what had taken its place. Césaire jolted the world by announcing, "Europe is

THE BLACK ANTIFASCIST TRADITION

21

indefensible," not only because of what it had done to the Jews but also because the Holocaust had exposed what Cedric Robinson called the "internal logic" of Fascism as the fulfillment of "racial destiny":

> It would be worthwhile to study clinically, in every detail, the steps taken by Hitler and Hitlerism and to reveal to the very distinguished, very humanistic, very Christian bourgeois of the twentieth century that without his being aware of it, he had a Hitler inside him, that Hitler inhabits him, that Hitler is his demon, that if he rails against him, he is being inconsistent and that, at bottom, what he cannot forgive Hitler for is not crime in itself, the crime against man, it is not the humiliation of man as such, it is the crime against the white man, the humiliation of the white man, and the fact that he applied to Europe colonialist procedures which until then had been reserved exclusively for the Arabs of Algeria, the coolies of India, and the blacks of Africa.[46]

Césaire's essay located Fascism's origins in slavery, colonialism, and anti-Blackness as a deep font in the psyche of Western bourgeois society. As Robin D. G. Kelley notes, Césaire's essay promised that the revolution to challenge Western civilization necessitated "the complete and total overthrow of a racist, colonialist system that would open the way to imagine a whole new world."[47] Fighting Fascism and fighting anti-Blackness was a way to unite the fight of non-white peoples everywhere against racial capitalism in all its forms while imagining emancipatory alternative futures to it.

Césaire's essay might be considered the first global manifesto of the Black Antifascist Tradition. *Discourse on Colonialism* demanded no less than a world revolution against Western definitions of the "human," which depended on the exclusion and abjection of non-white people, what Césaire called "pseudo-humanism." Thus, for Césaire, the fate of humanity rested in part on the eradication of all forms of anti-Blackness: "And that is the great thing I hold against pseudo-humanism: that for too long it has diminished the rights of man, that its concept of those rights has been—and still is—narrow and fragmentary, incomplete and biased, and, all things considered, sordidly racist."[48] Just one year after Césaire's essay appeared, a second Black Antifascist manifesto appeared on another side of the world. On December 17, 1951, the US Civil Rights Congress, headed by Communist attorney William Patterson, presented a 240-page petition to the United Nations general assembly, entitled "We Charge Genocide." Inspired by the UN Convention on the Prevention and Punishment of the Crime of Genocide adopted by the General Assembly on December 9, 1948, in response to the Nazi Holocaust, the petition applied the convention's definition of genocide, as "killing members of the group," to charge the US government with "mass murder of its own nationals, with institutionalized oppression and persistent slaughter of the Negro people in the United States on the basis of race." The petition cited the US history of slavery, lynchings, police killings, and murders committed in a war against Black people as evidence of a continuous strain of anti-Black Fascism in America analogous and akin to Hitler's decimation of European Jewry. Like Césaire, the authors of "We Charge Genocide" also argued that anti-Black Fascism was a crime against "humanity" and called for an end to it in order to save the world from future destruction: "If our duty is unpleasant it is historically necessary both for the welfare of the American people and for the people of the world. We petition as American patriots, sufficiently anxious to save our countrymen and all mankind from the horrors of war to shoulder a task as painful as it is important."[49]

"We Charge Genocide" might be considered *Discourse on Colonialism*'s American *doppelgänger* and fellow traveler. In combination, the two works constitute twin pillars of the Black Antifascist Tradition. Both share an analytic rage at Anti-Black Fascism as the cause of what "We Charge Genocide" named—in a phrase resonant of our own moment—the "premature death" of Black citizens. Their place in the Black Antifascist Tradition is also elevated because of their accompanying organizing visions for how to achieve a "whole new world." For example, in tandem with their petition, the authors of "We Charge Genocide" launched an organization, the Civil Rights Congress (CRC), dedicated to a full-scale war on Anti-Black Fascism. We will take up their history and work in detail in chapter 4. Meanwhile, prior to writing *Discourse on Colonialism*, Aimé Césaire had been trained as a Marxist, identified as a Communist, and cofounded the Negritude movement, an important stream in twentienth-century Pan-Africanism. As early as 1932, Césaire was among a circle of young Martniquian radicals drawing attention to the Scottsboro Boys trial in the US, the case of nine young Black men and boys falsely accused of rape in Alabama. Here, the history of the Black Antifascist Tradition finds an important intersection and crossroads: prior to helping to draft the "We Charge Genocide" petition, attorney William Patterson was a member of the International Labor Defense (ILD), which defended the Scottsboro Boys. As of 1929, the ILD was already identifying analogies between rising Fascism in Europe and racism in the Jim Crow South. In their reporting on the Scottsboro case in 1932 and 1933, Patterson and the Communist Party drew direct parallels between the railroading of Black working-class African Americans in the US and the arrest, internment, and growing racist repression of Jews and political dissidents in Nazi Germany.

Césaire, Patterson, and other antilynching trailblazers like Ida B. Wells-Barnett thus demonstrate the prescient antifascism that characterizes the Black Antifascist Tradition. Their experiences as Black people rising in the centers of capitalist modernity attuned them to Fascism's contours even as it remained a shadow on much of the global screen. Their proto-antifascism also bears out and anticipates Angela Davis's much later claim that "Blacks and other Third World peoples are the first and most deeply injured victims of fascism." Indeed, Davis's own antifascism would itself be shaped by contact with William Patterson and the Black Antifascist Tradition. In 1970, Davis accused the United States of incipient "fascism" after she was arrested and charged with conspiracy when weapons she had legally purchased were used in a deadly attempt to free Folsom Prison inmates on trial in the Marin County Courthouse. The Committee to Free Angela Davis that sought her exoneration was modeled on the ILD's Scottsboro Defense Committee. In fact, William Patterson served as trustee of the Angela Davis

24   **THE BLACK ANTIFASCIST TRADTION**

Legal Defense Fund. His wife, Louise Patterson, served as chair of the New York Committee to Free Angela Davis.

Césaire, Davis, and Patterson represent three of the vital roots and routes of the Black Antifascist Tradition. This book eagerly builds upon and honors their legacies by placing them in conversation with and in an historical narrative alongside a host of other Black Antifascists who have long animated the history of modern Black liberation struggles, from Lorenzo Kom'Boa Ervin and George Jackson to Assata Shakur and Ruth Wilson Gilmore. We will show how the history of twentieth- and twenty-first-century Black radicalism is inseparable from and organically linked to a long history of Black Antifascist organizing, writing, and theorizing. One shining example from the catalog to come: in 2014, a group of Chicago Black youth, under the leadership of radical activist Mariame Kaba, formed the Abolitonist group We Charge Genocide. Like its CRC namesake, We Charge Genocide set out to document and enumerate killings, tortures, and civil rights violations, mainly of Black and Brown youth, perpetrated by the notorious Chicago Police Department. In November 2014, a delegation of six organizers from We Charge Genocide presented their findings to the UN Committee Against Torture in Geneva. The committee, in turn, condemned the US for violating international bans on torture. We Charge Genocide's homage to the tactics, strategies, and arguments of the CRC demonstrates the unyielding, reflexive, and circular nature of the Black Antifascist Tradition. From the US antilynching movement of the late nineteenth century to the international organizing of the twenty-first, the Black Antifascist Tradition remains a vital link in the struggle for Black liberation and for alternative conceptions of human emancipation.

Overview

This book connects people and networks who make up the Black Antifascist Tradition, extending it into our living present.

In chapter 1, "Premature Black Antifascism: Ida B. Wells-Barnett, 'Lynch Law,' and the Conspiracy of Anti-Black Fascism," we show that the "Southern horrors" and "lynch law" described by antilynching movement architect and organizer Ida B. Wells-Barnett were indicative of much more than the phenomenon of lynchings across the South—Wells-Barnett's analysis illustrated a sophisticated understanding of how the law, or the intentional absence of the law, aided in the construction and justification of Fascism. Drawing on this early understanding of anti-Black violence, this chapter demonstrates how the antilynching movement served as one of the early formations of Black Antifascist organizing and resistance.

Chapter 2, "Communist, Anticolonial, and Pan-African Antifascism," details the global rise and spread of the first major Black Antifascist movement. Inspired by the fight against racism in the colonies and in the metropole, Communist, anticolonial, and Pan-African Antifascists organized their movements for Black liberation in and through the fight against Fascism in all its forms. The tradition of Black revolutionary thought in the first half of the twentieth century, we will show, is inextricable from the rise of Anti-Black Fascism.

Chapter 3, "Double V Antifascism and World War II," shows how the first mass popular Antifascist movement in the United States was created and led by African Americans. The "Double Victory" campaign, aimed at ending racism in the US and Fascism around the world, tied together strands of Black radicalism from the prewar period into a new wartime militancy against anti-Blackness. Writers, artists, and cultural workers of all stripes joined the fray to create one of the most important movements for social justice in the history of Black arts and in the name of Antifascism.

Chapter 4, "Legal Antifascism: The 'We Charge Genocide' Campaign," details the campaign by the Civil Rights Congress (CRC) to indict the United States as a Fascist threat to Black Americans. The CRC's petition to the United Nations sought to deploy the UN's newly minted definition of genocide to apply to the lynchings, police shootings, and mob violence running through American history. "We Charge Genocide" would also become a touchstone for future Black Antifascist fighters.

Chapter 5, "Black Power Antifascism," demonstrates how Black Power's commitment to self-organizing and self-defense of Black life was inextricably tied to a theory of state-sponsored white supremacy as Fascist. Leading writers and organizers from Robert F. Williams to Huey P. Newton, George Jackson, and Angela Davis devoted some of their most important writing and organizing to combating Anti-Black Fascism in their theory of liberation.

Chapter 6, "4A Black Antifascism: On Anarchy, Autonomy, Antagonism, and Abolition," traces the trajectory of Black Antifascism from the end of the Black Power movement through the 1990s, with the rise of Anarchist and other direct-action forms of resistance to Anti-Black Fascism. Groups like the Black Liberation Army both built and revised theories of Antifascist organizing inherited from the Black Power movement. Assata Shakur's important place in the Black Radical Tradition derives in large measure from her contributions to Black Antifascism.

Chapter 7, "Abolitionist Antifascism," shows how Black Antifascist analysis of anti-Blackness and racial capitalism has been inherited and advanced by the mass movement for abolition. Abolitionist groups, such as Chicago's We Charge Genocide, and leading Abolitionist thinkers and organizers, such as Angela Davis and Ruth Wilson Gilmore, have kept alive a tradition of writing and thinking on the relationship of Black life to Fascism as both a theory of anti-Blackness and a structure of oppression. Abolition might also be the most recent revolutionary horizon in the Black Antifascist Tradition.

A Note on Method

In tracing the history of Black Antifascism and Anti-Black Fascism, we found it necessary to work on multiple fronts and develop an extensive archive of study. Our book is both historical and contemporary in nature. We engage scholarly and organizing/movement-building texts, centering the narratives and writings of revered historical figures like Ida B. Wells-Barnett and W. E. B. DuBois, while simultaneously highlighting some of the underdiscussed works of Black Anarchists like Lorenzo Kom'Boa Ervin and Martin Sostre. We turn to literature and autobiographies, cultural texts, political organizing materials, newspapers, oral histories, and social media archives to begin to recast

THE BLACK ANTIFASCIST TRADITION

American history as one deeply rooted in Anti-Black Fascism and, more important, to capture the multifaceted Black Antifascist Tradition from Reconstruction to the present.

At the center of this work are a multitude of writings that are explicitly Black Antifascist texts as well as those that we have *recast* as being part of the broader Black Antifascist Tradition. Among the earliest texts we engage are Ida B. Wells-Barnett's articles and pamphlets detailing the history of lynchings during and in the immediate years following Reconstruction. In examining Wells-Barnett's work through the lens of Anti-Black Fascism, we offer that her pamphlets not only were integral to illuminating the history of lynchings, but they also pointedly captured how lynchings were part of a larger apparatus of post-slavery white supremacy that relied upon law and authoritarian governance to maim, kill, and retrap Black people into bondage. Furthermore, her pamphlets challenged readers to take action and write their own counternarratives to challenge scientific racists, eugenicists, and law enforcement that presumed Black people to be criminals, deserving of legal and extrajudicial killings. Thus, we understand Wells-Barnett to both be a "crusader for justice" and a "premature Black Antifascist."

While our work largely focuses on American Anti-Black Fascism, the anticolonial writings of Frantz Fanon and Aimé Césaire, among others, were critical to helping us draw connections between colonization and Fascism. It was Césaire who surmised that European Fascism was the practice of colonization on Europe's own people. Additionally, Black internationalist writings and experiences, including those of Paul Robeson, Mary McLeod Bethune, and members of the Abraham Lincoln Brigade, helped underscore how African Americans understood US racial politics through the lens of Fascism. They returned home unapologetically proclaiming that the US was more alike than different from the Fascists of Europe. They considered the question: What good was it to fight Fascism abroad, only to be met with anti-Black Fascism at home?

The more explicit Black Antifascist figures and organizations of the Black Power era, such as the Black Panther Party (BPP), Robert F. Williams, Angela Davis, Assata Shakur, and George Jackson, wrote and organized extensively under the banner of Antifascism. We consider how the politics of Black Power uniquely shaped the Black Antifascist response to the inequality of the immediate post–civil rights era via the culmination of a "united front against Fascism," mutual aid work, self-defense, and the prison abolition movement. Over the last decade, there has been a major proliferation of scholarship and movement work taking up abolition as a serious framework for racial justice and addressing systemic racism and anti-Blackness. Abolition has long been a rallying cry and strategy used to upend systems rooted in Black death and suffering—Anti-Black Fascism, in other words—in an effort to radically reimagine them. We see the work and writings of Abolitionists like Mariame Kaba, Ruth Wilson Gilmore, Patrisse Khan-Cullors, William C. Anderson, Aviah Sarah Day, Shanice Octavia McBean, among a host of others, as indicative of the Black Antifascist Tradition.

We have drawn upon primary-source archival materials in hopes of restoring and recreating the Black Antifascist Tradition to public view. These include the Civil Rights Congress papers at the Schomburg Center for Research in Black Culture in New York City, the Thyra Edwards Collection at the Chicago History Museum, the Black Panther Party News Service Collection at the Oakland African American Museum and Library, and the digital repository the Freedom Archives. We are grateful to the archivists at these collections for their assistance in our work.

We want this book to be much more than a "historical reframing." For this reason, our work foregrounds various strategies and tactics employed by Black Antifascists, including anarchy, mutual aid, antagonism, abolition, and consciousness-building. The Black Antifascist Tradition tells us that Fascism cannot be reformed or legislated away; thus, in our examination of anarchists like the Black Liberation Army (BLA), we consider the role of anarchy in challenging Anti-Black Fascism. By further illuminating these responses to Fascism, we hope this text can also serve as a generative tool for grassroots organizers and activists.

Finally, much of our book takes up the law as a major tool in the Anti-Black Fascist toolbox. We work on both fronts, interrogating how Fascism is embedded within the law and simultaneously examining how

Black Antifascists have leveraged the law and legal systems (both domestic and international) to challenge Anti-Black Fascism.

The Black Antifascist Tradition aspires to be a body of work that compiles and animates the dynamism of Black activism that has always resisted and pushed back on the boot of Fascism. Acknowledging and remembering this long tradition that spans both space and time, we hope this work not only sparks renewed interest in studying Fascism, particularly within Black studies, but also empowers those at the grassroots to take up the tradition and become Antifascists themselves.

— CHAPTER 1 —

PREMATURE BLACK ANTIFASCISM

Ida B. Wells-Barnett, "Lynch Law," and the Conspiracy of Anti-Black Fascism

I**N 1892**, Frederick Douglass, abolitionist and women's rights advocate, wrote to "brave woman" Ida B. Wells-Barnett, praising her for the recent publication of *Southern Horrors: Lynch Law in All Its Phases*, offering proverbial flowers for the pioneering work. Douglass aptly captured the significance of Wells-Barnett's pamphlet, a body of work that both documented lynchings that occurred across the American South following Reconstruction and uncovered the major underpinnings of racial terrorism and violence. A number of Black women historians and Black feminists, including Paula Giddings, Mia Bay, Beverly Guy-Sheftall, Darlene Clark Hine, Brittney Cooper, Daina Berry and Kali Nicole Gross, to name a few, have long named Wells-Barnett's life and work as being foundational to the twentieth-century campaign against lynching, integral to the canon of Black feminist writings and politics, and at the center of the Black women's club movement.[1] Indeed, Wells-Barnett is unequivocally the "race woman" and "mother of the anti-lynching movement." However, Douglass's last remark in his correspondence to Wells-Barnett, "Even crime has power to reproduce itself and create conditions favorable to its own existence,'" picks up on an often underexamined aspect of her archive of work. Beyond documenting lynchings, Wells-Barnett uncovered something even more sinister. She painstakingly traced the unwritten rule of lynch law to the emergent formal legal system, detailing how state governors, jailers, and other levels of law enforcement aided white mobs' implementation of "lynch law in America."[2] Wells-Barnett understood lynch law to be part of a larger apparatus, both judicial and extrajudicial, explicitly born out of anti-Blackness. Both Douglass and Wells-Barnett foresaw the emergent legal system and phenomenon of lynching as major obstacles for the Reconstruction era and beyond.

Robin D. G. Kelley has noted that Cedric Robinson's Black Radical Tradition includes what Kelley calls "premature antifascists," a recognition of pre-WWII Black consciousness and political awareness that foresaw the rise of Fascism.[3] Drawing on their own lived experiences, Black people understood that the veneer of Fascism, which captivated many white elites and working class early on, would soon reveal itself to be antidemocratic and white supremacist in nature, an authoritarian monstrosity whose gaze would one day shift away from colonies, plantations, and Black communities.[4] Wells-Barnett's groundbreaking newspaper reporting in the *Chicago Daily*, the *Conservator*, the *Memphis Free Speech and Headlight* (which she co-owned and edited), among others, as well as her work in helping found the National Association for the Advancement of Colored People (NAACP) and the National Association for Colored Women (NACW), are often the major points of entry to engaging with her life as a "crusader for justice"; however, we see her body of work as an early clarion call against the strategies and tactics of Fascism. She is *the* premature Black Antifascist, who laid the foundation for the more explicitly Antifascist (in name) work of Du Bois, the National Negro Congress (NNC), Claudia Jones, Thelma Dale Perkins, Esther Cooper Jackson, Thyra Edwards, William Patterson, and others mentioned throughout this book. Lynchings were, and still are, one of several violent techniques of Fascism. Wells-Barnett recognized that these were not just wanton, isolated acts of white supremacist violence. Lynchings aided in the denial of civil rights and the overall suppression of democracy to Black people. At the time, the threat of lynching was weaponized as a means of forcing Black people back into subservience and bondage, at best; at worst, as a means of systematic eradication.

Wells-Barnett's writings detail the US genealogy of Fascism decades prior to the formal introduction of the term by Benito Mussolini.

Through her newspaper the *Free Speech*, pamphlets, lobbying to the federal government, and an international speaking tour, Wells-Barnett offered counternarratives to resist the erasure of the "strange fruit" phenomenon from the national and international press, as she vehemently believed that "the way to right wrongs is to turn the light of truth upon them." In *A Red Record*, Wells-Barnett's follow-up to *Southern Horrors*, she connected the early seeds of Fascism being sowed abroad to what Black people had long endured in the American South. She challenged, "Surely the humanitarian spirit of this country which reaches out to denounce the treatment of the Russian Jews, the Armenian Christians, the laboring poor of Europe, the Siberian exiles and the native women of India—will not longer refuse to lift its voice on this [lynchings] subject."[5] Wells-Barnett saw what was happening across the American South as having an uncanny resemblance to the pogroms ravaging Russian Jews and other acts of ethnic cleansing and genocide that were sweeping parts of Europe and Asia. Her observations helped draw international attention to these acts of terror and foregrounded that they did not happen in a vacuum but were influenced by a swirl of overlapping authoritarian, white supremacist, and religious politics within the state. In this regard, Wells-Barnett's archive of counternarratives represents one of the first major strategies of Black Antifascism—amplification: sounding the proverbial alarm alerting others to the rise of Fascism.

At the turn of the century, Wells-Barnett maintained great prominence and influence within various Black women's clubs, with many also taking up her antilynching campaign as hallmark initiatives. Part of Wells-Barnett's greater legacy, then, must be her foregrounding of Black Antifascism within Black women's activism. Black women's groups like the Neighborhood Union in Atlanta, Georgia, built upon Wells-Barnett's analytical framework, maintaining their own records on local lynchings and using them to lobby the federal government to sanction the extrajudicial crimes. Furthermore, Black women's clubs and Wells-Barnett rightly named gendered violence and misogyny/misogynoir as intrinsic features of Anti-Black Fascism. In this way, the Black women's club movement acted as an Antifascist chorus in helping

34 THE BLACK ANTIFASCIST TRADTION

amplify one of the early ills of Anti-Black Fascism. Black women's activism in this capacity stands as one of the most enduring post-slavery challenges to Anti-Black Fascism. From Wells-Barnett, Dorothy Height, Lugenia Burns Hope, and Mamie Till to the women and nonbinary organizers, leaders, and activists of #blacklivesmatter, Black women have passed the torch generation after generation, paving the way to the passage of the belated Emmett Till Antilynching Act of 2022. This chapter re-examines the history of the antilynching movement through the lens of the Black Antifascist Tradition, recasting the work of Wells-Barnett and the organizing within Black women's clubs as premature Black Antifascist activism.

Setting the *Red Record* and Uncovering the Conspiracy of "Lynch Law"

Between 1877 and 1950 an estimated 4,084 recorded lynchings—violent, often public, extrajudicial killings of an individual for the sake of terrorism, intimidation, or alleged punishment—occurred throughout the US South, with primarily Black women, men, and children as victims.[6] Countless lynchings went unrecorded. Following the abolition of slavery, lynchings became a phenomenon ingrained in the racial status quo of the Reconstruction era and among the most brutal techniques of violence employed as a means to intimidate the formerly enslaved and reassert white dominance across the American South and beyond. Public segregation, race riots, the rise of the Ku Klux Klan (KKK) and racial animus, Jim Crow laws, and incarceration were other modes in which white supremacy took shape during this period, and Wells-Barnett experienced and bore witness to them all. In May 1884, she boarded a train in Memphis, Tennessee, headed to Nashville, where she attended Fisk University, with a first-class ticket in hand. She was swiftly denied a seat in the first-class car and redirected to a second-class smoking car.[7] In a disavowal of early de facto and de jure racial segregation, Wells-Barnett refused the demands of the train crew and was forcibly removed; she bit one of the crew members on the way out. She later sued the railroad company and won five hundred dollars. The company appealed the decision, and the case was sent to the Tennessee Supreme Court, where the original decision in Wells-Barnett's favor was overturned. This was a seminal moment for Wells-Barnett, as she experienced the contradictions in the law, which effectively endorsed anti-Blackness and the treatment of Black people as a second-class citizenry undeserving of the same civil and human rights as their white counterparts. Wells-Barnett's case was tried just twelve years prior to the landmark Supreme Court decision in *Plessy v. Ferguson*, which would codify racial segregation in the supposed spirit of "separate but equal."

Prior to *Plessy*, Wells-Barnett worked as a public school teacher in Memphis and began her career as a journalist under the pseudonym "Iola," offering dissenting commentary on the conditions of the segregated schools at which she was employed. In 1891, she was fired from her teaching post by the Memphis Board of Education over her criticisms. This moment confirmed for Wells-Barnett that she needed to continue writing in an effort to provide counternarratives that would challenge the white supremacist status quo that she encountered at every turn. The following year, three of her friends—Thomas Moss, Calvin McDowell, and William "Henry" Stewart—were lynched by a mob. The three Black men owned and worked at a grocery store in Memphis, People's Grocery, the success of which drew the ire of nearby white business owners. The Black owner and store clerks were threatened with violence, should they continue to operate. During the initial attack, the men defended themselves by shooting a white male intruder. The three Black men were later arrested for their use of armed self-defense, and, before formal court proceedings could take place, they were dragged out of jail by a white mob and lynched. No one was ever punished for the extrajudicial crime. The brutal death of Wells-Barnett's friends was a turning point that deepened her crusade against lynchings. She would also go on to be the foster mother for Thomas Moss's daughter, Maureen Moss Browning.[8] In a speech she delivered to Tremont Temple in Boston, Massachusetts, on the aftermath of the lynching, she described the toll the event had on Black Memphians and spoke of a larger conspiracy at play:

> I have no power to describe the feeling of horror that possessed every member of the race in Memphis when the truth dawned

upon us that the protection of the law which we had so long enjoyed was no longer ours; all this had been destroyed in a night, and the barriers of the law had been thrown down, and the guardians of the public peace and confidence scoffed away into the shadows, and all authority given into the hands of the mob, and innocent men cut down as if they were brutes—the first feeling was one of utter dismay, then intense indignation . . . The power of the State, country, and city, the civil authorities and the strong arm of the military power were all on the side of the mob and of lawlessness . . . It was our first object lesson in the doctrine of white supremacy.[9]

Of the lynching cases documented and the statistical analysis included in A *Red Record*, Wells-Barnett surmised that an overwhelming number of the Black victims had been charged with murder, rape, or barn burning. She also recognized that successful Black businesses and business owners were frequent targets, as whites sought to stifle Black upward mobility. A significant portion of Wells-Barnett's writings spoke to the charge of rape, which she found to be particularly erroneous, suspicious, and indicative of a broader conspiracy. Allegations of violence, often sexual and against white women, were the most common unfounded justification for lynching Black men—"the myth of the Black rapist."[10] Wells-Barnett maintained that there was no intrinsic "character flaw" in Black men that predisposed them to sexual predation, underscoring that the narrative of Black sexual violence was not promoted to such

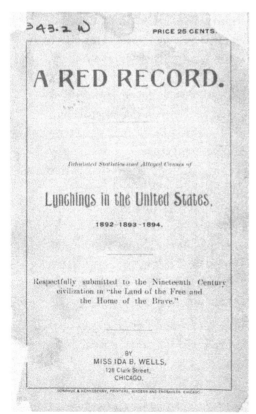

A Red Record by Ida B. Wells, circa 1894, Schomburg Center for Research in Black Culture, Manuscripts, Archives and Rare Books Division, The New York Public Library Digital Collections.

extents prior to the Civil War. Post Civil War, however, this was certainly a narrative promoted by KKK propaganda, eugenicists, and, most notoriously, in D. W. Griffith's film *The Birth of a Nation*. In both of her pamphlets and in many articles, Wells-Barnett refuted the allegations of sexual violence, noting that many were false claims and that the allegation of rape had been weaponized, as white men and mobs turned to violence in their quest to "chivalrously" protect white women and their presumed docility.[11] Lynchings were thus a response to white male fragility, which was also foundational to Anti-Black Fascism.

Wells-Barnett went even further, challenging notions of "true womanhood" (namely, white womanhood), arguing that some of the relationships between Black men and white women were consensual and, at times, instigated or coerced by the alleged white women victims. The 1892 incarceration of a Black man, Mr. Underwood, in Elyria, Ohio, for raping a white woman exemplified these claims. Several years into Mr. Underwood's prison sentence, the "victim" admitted to having personally invited Mr. Underwood inside her home. Soon after, she sat on Mr. Underwood's lap and consented to having sex with him. She had only shared this indiscretion with her husband out of fear that she had contracted a "loathsome disease" and/or would give birth to a Black baby.[12] As the victim's husband sought a divorce, Mr. Underwood was sentenced to over fifteen years in prison. Wells-Barnett deemed that there were "thousands of such cases throughout the South," and, while Mr. Underwood's life was spared (albeit forced back into bondage), other Black people would fare worse under similar conditions.[13]

Wells-Barnett's documentation is a reminder that Fascism as a political movement has always been profoundly racist *and* sexist, emboldened by appeals to defend and extend white supremacy and racial purity.[14] Fascism constantly looks for new ways to bolster or "purify" the white race while simultaneously eradicating, repressing, and commodifying all non-white human life. Thus, lynchings were not just about relegating Black people to a second-class citizenry; those motivated by unfounded anxiety around Black sexual prowess were very much invested in the control of women's bodies and the reproduction of white children, and whiteness by extension. As Ruwe Dalitso argues, eugenicists aided in the proliferation of anti-Black, particularly anti–Black male, rhetoric that called for the sterilization of Black people. While eugenicists would push for greater use of "non-lethal violence" like castrations, forced vasectomies, and female sterilization, their work is inextricably linked to the phenomenon of lynchings, Anti-Black Fascism, and European Fascism.[15] For example, American biologist and eugenicist Charles Davenport deemed "race mixture, unselected immigrants, and unequal rates of reproduction in various native groups" as being detrimental to the welfare of the nation and provided academic grounds to justify an ethos of anti-Blackness and anti-miscegenation, further influencing mob violence and legislation that allowed lynchings.[16] Davenport's work was so influential that he was later appointed to the editorial boards of two German "racial hygiene" (eugenics) journals, *Zeitschrift für Rassenkunde und ihrer Nachbargebiete* and *Zeitschrift für menschliche Vererbungs- und Konstitutionslehre*, thus directly connecting US eugenic practices and European blood-purity doctrine.[17]

As a Black woman, Wells-Barnett stood in direct opposition to many nineteenth-century notions of womanhood. She prided herself in working outside the home, she frequently traveled alone, and she vehemently challenged male journalists and politicians head-on when it came to seeking justice for victims of lynchings and the education of Black youth. However, her gendered analysis of lynchings and activism made her especially radical, even within the Black women's club movement. She aptly pointed out that the extreme efforts to protect white women's chastity, docility, and virtue had not been afforded to Black women and girls. In *Southern Horrors*, Wells-Barnett documented the rape of several Black girls by white men as a counterpoint and means of amplifying their stories in the name of justice. Throughout and following slavery, Black women and girls had been subjected to sexual violence at the hands of white men, yet seldom was the offense regarded as a crime, and it was certainly not seen as an act deserving of lynching.[18] In the case of Pat Hanifan, a white man who raped a young Black girl in Nashville, Hanifan was jailed for just six months and offered a job as a

PREMATURE BLACK ANTIFASCISM

detective in the city shortly after his release. In a second case of the rape of a Black girl in Nashville, the white male perpetrator was set to be lynched by a Black mob after the legal system failed to bring about justice. To thwart the Black mob, the state militia mounted cannons, and white citizens stood guard outside the perpetrator's home.[19] There was no justice, even extrajudicial, for Black women and girls, as they existed at the intersection of marginalized race and gender identities and were stereotyped as "promiscuous" and deserving of sexual violence by both Black and white men. Indeed, Anti-Black Fascism is emphatically both sexist and racist, maintaining a particular disdain for Black women and exemplifying what Moya Bailey has coined as *misogynoir*.[20] The double standard applied to sexual violence, the sexualized depiction of Black womanhood and girlhood, and the overall brutality of lynching would especially engender the activism of Black women in the antilynching campaign and the fight against Anti-Black Fascism.

The conspiracy of "lynch law" that Wells-Barnett outlines was not some far-fetched conspiracy but Anti-Black Fascism at work. At every turn, she uncovered fundamental characteristics of Fascism coalescing to bolster the overall movement, from the dual application of the law, an undergirding belief in white racial purity and superiority, state-supported white terrorism and violence, authoritarian governance, and suppression of democracy to sexism. The pattern of violence detailed by Wells-Barnett connected lynchings to how the Black individual had been "cheated of his ballot, deprived of civil rights or redress therefor in the civil courts," and "robbed of the fruits of his labor."[21] She understood how all these forms of anti-Black violence and injustice worked together, rendering Black life as one rooted in a second-class treatment.

Organizing against "Lynch Law"

In February 1898, Frazier Baker, the postmaster of Lake City, South Carolina, and his daughter were lynched. Wells-Barnett elevated her strategy of providing counternarratives in local newspapers and via her pamphlets, using those materials as evidence to lobby the federal government to introduce bold legislation that would outlaw lynchings. This

40   THE BLACK ANTIFASCIST TRADTION

strategy of appealing to presidents and members of Congress directly would continue for over a century and was largely led by Black women. In addition, Black Antifascists such as William Patterson would turn to international governing bodies to call for similar sanctioning after WWII and at the outset of the #blacklivesmatter movement. With the Baker case gaining attention in the Black press and organizing spaces, including the Ida B. Wells Woman's Club, Wells-Barnett appealed directly to President McKinley:

> For nearly twenty years lynching crimes, which stand side by side with Armenian and Cuban outrages, have been committed and permitted by this Christian nation. Nowhere in the civilized world save the United States of America do men, possessing all civil and political power, go out in bands of 50 and 5,000 to hunt down, shoot, hang or burn to death a single individual, unarmed and absolutely powerless. Statistics show that nearly 10,000 American citizens have been lynched in the past 20 years. To our appeals for justice the stereotyped reply has been that the government could not interfere in a state matter. Postmaster Baker's case was a federal matter, pure and simple. He died at his post of duty in defense of his country's honor, as truly as did ever a soldier on the field of battle. We refuse to believe this country, so powerful to defend its citizens abroad, is unable to protect its citizens at home. Italy and China have been indemnified by this government for the lynching of their citizens. We ask that the government do as much for its own.[22]

For Wells-Barnett, Anti-Black Fascism was a global phenomenon, as she once again drew comparisons to the atrocities happening in Armenia, Italy, and elsewhere, calling it reprehensible for the US to condemn lynchings that happened abroad while ignoring those in the American South. This sentiment was echoed in the activism of Mary McLeod Bethune, Wells-Barnett's contemporary, instrumental Black club woman, humanitarian, and pioneering educator. Bethune was elected to the National Association of Colored Women's Clubs (NACWC) in

1924 and was the founding president of the National Council of Negro Women (NCNW). Under her leadership, the NCNW emphasized forming connections with women activists from around the world, "maintained that human rights started at home," believed that "racism and sexism transcended national boundaries," and "saw an international mind as the pathway to solidarity, justice, and freedom for Black women both within the United States and without."[23] Bethune was in no way a radical leftist like Black women communists of the time, such as Claudia Jones and Grace P. Campbell.[24] Bethune was part of a cohort of Black middle-class women who defined "ideal" Negro womanhood, laying the groundwork for what Evelyn Brooks Higginbotham has called the "politics of respectability."[25] Bethune's notion of Black womanhood afforded her access to both national and international powers, including a friendship with first lady Eleanor Roosevelt and membership in the US delegation that chartered the United Nations. At the national level, Bethune was an ardent defender of democracy, recognizing that the full promise of democracy had never been extended to Black people. At the international level, she aligned herself with other Black delegates like Du Bois, who "connected colonialism with Jim Crow and America's fight against fascism with the fight against racism at home."[26] However, where Bethune often diverged from her Black male counterparts was around gender politics, bemoaning the all-white and/or all-male spaces, advocating for the explicit inclusion of Black women. Bethune challenged both misogynoir and the antidemocratic nature of the US—Anti-Black Fascism—head on. Her work is also a pointed example of how later Black feminists understood that Fascism "degrades women," as we discuss in the next chapter. As Michael O. West stated, "The struggle against imperialism, racism, and fascism intersected worldwide, and the African American woman activist, as a composite figure, was in the middle of it, battling patriarchy as well."[27]

Although Wells-Barnett's appeal to President McKinley was unsuccessful, similar appeals to Congress and future presidents continued for decades, coming from various parts of the country, largely authored by Black women's organizations. As documented in the work of Black women historians Mia Bay and Brittney Cooper, Wells-Barnett was integral to the development of the club movement, helping found several regional and local organizations, including the Alpha Suffrage Club and the aforementioned Ida B. Wells Woman's Club. In 1896, she co-founded the NACW alongside Mary Church Terrell, Frances Watkins Harper, Harriet Tubman, and others, with the mission to "Lift as We Climb." These organizations were much more than leisurely social groups, although they often gestured toward notions of Black elitism and respectability. Many of the organizations were heavily influenced by the early integrationist and assimilationist politics of the major race men of the twentieth century, W. E. B. Du Bois and Booker T. Washington, which often put Wells-Barnett, who was arguably much more radical than her peers, at odds with some of them. While those around her sought to work within the law and turned to the courts for justice, or like Bethune, leveraged international diplomacy, Wells-Barnett had no problem calling Southern whites "lawless liars," and she denounced proposals for racial integration. She was also a proponent of armed self-defense, having bought a pistol following the People's Grocery lynching, and called upon others to do the same, passionately asserting, "One better die fighting against injustice than to die like a dog or a rat in a trap."[28] Here, Wells-Barnett was also a "premature" Black Antifascist, anticipating the self-defense strategies of later Black Antifascists like Robert F. Williams and the Black Panther Party.

Despite these differences, Wells-Barnett's influence was undeniable. In 1918, the anti-lynching movement was in full swing, and Black women's efforts to lobby Congress were finally making some headway. Lugenia Burns Hope and other Black women affiliated with the Neighborhood Union, an Atlanta-based Black women's club largely comprising faculty wives from nearby Historically Black Colleges and Universities (HBCUs), lobbied Congress, again decrying the conditions and inhumanity produced by lynch law and Anti-Black Fascism. They argued that lynchings were "worse than Prussianism" and the lawlessness of lynching "decreased faith in the boasted justice of our so-called democratic institutions."[29] The women foregrounded early twentieth-century anti-Blackness, declaring, "We are the one group of American people, than whom there is none more loyal, which is marked out for discrimination, humiliation, and abuse. In great patriotic and humanitarian movements, in public carriers, in federal service, the treatment accorded us is humiliating, dehumanizing and reprehensible in the extreme."[30] The Neighborhood Union's letter called for the right to vote and the introduction of legislation that would sanction lynching, uniting the two major initiatives of the Black women's club movement.

Later in 1918, Missouri representative Leonidas Dyer introduced the first antilynching bill to Congress—the Dyer Bill. Dyer represented a St. Louis community that neighbored the predominantly Black and industrial city of East St. Louis, Illinois. Dyer's bill was a direct response to a race riot that had occurred the previous summer as well as to the decades of lobbying led by Wells-Barnett, Black club women, the nascent NAACP, and others. East St. Louis was a major settling point for Black people fleeing the South during the early part of the Great Migration, as many were able to secure work in factories. Throughout the summer of

Mrs. Lugenia Burns Hope and Neighborhood Union Group, circa 1920, Neighborhood Union collection, Atlanta University Center Robert W. Woodruff Library.

44 **THE BLACK ANTIFASCIST TRADTION**

1917, racial tensions were high, as striking white workers were replaced by Black workers. In July, the whole ordeal erupted. For three days, the city of East St. Louis was ravaged by a white mob, aided by law enforcement and the military. In the early hours of the massacre, homes were burned and shot up, Black citizens were yanked out of trolley cars on their way home and bludgeoned. Many attempted to flee the community in search of refuge; however, local police shut down a nearby bridge, trapping people in the ongoing slaughter. In a desperate attempt to escape, some tried to swim across the Mississippi River, which resulted in several drownings. A local reporter called the event "a man hunt, conducted on a sporting basis," revealing that "'get a nigger' was the slogan" shared across the mob as Black people in the city were massacred.[31] More than one hundred Black men, women, and children were killed, and the city was completely leveled, reduced to ashes. W. E. B. Du Bois would call the incident a "pogrom."[32] Race riots represented an evolution of lynchings, and this advanced technique of Fascist violence exploded during the 1910s and 1920s. This evolution illustrated that lynchings were indeed genocidal acts, as entire communities of Black people were killed. Harry Haywood, an influential Black Communist activist, later called the 1919 Chicago race riot—and the overall inequality that Black people experienced in the city—a "holocaust."[33] At every turn, major Black activists and thinkers of the time were building on Wells-Barnett's archive of lynching violence and the conspiracy of lynch law. Moreover, signaling their commitments as "premature Black Antifascists," they used language (*holocaust*, *pogrom*) that would later be used to explicitly underscore the atrocities of European Fascism.

The legislation proposed in the Dyer Bill quickly became the focus of the antilynching movement. Many Black activists saw the bill as having the potential not only to sanction white mob violence but also to challenge the authoritarian state governments and local law enforcement that colluded with mobs, thus issuing a major blow to Anti-Black Fascism. In the aforementioned letter from the Neighborhood Union, the members referenced both the East St. Louis and Houston race riots of 1917, pleading, "We cannot help seeing white soldiers who massacred our black brothers and sisters in East St. Louis have gone scot free. We cannot help seeing that our black brothers who massacred white citizens in Houston have paid the most ignominious penalty that can come in this country to a man in uniform."[34] In 1922, as KKK membership and white terrorism ballooned, the Dyer Bill died on the Senate floor after being filibustered by Southern Democrats. Similar proposed legislation, like the 1935 Wagner-Costigan bill, would be introduced later, with similar aims of protecting Black people from white-mob and state-sanctioned violence.

More than a century after Wells-Barnett's friends were lynched in Memphis, the US Senate has only now, in 2022, passed key legislation criminalizing lynchings.[35] Even with its passage, lynchings continue to occur unchecked, many in the form of anti-Black, state-sanctioned police violence. Wells-Barnett understood that what law enforcement was not able to do, the mob would, and vice versa, creating a symbiotic bond between the two. This insidious relationship has become more pronounced, as government watchdog groups and investigative journalists have detailed how law enforcement ranks have increasingly been infiltrated by far-right and neo-Nazi members over the last twenty years, signaling that Anti-Black Fascism is very much alive and well.[36] These findings have been echoed by a number of anti–police brutality grassroots groups, such as the Every 36 Hours Campaign and Malcolm X Grassroots Movement (MXGM), which organize "in the tradition of *On Lynching* by Ida B. Wells-Barnett and *We Charge Genocide* by William Patterson." In the 2012 report *Operation Ghetto Storm*, Kali Akuno, cofounder of Cooperation Jackson, and members of MXGM provide a detailed report on the "extrajudicial killings of 313 Black people by police, security guards, and vigilantes," arguing, "like in the years of lynching, there is no geographic sanctuary," decrying this phenomenon as an epidemic of "modern day lynchings" that some would suggest amounts to systematic genocide.[37] The 2014 killing of Michael Brown Jr. by Ferguson, Missouri, police officer Darren Wilson served as a major catalyst for the #blacklivesmatter movement and reinforced the conclusions of *Operation Ghetto Storm*. The fact that police officers were allowed to act as "judge, jury, and executioner," disproportionately killing Black people, often over petty or nonviolent offenses, while receiving special protections under state and federal laws, like California's Police Officers' Bill of Rights (POBR), indicated yet again that lynch law, or Anti-Black Fascism, was still in effect, had evolved, and was escalating.

As Anti-Black Fascism has evolved since Reconstruction and the race riots of the 1910s, so has the tradition of Black Antifascism, and much credit must be given to Wells-Barnett's pioneering work. There is no NAACP antilynching crusade, Deacons of Defense and Justice, We Charge Genocide, *Operation Ghetto Storm*, or #blacklivesmatter without Wells-Barnett. Furthermore, many of the Black Antifascists explored in later chapters of this work, including W. E. B. Du Bois, Paul Robeson, William Patterson, and Robert F. Williams, rightly hark back to her work during their own political formations. There is much we owe to Ida B. Wells-Barnett—race woman, mother of the antilynching movement, crusader for justice, *and* premature Black Antifascist.

— CHAPTER 2 —

ANTICOLONIAL, PAN-AFRICANIST AND COMMUNIST ANTIFASCISM

"Being aware of what the Fascist Italian government did to the Ethiopians, and also the way that I and all the rest of the Negroes in this country have been treated ever since slavery, I figured I had a pretty good idea of what fascism was."

> **—Crawford Morgan,** Young Communist League and Abraham Lincoln Brigade[1]

"Every colonial nation carries the seeds of fascist temptation in its bosom . . . There is no doubt in the minds of those who have lived through it that colonialism is one variety of fascism."

> **—Albert Memmi,** *The Colonizer and the Colonized*[2]

"Today 150 million Negroes, knit into the world economy infinitely more tightly than their ancestors of a hundred years ago, will far surpass the work of that San Domingo half-million in the work of social transformation. The continuous risings in Africa; the refusal of the Ethiopian warriors to submit to Mussolini; the American Negroes who volunteered to fight in Spain in the Abraham Lincoln Brigade . . . these lightnings announce the thunder."

> **—C. L. R. James,** "Revolution and the Negro"[3]

"Fascists is Jim Crow peoples, honey."

> **—Langston Hughes,** "Love Letter from Spain"[4]

48   THE BLACK ANTIFASCIST TRADTION

IN OCTOBER 1896, Ethiopian troops defeated Eritrean Italian forces attempting to turn Ethiopia, then known as Abyssinia, into an Italian protectorate. The defeat represented the first time since the Haitian Revolution of 1804 that a Black nation had defeated a European power set on cannibalizing its independence. In the same year, the US Supreme Court in its decision in *Plessy v. Ferguson* legally enshrined "separate but equal" conditions in the American South, ruling that interstate train cars could be separated by race. The decision formally launched the brutal US racist system of segregation known as Jim Crow and swung open even wider the door for the terrors and lynchings that had inflamed the South with the collapse of federal Reconstruction in 1877.

The Black Antifascist Tradition that emerged in the twentieth century sprang from these twinned moments. Those African Americans who traveled to Spain to fight Franco's Fascist forces in the 1930s, like Crawford Morgan, quoted earlier, were often spurred by memories of European aggression against the African homeland and the brutalizing experiences of Black Americans in the United States. Langston Hughes spun this history into poetry when he declared that Fascists were "Jim Crow peoples," but he also meant to signify what Black people understood about Fascism that others did not: that it was a sequel to the immiserations of Africans in the diaspora under capitalist modernity, offering them incipient awareness of Aimé Césaire's notion that Fascism was the political violence of the white Western world come home to roost.

This chapter will examine Black radicals in the African diaspora who developed and braided three currents of thought and organizing practice into the first momentous phase of the Black Antifascist Tradition: the Anticolonial Movement, begun after the 1885 partition of Africa; the Pan-African Movement, formally launched in the immediate wake of both the Italian defeat in Ethopia and the emergence of US Jim Crow; and the Black Communist Movement, spurred by the 1917 Bolshevik Revolution in Russia. Together, these moments produced an explosion of political practice, cultural innovation, and organizing strategy for dismantling the system of racial capitalism upon which Fascism as a world system depends. Black Antifascism at its inception should be understood as the beginning of a long strand of independent Black political imagining of how to create the conditions for overthrowing racial capitalism itself.

In 1915, W. E. B. Du Bois wrote in the *Atlantic Monthly*, "In a very real sense, Africa is a prime cause of this terrible overturning of civilization which we have lived to see."[5] Du Bois was referring to the world war then raging across Europe, but his carefully chosen phrase "overturning of civilization" also indexed what Albert Memmi calls the "fascist temptation" represented by the war itself. Du Bois, who, in 1900, had cofounded the Pan-African Federation in London in response to Europe's partition of Africa, described Germany's annexation of African territories as compensation for being shut out of the colonizing game by the US Monroe Doctrine—which employed the very argument Hitler made later to justify the annexation of Eastern Europe in the Nazis' notorious *Lebensraum* ("living space") plan. He also cited Italian wars already waged in Ethiopia and Tripoli, as well as German and Dutch wars against South Africa, as examples of what Marx and Engels called "primitive accumulation" intended to generate wealth for Europe's capitalist states. Yet, it was Du Bois's attention to the *means* of African conquest that spoke most directly to the essay's prediction about the shape "not simply . . . of war to-day but the menace of wars to-morrow":

> The methods by which this continent has been stolen have been contemptible and dishonest beyond expression. Lying treaties, rivers of rum, murder, assassination, mutilation, rape, and torture have marked the progress of Englishman, German, Frenchman, and Belgian on the dark continent.[6]

For Du Bois, World War I's annihilative methods of civilizational "overturning" were the African seeds of Fascist governmentality now flowering in Europe. In 1941, as Hitler rampaged through Europe, Du

Bois returned to this theme: "If Hitler wins . . . Africa will be parceled out between Germany and Italy. Its people will be subjected to an attempted caste system resembling slavery, except that they will be trained to certain modern techniques; techniques which if they are at all valuable to the conqueror, will mean his eventual disaster."[7] Du Bois's prescience helps explain how and why, between the writing of these essays (1915 and 1941), the Black Antifascist Tradition developed an African-centered political epistemology to define its understanding of and opposition to Fascism. Black citizens of the world watched in horror as Germany committed the first twentieth-century genocide in its newly annexed colony of Southwest Africa (now Namibia). Between 1904 and 1907, Germany attempted to enslave and exterminate the Indigenous Herero and Namaqua people, as well as groups of rebellious Khoikhoi, using techniques of murder, rape, and medical experimentation. Germany likewise created the twentieth century's first "internment camps"—modeled, in part, on the camps created by the US to restrict Native Americans violently removed from their territories—and submitted the Indigenous population to forced labor. This technique would be used against Jews, Slavs, and others by the Third Reich.[8] After World War I, the League of Nations assigned the German colony to become a mandate of South Africa, prompting Hitler to proclaim later that there would never be "another 1918."

Also during World War I, Black Americans and Black colonial subjects witnessed portents of Fascism as ground troops in segregated armies fought on the side of ruling elites. French Senegalese soldiers assigned to the Rhineland were accused of sexual crimes against white German women, triggering a racist panic dubbed by the Nazis the "Black Horror" or "Black Disgrace." Hitler later blamed Jews for bringing Blacks into German lands and used the threat of "negrification" to whip up anti-Black racism as a component of Third Reich ideology.[9] Meanwhile, soldier Harry Haywood, soon to be a member of the US Communist Party, discovered the US Army's *Secret Information Bulletin Concerning Black American Troops* while serving on the European Front in a Jim Crow military unit. As Haywood recalled later, the *Bulletin*

ANTICOLONIAL, PAN-AFRICANIST, AND COMMUNIST ANTIFASCISM 51

read, in part: "Although a citizen of the United States, the black man is regarded by the white American as an inferior being with whom relations of business or service only are possible . . . Familiarity on the part of white women with black men is furthermore a source of profound regret to our experienced colonials, who see in it an overweening menace to the prestige of the white race."[10] Upon his return to the US after the war, Haywood was caught in the crosshairs of the Chicago race riot of 1919, in which whites murdered twenty-three Black people and injured more than three hundred over a six-day rampage on the city's South Side, one of twenty-six such pogroms in the US during that "Red Summer." In his autobiography, *A Black Communist in the Freedom Struggle*, Haywood described the Chicago riot as a "holocaust"; it was, he wrote, a "pivotal point in my life . . . I began to see that I had to fight; I had to commit to struggle against whatever it was that made racism possible."[11]

Haywood's turn to Communism and his lifelong commitment to fighting Fascism were one and the same solution to his American holocaust. For Haywood and thousands of others, Black Antifascism became a way to rescue the world from a set of perilous, life-threatening, binary choices: capitalism or barbarism, colonialism or independence, Fascism or democracy. In turn, Pan-Africanism, Communism, and Anticolonialism became tools to build an independent Black Antifascism that would attempt a third way forward toward Black liberation. Not surprisingly, the first to enter this tradition in full force were Black former colonial subjects.

A leading example was George Padmore. Padmore was born Malcolm Ivan Meredith Nurse in Trinidad in 1903, then a British colony. He attended the HBCUs Fisk University and Howard University in the US before joining the Communist Party of the United States (CPUSA) in 1927. In 1929, he traveled to the Soviet Union, where he headed the Negro Bureau of the Red International of Labor Unions (RILU). In 1930, from posts in Austria and Germany, he began editing *The Negro Worker*, a journal of the International Trade Union Committee of Negro Workers (ITUCNW), formed by the Communist International (Comintern) in Moscow. It was the task of the ITUCNW and *The Negro*

Worker to bring workers from the Caribbean, Africa, and what was then known as the Third World into closer contact with the labor struggles of workers in Europe and the US. The journal covered conditions of Black unemployment in the US and accounts of the ongoing US military occupation of Haiti, begun in 1914. In 1933, *The Negro Worker* was shut down when ultranationalist gangs stormed its offices: the Nazis had come to power. Padmore was ordered to spend several months in a German prison before being deported to England.

Padmore used these experiences to help form the epicenter of a new Black Antifascism that would couple his Communist training to a rising Anticolonial and Pan-African movement. Padmore had joined the Comintern because he believed the Soviet Union would help build the workers' international that could defeat capitalism and incipient European Fascism. When Trinidad's Governor Hollis tried to ban circulation of *The Negro Worker* on the island in 1932 to prevent trade union organizing, the journal referred to him as "Trinidad's Mussolini."[12] But when the Comintern ordered closure of the ITUCNW in 1933, Padmore concluded that Stalin was trying to "put the brake upon the anti-imperialist work" and "sacrifice the young national liberation movements in Asia and Africa."[13] Padmore resigned from the Comintern. His disillusionment with Stalinism came to a head in 1935 when Italy invaded Ethiopia. Italy and the Soviet Union had signed a nonaggression pact in 1933. After the invasion, the Soviets continued to send oil to support the Italian invasion. Padmore felt that Stalin had undercut the very fight against Fascism to which Socialism remained the best alternative.

What was needed, Padmore decided, was an independent movement against Fascism built by Africans in the diaspora, what Minkah Makalani calls a "new discourse of black internationalism."[14] That discourse came about through Padmore's collaboration with his childhood friend and fellow Trinidadian C. L. R. James. James had moved to London in 1931, where he immediately established himself as a leader in the British Trotskyist movement and in the center of a community of radical Black diasporic intellectuals that included Marcus Garvey's widow, Amy Ashwood Garvey. In July 1935, as Italian troops gathered for their assault on Ethiopia, Garvey and James established in London the International African Friends of Ethiopia (IAFE). The IAFE followed the lead of West Africans and Caribbeans who had called for boycotts of Italian businesses to protest the invasion and encouraged Trinidadian and South African workers not to service Italian ships. The IAFE declared brazenly that it would "assist by all means in its power, in the maintenance of the territorial integrity and the political independence of Abyssinia."[15]

By the end of 1935, Padmore was in London working closely with the IAFE. For Padmore, Italy's invasion of Ethiopia revealed race as central to Europe's Fascist and colonial projects. For the NAACP's journal, *Crisis*, Padmore wrote that the invasion was part of a long history of "white nations . . . joining hands in assigning parts of Africa to whichever one stands in need of colonies"[16]—a statement planting Fascism's roots in the 1885 Berlin Conference, the partition of Africa, and the inter-imperial rivalry of World War I. Padmore's position was a revision of his Comintern line from 1931 that Ethiopia (then Abyssinia) was a "feudal oligarchy" in need of proletarian internal revolution, a line also heralded by Black Communist James Ford until the time of Italy's invasion.[17] This shift, from a Comintern-directed to a Pan-African analysis, was a key tipping point in the creation of a Black Antifascist international. In fact, also working with the IAFE in London at this time was a young Jomo Kenyatta, later to lead the independence struggle of Kenya and become both its first president and a leader of the Pan-African Movement. Writing as an IAFE representative in *Labour Monthly*, the newspaper of the Communist Party of Great Britain, Kenyatta proclaimed, "To support Ethiopia is to fight Fascism."[18]

The work of the IAFE in London was part of a rapidly emerging Black Antifascist international. In September 1935, two thousand people attended a meeting in support of Ethiopia at Glover Memorial Hall in Lagos, Nigeria.[19] In Port Au Prince, Trinidad, in October, the National Welfare Culture and Social Association met and "called on all Negroes to boycott French and Italian goods and stevedores were asked to refuse to unload Italian ships."[20] In Morocco, the Caribbean poet Claude McKay took part in a boycott of Italian businesses.[21] These actions resounded with C. L. R. James's calls from London for "workers' sanctions" against Italy. Seeking to build a Pan-African workers' international against Fascism, the Trotskyist James exhorted workers of the world, "Organize yourselves independently, and by your own sanctions and the use of your own power, assist the Ethiopian people."[22]

By 1937, organizing against Italy's invasion of Ethiopia had produced permanent structures that connected the links between Fascism, capitalism, and colonialism. In that year, Padmore, Garvey, and Kenyatta became chair and vice chairs of the new International African Service Bureau (IASB) based in London. Its slogan was to "Educate, Co-operate, Emancipate" millions of Black workers in the diaspora under threat from European aggression and colonial exploitation. In the same year, Padmore spelled out the IASB analysis of fascism in *Crisis*, the journal of the NAACP. In "Hitler, Mussolini and Africa," published in September, Padmore argued that Germany and Italy sought to resolve capitalist crises within their national borders by exporting "surplus" populations to their African colonies while extracting African resources and exploiting African labor to build their war machines. In an uncanny echo of Du Bois's 1915 "African Roots of War" essay, Padmore wrote, "It is no exaggeration to say that there never was a period in the history of postwar Europe when the issue of peace or war has been so inseparably bound up with the scramble for colonies as at the present time."[23] Padmore's essay and the formation of the IAFE showed that Black Antifascism was beginning to merge Pan-Africanism and Marxism into a programmatic whole that equated Fascism and colonialism and saw mass Black organizing across the diaspora as the only solution. Those messages would reach far and wide, continuing to take new shape, including within the shores of North America.

James Yates had just left a speech by New York congressman Adam Clayton Powell in Harlem's Abyssinian Baptist Church on October 2, 1935, when he noticed an "electric feeling in the air."[24] A crowd was

ANTICOLONIAL, PAN-AFRICANIST, AND COMMUNIST ANTIFASCISM 55

rapidly assembling at a nearby park, and an unusually large number of cops swirled in the streets. Yates stopped and asked a man what was happening. "Why, man, don't you know," he responded, "that Italy has invaded the homeland of Ethiopia?"[25] Yates was born in a small mill town in Mississippi. His grandmother was enslaved. When he was six years old, a KKK lynching took place in Shubuta, near his home. When he was about twelve, his Uncle Willie was nearly lynched by a white mob, saved only when members of the family armed themselves with guns to fend off the lynchers. From these lessons, Yates determined to go up North, where "[he'd] heard some freedom was."[26]

Yates's crash course in Klan racism, working-class Black life, and self-defense drew him up North into political radicalism and labor organizing. Inspired partly by the case of Angelo Herndon—a Black Communist sentenced to a chain gang, freed in part by the defense of the Communist Party—Yates joined the CPUSA and became an organizer with Dining Car Employees Union 370.

Just six weeks before Yates walked out of Abyssinian Baptist in Harlem, the Seventh World Congress of the Comintern had met in Moscow to declare its "Popular Front" policy to unite classes across the world in an effort to defeat Fascism and protect the Soviet Union. Yates explained his own Antifascist sympathies this way, while watching an Antifascist speaker at a Communist rally in New York City:

> We Blacks had our own fascism to contend with. The Ku Kluxers and lynchers here at home were an ever-present threat. All the time he was speaking, I was back in Mississippi as a boy, seeing five men and four women dangling from a bridge—lynched.[27]

For African Americans, well before Mussolini's invasion, Ethiopia had become a symbol for the "homeland" that slavery had taken from them. It was also a symbolic touchstone for Black Christians, the so-called African Jerusalem, as one of the first countries in the world to adopt Christianity. The great eighteenth-century African American poet Phillis Wheatley, kidnapped from West Africa, brought to America as a slave, and converted to Christianity, called herself an Ethiopian,

56   **THE BLACK ANTIFASCIST TRADTION**

in reference to the biblical injunction that Ethiopia "shall soon stretch out her hands to God" (a reference to Psalm 68:31), an image meant to bridge and lament her African free past and exilic status as an American slave. David Walker's 1830 "Appeal" to "Coloured Citizens of the World," the first important Black Nationalist text of the nineteenth century, summoned the "God of the Etheopeans" for assistance against "white Christians of America, who hold us in slavery."[28] James Yates's stroll that day from the Abyssinian Baptist Church to a Harlem rally to save Ethiopia was, thus, also a journey along a diasporic timeline of Black Antifascism taking root in America.

Indeed, Italy's attack on Ethiopia lit the fuse of Black Antifascism in the US. As Robin D. G. Kelley has put the matter, "The defense of Ethiopia did more than any other events in the 1930s to internationalize the struggles of black people in the United States."[29] On July 10, 1935, an emergency meeting for Ethiopia of Southside Communists in Chicago drew more than 1,100 delegates, including members of the Black YWCA, Unemployed Councils, the League Against War and Fascism, and Black Nationalist groups.[30] At that conference, the Joint Committee for the Defense of Ethiopia was formed. Plans were made for a mass Hands Off Ethiopia! Parade, on August 31, 1935. A demonstration was also called in front of the Italian consulate on before the parade. On the day of the parade, ten thousand "Negro and white enemies of war," as described by the Communist Party's *Daily Worker*, marched in solidarity against the Italian Fascist threat. Chicago police, especially the notorious anticommunist "Red Squads," turned out in full, beating protesters at every turn. Despite the attacks, Harry Haywood exhorted demonstrators to march on, "scoring Chicago's Mayor Kelly and Chief Allman for importing Mussolini's tactics into the Southside."[31] Meanwhile, C. L. R. James's call for "workers' sanctions" was heeded by the multiracial US National Maritime Union (NMU), which refused to load steel-laden ships headed to Italy.[32]

The most significant permanent development for Black Antifascism to emerge from the 1935 protests was the formation, in February 1936, of the National Negro Congress (NNC). Organized by the Communist

ANTICOLONIAL, PAN-AFRICANIST, AND COMMUNIST ANTIFASCISM 57

Party, the NNC was headquartered on Chicago's South Side and became a primary organ for radical Black opposition to Italian Fascism. Socialist labor leader and journalist A. Philip Randolph delivered the keynote address at its opening session. The NNC also called for increased support for Ethiopia, linking the request to a resolution opposing lynching and calling for continued support for arrested Communist labor organizer Angelo Herndon and the Scottsboro Boys. By 1936, the Scottsboro case of nine Black working-class boys falsely accused of rape in Alabama had become a dominant focus of the Black Antifascist struggle. In 1933, a "Local Antifascist Conference" organized in Rockford, Illinois, by the Unemployed Council there had passed a resolution condemning the arrest and false conviction of the Scottsboro Nine. Albert Einstein, soon to be a leading voice against German Fascism, signed a letter from Berlin in 1931 pleading for the state of Alabama not to execute the Scottsboro Boys.[33]

Support for Ethiopia also charged through Black cultural communities. As early as 1922, the Ethiopian Art Theater had been founded in Chicago as an African American theater company. Two years later, a National Ethiopian Art Theater was founded in New York City. Italy's 1935 invasion prompted the "living newspaper" project within the New Deal's Federal Theater Project (FTP) to attempt to stage a theatrical documentary play, *Ethiopia*, to rally support against Mussolini's invasion. According to scholar Benjamin Balthaser, the production was to have included Ethiopian actors participating in the Negro Theater Unit of the FTP.[34] But the play was censored when the federal government issued an order prohibiting the representation of heads of state.[35] In January 1936, radical Communist sympathizer, singer, and actor Paul Robeson, en route to England to make a film about the Portuguese exploitation of Africa, told the *New York Herald Tribune*, "My sympathy is all with the Ethiopians. It would seem that those people could get along without the kind of 'civilizing' that European nations do with bombs and machine guns . . . I believe that African states will be free some day. It may come about through partial withdrawal of European power, or there may be a sudden overturn."[36]

THE BLACK ANTIFASCIST TRADTION

Robeson's invocation of the battle for Ethiopia as the starting point for a possible African anticolonial revolution captured the imaginative Zeitgeist of a new Black Antifascist moment in history. For political radicals like Robeson, Italy's Fascist invasion was a call to put their political education to use in a broader assault against racial capitalism. An unheralded but representative example of how African Americans answered this call is Thyra Edwards. Edwards was born into poverty in Texas in 1897, the granddaughter of runaway slaves. She was teaching high school in 1917, after graduating from Houston (Texas) Colored High School, when the so-called Camp Logan Riot occurred. As described by the Zinn Education Project, the "riot" was an organized pogrom against Black soldiers stationed at Houston's Camp Logan, after Corporal Charles Baltimore was beaten by police for attempting to investigate a case of police brutality against an African American woman dragged by cops from her home. Outraged by the beating, Black soldiers rose up. A lynch mob soon formed. At Fort Sam Houston in San Antonio, more than one hundred Black soldiers from Camp Logan were convicted of crimes, and nineteen Black soldiers were executed outside San Antonio, thirteen by hanging.[37]

Like Harry Haywood's experience of the "Red Summer" of 1919 and James Yates's proximity to the Shubuta lynching, the Houston holocaust was a turning point in the life of Thyra Edwards. She and her sister Thelma moved north to Gary, Indiana, in 1920, seeking escape from Jim Crow. There, Edwards moved from teaching to social work, helping to organize Black steelworkers after U.S. Steel used Black strikebreakers to bust the 1919 steel strike. In the aftermath of the strike, KKK officials swept into office in Gary's local elections. Edwards committed herself to fighting this local form of Anti-Black Fascism. She moved to Chicago and began an independent study of Marxism, including the works of Lenin, Trotsky, and Emma Goldman. She studied labor and befriended A. Philip Randolph, becoming a regular reader of his Socialist magazine, *The Messenger*. Eventually, Edwards earned a fellowship from Randolph's Brotherhood of Sleeping Car Porters to conduct field investigation on labor and housing conditions in Denmark. From

ANTICOLONIAL, PAN-AFRICANIST, AND COMMUNIST ANTIFASCISM 59

1933 to 1934 she traveled across Europe, including one week in Nazi Germany, where she wished to see and report up close on the rise of Fascism. Traveling alone by train near Hamburg, she spied a Nazi passenger and got a whiff of Fascism back home, writing, "He might have been a Holy Roller, Jumper or Grand Kleagle of the Klu Kux Klan."[38] She traveled to Oxford, England, in the same year to meet with Indian students to discuss the Anticolonial Movement, noting, while there, that "Fascism was growing openly like a virulent sore in England under the dramatic direction of Sir Oswald Mosley."[39]

Edwards was already a committed Antifascist when Black Americans rose up for Ethiopia. In 1936, after returning from Europe, she spoke at an NNC meeting, at which she praised Danish workers for contributing fifty thousand dollars to support Ethiopia and warned that Italy's invasion would encourage Nazi Germany to attack Liberia.[40] Like her counterparts C. L. R. James and George Padmore in the UK, Edwards understood European Fascism as a colonial and imperial weapon against workers in the African diaspora. For Edwards, the outbreak of Spain's civil war against its democratically elected Republic came as no surprise: the revolt against the Republic of Fascist Spanish troops in its occupied Moroccan colony seemed a sequel to Mussolini's war against Ethiopia—Europe's colonial fever again coming home to roost.

In 1937, Edwards leaped into the international fray of Black Antifascism: she traveled to Paris to participate in the Anti-Imperialist International Congress. There, she met American Communists William and Louise Patterson, Afro-Cuban poet Nicolás Guillén, and the African American poet Langston Hughes and watched the unveiling of Pablo Picasso's painting *Guernica*, commemorating the recent Fascist bombing massacre in that Spanish town.[41] In October, Edwards entered Spain from France on behalf of the Social Workers' Committee to Aid Spanish Democracy. Her mission was to report on the conditions of children in Valencia, Barcelona, and Puigcerda who had been separated from their families by Fascist bombing campaigns. In Barcelona, Edwards stayed at the Rosa Luxemberg children's colony under nightly Fascist bombardment. About the ongoing war, she wrote:

It is interesting mainly because we are not on an inter-racial, save the Negro crusade but rather on an inter-national commission concerned with freedom and democracy for all kinds of people. Just now the Spanish people happen to be symbolic of all the rest of us. And certainly there isn't going to be any freedom and equality for Negroes until and unless there is a free world.[42]

In the same month, Edwards attended the National Assembly of Spanish Women Against War and Fascism as a delegate of the NNC. Also attending, according to Edwards's biographer Gregg Andrews, was the iconic Spanish Antifascist Communist Dolores Ibarurri, who urged the crowd to cheer, "Viva la raza Negra! (Long live the Black Race!)"[43] Before leaving for Spain, Edwards had written for the League Against War and Fascism, "No force in the world today so threatens the position and security of women as does the rising force of fascism. Fascism degrades women."[44] Edwards was likely referring to Fascist policies, such as in Mussolini's Italy, where abortion had been criminalized as a threat to the reproduction of the Italian citizens needed to build the Fascist state. Her presence in Spain, like that of her compatriots Louise Thompson and Salaria Kea, was part of her commitment to building what scholar Erik S. McDuffie calls the "black women's international."[45]

Edwards also interviewed Black soldiers at the front who had joined the Abraham Lincoln Brigade volunteers to fight with the Loyalists to the Republic. Among her interviewees was Basilio Cueria y Obrit, a Cuban-born professional baseball player who had moved to New York City and joined the Communist Party. "In our trenches we fight fascism," he told Edwards. "If we're defeated the working class of the world is defeated."[46] This would not be the last of Edwards's Antifascist organizing efforts.

Black Volunteers in the Abraham Lincoln Brigade

A still hidden beating heart of twentieth-century Black Antifascism is the African Americans who traveled to Spain to fight the Fascist Franco government during the Spanish Civil War. Nearly one hundred Black

Americans, and others in the diaspora, arrived in 1937 to take up arms in integrated militias named in the US for the American president who had formally emancipated the enslaved. As Abraham Lincoln Brigade volunteer Crawford Morgan said in an epigraph to this chapter, the lived experience of Black Americans growing up under Jim Crow and attentive to Western imperial warmongering in Africa made fighting Spanish Fascism a logical internationalization of the Black freedom struggle.

Morgan was born in 1910 in Rockingham, North Carolina, and joined the Young Communist League in 1932. In March 1937, he boarded the ship *Washington* and sailed to Spain, assigned to the infantry attached to the Mackenzie-Papineau battalion. "From the time I arrived in Spain until the time I left, for that period of my life, I felt like a human being, like a man," Morgan later said.[47] Like Morgan, Black volunteers to the Abraham Lincoln Brigade typically came to Spain with their political consciousness against Fascism sharpened by membership in the Communist Party, trade unions, or proletarianization. They also had their appetites whetted for Spain by rooting from afar for Ethiopia after Italy's 1935 invasion, yearning but unable to fight there. For James Yates, these factors worked in combination. Yates immediately jumped at the chance to serve when the brigades were formed. He sailed with ninety-six brigade volunteers, Black and white, in February 1937, carrying books by Gorky, Claude McKay, and Langston Hughes. As did all brigade volunteers, he entered Spain from France, struck by the uphill chances of winning Franco's defeat. "French and English capitalists were not only lending the Fascists moral support but continued to supply them with guns and planes and tanks. From America, and from the big oil companies, the Fascists, including Hitler, got oil without which they couldn't have maintained their huge war machines. We were set up to lose. This was in spite of the thousands of sympathetic Americans for the cause of Spain."[48] Yates was in Madrid as Fascist bombs fell and worked as an ambulance driver. On one excursion he surprised himself by driving a car for Ernest Hemingway.

Yates and Morgan were motivated by a comradeship sparked by participation in an international, multiracial army, in sharp contrast to the

THE BLACK ANTIFASCIST TRADTION

Jim Crowed life—and military life—at home. Albecete, a key site of brigade combat, wrote Yates, had become by 1937 a "United Nations of a special kind."[49] There, Black Lincolnites battled side by side with Germans, Italians, Irish, and even volunteers from Uganda, Cuba, and Ethiopia.[50] Like their international comrades, Black Lincolns also fought, were wounded, and died. Walter Garland from New York City, for example, was appointed Section Commander of the Seventeenth Internal Column because of his two years of experience in the US Army. He was wounded on February 27, 1937, during an attack on Pingaron Hill during the bloody battle of Jarama. He recovered and took command of two other campaigns. Yates and Garland became fast friends in battle. When Yates pondered one day whether President Franklin Roosevelt would take the US out of the embargo against the Republican government, Garland quipped, "It will never happen. They'd [the U.S. government] be much more comfortable with a Nazi and fascist victor."[51] In August 1937, Garland joined Langston Hughes and Harry Haywood in a radio broadcast from Madrid to the US. It was also Garland who put perhaps the clearest verbal stamp on why he and other African Americans joined the Lincoln Brigade: "We can't forget for one minute," he said, "that the oppression of the Negro is nothing more than a very concrete form, the clearest expression of fascism . . . In other words, we saw in Spain . . . those who chain us in America to cotton fields and brooms."[52]

Less fortunate, but of equal historical consequence to Garland, was Milton Herndon. Herndon was born in Wyoming, Ohio, in 1908, one of three brothers to Angelo Herndon, the Communist Party leader sentenced to death in 1932 (later reversed). Milton's mother was a domestic worker, his father was a coal miner. After joining the Communist Party himself, he sailed for Spain in 1937. A former National Guardsman, Herndon joined up with the same Mackenzie-Papineau Battalion as James Yates. During the battalion's first action, on October 13, 1937, at Fuentes de Ebro, Herndon was ordered to move a machine gun to support a battalion advance. He and his entire gun team were killed in the process by long-range machine-gun fire. Herndon's death was reported in the *New York Times*, conveyed by of the Friends of Abraham Lincoln

ANTICOLONIAL, PAN-AFRICANIST, AND COMMUNIST ANTIFASCISM 63

Brigade organization in New York City, as "Brother of Angelo, Freed From Georgia Chain Gang, Is One of Nine Americans Slain."[53]

An equally monumental biography is that of brigade member Oliver Law. According to scholar Chris Brooks, Law was the first African American in US history to lead an integrated military force. He was born in West Texas and joined the US Army as a teenager in 1919, serving in an all-Black regiment on the Mexican border. Law eventually joined the radical International Longshoremen's Association and later the ILD and Communist Party. Before leaving for Spain, Law was arrested for leading a rally to protest Italy's invasion of Ethiopia. He left for Spain in January 1937 and was eventually promoted to commander and later captain of a machine-gun company. On July 10, 1937, Law led the brigade in the Brunete Offensive and was killed in an assault on Mosquito Ridge.[54]

Another extraordinary Black woman formally participated in the brigade, responding to Thyra Edwards's insistence that "Fascism degrades women." Salaria Kea (also spelled Kee) lost her father at a young age; her mother took Salaria and her brother to Akron, Ohio, to live. Around 1930, Salaria moved to New York City, where she enrolled in Harlem Hospital Training School, the only nursing school in the city accepting African Americans. Her initial political education unfolded there. Protesting shoddy work conditions, the students had organized themselves and were ready with certain basic demands. These were as follows: 1) Discontinue racial discrimination in the dining room; 2) Appoint one Negro dietician to the staff now composed of five white; 3) Grant more authority to the charge nurses who now function merely as straw bosses and petty foremen.[55]

In her memoir *While Passing Through*, Kea reflected on how her experiences in Spain were shaped by struggles in Harlem. "The [Spanish] peasants had been psychologically just as imprisoned, had accepted the belief that nothing could be done about their situation as had the Harlem nurses earlier accepted racial discrimination in their dining room," she wrote. "Like the Harlem nurses, too, the peasants were now learning that something could be done about it. . . . There was nothing inviolable about the old prejudices . . . they could be changed and justice established."[56] After Italy's invasion of Ethiopia, Kea and other nurses gathered blankets and medical supplies to send to Italy's new Fascist subjects. Kea wished to travel to Ethiopia herself, but Emperor Haile Selassie had stopped taking foreign volunteers. In addition, as Robin D. G. Kelley notes, potential volunteers were warned that they would be in violation of a federal statute of 1818 governing the enlistment of US citizens in a foreign army. As a result, during this time, only two African Americans ever reached Ethiopia—airmen John C. Robinson of Chicago and Hubert F. Julian of Harlem.[57]

On March 27, 1937, persisting in her desire to join the fight against Fascism, Kea sailed with the Second American Medical Unit to Republican Spain, part of the larger Medical Bureau and North American Committee to Aid Spanish Democracy. The only African American in the group of twelve nurses and physicians, Kea was also the first Black woman from the US to go to the war in Spain. A year later, the Negro Committee to Aid Spain, along with the Medical Bureau, issued a pamphlet describing Kea's work and experiences. The Negro Committee to Aid Spain had been established when the war began, with Edwards as one of its architects. It fundraised in Black communities to provide medical supplies and other resources, including trucks and ambulances.

In Spain, Kea was assigned to a hospital base at Pueblo de Canada. The pamphlet dramatized in her own words the work done as Fascist planes buzzed overhead:

> That evening about seven o'clock patients began to pour in by hundreds. All that night we worked to treat well as many as possible and start them on the way further behind the front lines. When morning came we had nineteen patients left. These were wounded so badly that it did not seem safe to move them. By eight o'clock that morning we were visited by five fascist planes. These flew very low and slowly over our unit. For about twenty minutes they circled, close above us then flew away. Within an hour they were back. This time they were ten. They

turned their machine guns on us and began firing—terrifically, continuously. This time they were confronted by seven Government planes and together they battled just over our hospital unit. We could hear the stray bullets as they fell through the olive trees.[58]

In another memoir recollecting the war, titled *Health and Medicine*, Kea described a kind of medical international in Spain:

The beds of Villa Paz were soon filled with soldiers of every degree of injury and ailment, every known race and tongue from every corner of the earth. These divisions of race, creed and nationality lost significance when they met in a united effort to make Spain the tomb of Fascism. I saw my fate, the fate of the Negro race, was inseparably tied up with their fate: the efforts of the Negroes must be allied with those of others as the only insurance against an uncertain future.[59]

Kea served in nursing units in various locations, including Aragon and Barcelona. After being wounded by a bomb, she traveled to France to convalesce, returning to the US in 1938 and volunteering for the Medical Bureau in New York. Along the way, she married John Patrick O'Reilly, a member of the Irish American Lincoln Brigade. It would be two years after Kea's return to New York until he would be able to join her.

Black on Black: Moors in the Spanish Civil War

Franco's July 1936 coup produced the first Spanish aerial transport of troops to protect the new Fascist state. Franco's airlifted "African Army" was comprised of Foreign Legionnaires and thousands of Moroccan soldiers living in Spain's North African protectorate—a colony by another name. These thousands were among the first to die for Fascism. The experience of African American International Brigade volunteers encountering their Moorish brothers as the enemy served as a stark illustration of the dual racism that motivated Black Antifascism: directed like a gun, both at the Black African troops in the Spanish colony and at the Black Americans who came to fight them.

It was in part this aspect of the Spanish Civil War that drew the American poet Langston Hughes to Spain and to Black Antifascism. Hughes arrived in Spain in 1936 as a correspondent for two Black newspapers, the *Baltimore Afro-American* and the *Cleveland Call and Post*. He arrived already a committed Anticolonialist and a Communist sympathizer. In 1932, he had traveled to the Soviet Union, intending to make a film inspired by Bolshevik support for Black American self-determination and African decolonization. The trip inspired Hughes's famous poem "Lenin," a paean to the Soviet leader, and the poem "Good Morning Revolution," an internationalist ode to workers in Africa, China, Poland, and the US. In Spain, Hughes trained his poetic sights on Fascism as the newest obstacle between the Black diaspora and freedom:

> Why had I come to Spain? To write for the colored press. I knew that Spain once belonged to the Moors, a colored people ranging from light dark to dark white. Now the Moors have come again to Spain as cannon fodder. But, on the loyalist side, there are many colored people of various nationalities in the International Brigade. I wanted to write about both Moors and colored people.[60]

Hughes's best-known attempt to describe "Moors and colored people" was his poem "Letter from Spain" (subtitled "Address to Alabama"), written in November 1937. The poem includes the header "Lincoln Battalion,/International Brigades,/November Something, 1937." It attempts to write across the two sides of war the tenuous prospect for Black international solidarity. The poem's speaker, an African American member of the brigades, writes to his brother at home: "We captured a wounded Moor today./He was just as dark as me./I said, Boy what you been doin' here/Fightin' against the free?" The Moor answers in a language the speaker can't understand, but someone else tells him that he is saying, "They nabbed him in his land/And made him join the Fascist Army." Now, he says he has a feeling "He'd never get home again."[61] Hughes analogizes "colored and Moor" through the comparative experiences of enslavement and dispossession: colonialism and Fascism bring

ANTICOLONIAL, PAN-AFRICANIST, AND COMMUNIST ANTIFASCISM   67

them together far from home, in a kind of conjoined Middle Passage. After hearing that the Moor "didn't know/the folks he had to fight," the speaker peers across the short symbolic distance from Spain to North Africa as the utopian space of the war's possible outcome:

And as he lay there dyin'
In a village we had taken,
I looked across to Africa
And see foundations shakin'.

Cause if a free Spain wins this war,
The colonies, too, are free—
Then something wonderful'll happen
To them Moors as dark as me.[62]

For Hughes, the defeat of Fascism in Spain was the potential portal to what Paul Robeson called African colonization's revolutionary "overturn." That's why, the soldier concludes, England and Italy "is afraid to let a workers' Spain/Be good to you and me/Cause they got slaves in Africa—And they don't want em' to be free."[63] It is telling that Hughes looks not to Nazi Germany but imperialist England to see in the mirror of Spanish Fascism the enemy of a Black Antifascist international. Thyra Edwards also zeroed in on the condition of the Moors in her reporting on the war to Black US readers. In a 1938 issue of *Opportunity*, the journal of the National Urban League, she published "Moors in the Spanish War." The report was based on an interview with a Señor Vicens, an official with the Republican Party. Edwards begins the report by saying she wishes to confront rumors and reports of Moorish soldiers as sexual predators against white women in Spain—a reiteration of the charges of "Black disgrace" hurled by the right-wing German press at Senegalese soldiers serving in the French-occupied Rhineland. Vicens responds that Moorish soldiers are of two kinds: elites turned into officers and ground soldiers from among the poor. He also notes that Franco has wooed the poorest Moors with promises of two hours of looting and return to their homeland for each battle won. When

Edwards asks Vicens about the Republican policy on Spain's African colonies, he replies that the Republicans would have freed the colonies if not for Franco's opposition. The report is framed to link Franco's plans for the fascisization of Spain to its colonization of North Africa.[64]

Edwards's interview underscores what might be called the Moorish contradiction within Black Antifascism in Spain and the challenge of holding solidarity for Africans in the diaspora doubly threatened by colonialism and Fascism. Franco's use of Moorish soldiers to win Fascism, the legacy of Spanish colonization of North Africa and race prejudice against "Moorish domination," and the refusal of the Republican government to consider granting independence to North Africans under Spanish rule all underscore the precarious position of diasporic Africans in the war against Franco. Of the Moors conscripted by Franco, wrote novelist Richard Wright, "The fascists have duped and defrauded a terribly exploited people."[65] At times, African Americans were shot at by Loyalists who confused them for Moors. The Communist Party of Spain even attempted to create a Hispano Moroccan Anti-Fascist Association to win North African support for the Republic, but with limited success.[66] Still, the search for Black diasporic solidarity within the Black Antifascist Tradition did not abate and would travel home with Black brigade veterans after the war.

Fighting the Good Fights Back Home

African Americans who returned from Spain brought their politics home to a landscape often as ideologically dangerous as the frontline of battle. Thyra Edwards returned to the US on November 8, 1937. She joined up as a field representative of the American Medical Bureau to Aid Spanish Democracy and the North American Committee to Aid Spanish Democracy. She undertook speaking tours to HBCUs to raise awareness and funding in support of the Republican cause. In 1938, after Salaria Kea's return, close friends Edwards and Kea traveled the country to raise Black funds to buy and send an ambulance to the Spanish front. Edwards also continued to write about the war, reporting on the deaths of Chicagoans Milton Herndon and Joe Dallett. She was an

ANTICOLONIAL, PAN-AFRICANIST, AND COMMUNIST ANTIFASCISM   69

invited speaker at the Women's Council established by the Brotherhood of Sleeping Car Porters, where she exhorted women to fight Fascist sexism: "The fascists believe that women have only one purpose and that is to bear children."[67]

In August 1939, Edwards traveled to Mexico to report on efforts of the Mexican and Soviet governments to resettle Spanish refugees, the only two countries in the world to do so. In 1940, she returned to the US, only to find herself hounded by the FBI for her Spanish travel and open work for Spanish refugees. With the 1940 passage of the Alien Registration Act, informally known as the Smith Act, the Red Scare had begun, and Black Antifascists were some of its first targets. In 1942, the Chicago Office of the FBI summoned Edwards for questioning, and its infamous "Red Squad" filed a report on her.[68] J. Edgar Hoover sent a special agent to Chicago to investigate her work in the American League Against War and Fascism. She also received a letter, dated December 19, 1942, from Perrin H. Lowrey, Executive Secretary, Subversive Personnel Committee, Federal Security Agency, Washington, DC, asking her, "Are you now or have you ever been a member of the Communist Party?" Edwards replied no.[69] After a brief stint working for the progressive *People's Voice* magazine in New York, Edwards met and married a Jewish Communist, Murray Gitlin. They would move to Italy, where Gitlin was helping resettle Jewish refugees from the Holocaust.

Salaria Kea also took up speaking tours for Spain: "Spain Unconquerable, Negro War Nurse Says" was the headline to a story reported in the *Midwest Daily Record* about her speech at the University of Chicago. "Under fascism, Negroes, Jews, and every other racial minority would have no other destiny than constant subjection to filthy ghettoes," Kea told audiences.[70] When World War II began, Kea joined up as a nurse while her husband, John Patrick O'Reilly, was conscripted to fight. The interracial couple faced racism throughout their marriage, and Kea later worried that her political commitments would put her on Richard Nixon's "enemies list."[71] Kea died in 1990 in Akron, Ohio, where she had spent her childhood.

The collapse of the Spanish Republic in 1938, followed by Franco's invasion of Catalonia, decimated the Republican cause; almost 70 percent of the Lincoln Brigade died in a losing effort.[72] Black Lincoln Brigadiers who survived returned to a hostile America: some, like James Yates, had their passports revoked for having traveled to Spain to fight. But they rarely sacrificed their political commitments. Walter Garland is a good example. After returning to the US, he traveled to Washington, DC, to lobby the State Department to lift the embargo on Spain. In 1938, he ran as the Communist Party's candidate for representative of the Sixth Congressional District of New York and was the Communist Party candidate for the New York State Assembly from the Seventeenth Assembly District, Kings County, Brooklyn, in 1940. He also fell under the state's Black Antifascism microscope: in 1941, the FBI classified him among "individuals believed to be the most dangerous and who in all probability should be interned in event of war"—a foreshadowing not only of the December 1941 internment of Japanese Americans after the attack on Pearl Harbor but also of the arrests, expulsions, detentions, and trials of American Communists with the passage of the 1940 Smith Act.[73]

Often jobless and without medical benefits upon their return, Black brigade veterans were sustained in part by the formation of the Friends of the Abraham Lincoln Brigade (FALB). FALB raised money to provide stipends and help pay medical bills. It provided Crawford Morgan with eyeglasses.[74] A more overtly political initiative was the formation of the Veterans of the Abraham Lincoln Brigade, an antiracist, Antifascist organization. Labeled a Communist front, it made the Dies Committee's list of subversive organizations, putting Black Antifascists further in the state's crosshairs. Black brigade veterans were, in turn, brought to testify before the House Un-American Activities Committee (also known as the Dies Committee) and the Subversive Activities Control Board. Not one turned informant.[75] Rather, brigadiers turned the tables on the procedures and made accusations of American Fascism. When asked by the Subversive Activities Control Board what the Veterans of the Abraham Lincoln Brigade thought of the US state's official recognition and embrace of the Franco regime, Crawford Morgan testified:

Well, we thought it was one of the most terrible things our government had ever done for the simple reason [that] we were the first Americans that felt fascism and later on a great section of the world was fighting for it, including America. Thousands of our sons and daughters died over on the other side fighting fascism, and now our government is embracing it, and because we don't want to embrace it with them they are persecuting us for it.[76]

Morgan's words turned out to be prophetic. Once the US officially entered World War II, the state would work even harder to repress the memory of the Abraham Lincoln Brigade in the name of national unity. At the same time, Communist, Anticolonial, and Pan-African Antifascism would be reborn as a new fight against Fascism, both within the borders of the United States and around the world. That fight would go under the name "Double Victory."

— CHAPTER 3 —
DOUBLE V ANTIFASCISM AND WORLD WAR II

"The democracy which the white world seeks to defend does not exist."
—**W. E. B. Du Bois**, *Dusk of Dawn*, 1940[1]

"The smell of death? I know it well.
At Buchenwald, you say?
I wasn't there. . . .
But here at home. . . . in Georgia
I smelled it once."
—**Grace Tompkins**, *Negro Story*, 1944[2]

"Who is the god of war? The god of war is greed. Money-hungry
mad men make the wars. Always the poor people are forced to fight
in the wars. This is not a people's war."
—**Margaret Burroughs**, "A Negro Mother Looks at War," 1940[3]

F WORLD WAR I, Ethiopia, and the Spanish Civil War helped lay the foundation for the Black Antifascist Tradition, World War II gave the tradition a name. Just weeks after the United States entered the war in 1941, African American newspapers, led by the *Pittsburgh Courier*, announced a "Double Victory" campaign for Black Americans: defeat Fascism abroad, defeat racism at home. Suddenly, C. L. R. James's prediction that colonized and diasporic Africans would enact a "social transformation" in the name of Antifascism had scale, scope, and voice. Black Americans, confronted with the specter of dying in a segregated armed forces against a Fascist enemy, exploded this contradiction by naming a condition of war itself as Anti-Black Fascism. Fascism, in turn, became the nominal terrain for Black struggle, domestically and internationally, against the global forces of racial capitalism. So wrote Langston Hughes about the American political landscape in August of 1945:

> Fascism is Bilbo and Rankin and Eastland who don't want Negroes or Jews or Italian-American to have job protection. Fascism is the President of Dartmouth College who doesn't want minorities to have an equal chance at education. Fascism is our Red Cross that follows Hitler's blood policy. Fascism is the force that would keep people ignorant and helpless in the face of economic greed, and that gathers its educational, economic, or military power to support its suppression of the people.[4]

Hughes's essay, written just days *after* the US declaration of victory in the war, used "Double Victory" logic to argue that, for many people, the fight against Fascism was far from over. Indeed, Hughes's analysis of "Double Victory" Fascism, published in the widely read Black newspaper *Chicago Defender*, implicitly recognized that thousands of Black Americans had been mobilized by the war itself into a renewed struggle for the goals that had generated the Black Antifascist tradition in the first place: the liberation of the world's Black colonies; the end of formal, legal, and informal Jim Crow; challenges to racial capitalism; and the destruction of a white supremacist world order. Thus, as the war officially ended, Black Antifascism pointed toward a futurity that could build from the victory over one set of Fascist enemies in Europe an emancipatory democracy to defeat the greater Fascist enemy worldwide: "No one," wrote Hughes, "will any longer be so undemocratic or boorish as to Jim Crow an African in his country."[5] This chapter will demonstrate how World War II became the crucible for the birth of a new epoch of global Black Antifascism and a foundation for postwar Black Antifascist struggles.

Black Antifascist organizing in support of Ethiopia and Spain in the 1930s produced a militant layer of radicals seasoned to perceive the coming war as a continuation of, rather than a break in, the Fascisization of the Western world. US neutrality in the Spanish Civil War, the League of Nations' indifference to Italy's Fascist crimes in Libya and Ethiopia, the ongoing colonization of Africa and Asia by European powers, lynchings of Black soldiers on US soil, the repression and ostracization faced by Black veterans of the Spanish Civil War, and continued Jim Crow policies in the US under a "progressive" New Deal Roosevelt administration all inspired W. E. B. Du Bois's 1940 lament about the death of democracy. Like Thyra Edwards, Du Bois had made an in-person study of Fascism well before the next world war began. In 1936, he spent five weeks in Germany as part of a world excursion that included Japan and China. Much of Du Bois's political education owed to German tradition: from 1892 to 1894, on a fellowship, he attended Humboldt University in Berlin, where he studied Hegel and wrote admiringly about Bismarck and the rise of the German state as a potential model for African Americans. His 1936 return visit was an effort to assess what had become of that Germany.

Du Bois's December 12, 1936, article for the *Pittsburgh Courier* was the first widely circulated Black American–written reportage on German Fascism. His piece, "Writings on National Socialism," reflected Du Bois's concentrated study of Marxism in the early 1930s, as demonstrated in his magnum opus *Black Reconstruction*, published in 1935. In that book, much like C. L. R. James in his 1936 opus *The Black Jacobins*, Du Bois argued that the end of Reconstruction had brought "counterrevolutions" of war and property by ruling white elites.[6] The seeds of both James's and Du Bois's subsequent analysis of Fascism as an international capitalist, ruling-class formation meant to destroy Black (and white) workers' movements lay in those respective texts. It follows that Du Bois's *Courier* article argued that National Socialism was a response to Bolshevism at Germany's door: "They sought to build a national, German socialism, to avoid international working-class movements, and to save capital and private profit by yielding enough to the German worker to keep him quiet and satisfied."[7] Du Bois also recognized National Socialism as a hyper-racist regime, "composed of pure Nordics, with no contamination of Jews, nor of inferior races."[8] In a second article a week later, Du Bois framed the prospects of a Jewish Holocaust within the broad context of Western capitalist and imperialist history. Nazi antisemitism, he wrote, "surpasses in vindictive cruelty and public insult anything I have ever seen; and I have seen much. There has been no tragedy in modern times equal in its awful effects to the fight on the Jew in Germany. It is an attack on civilization, comparable only to such horrors as the Spanish Inquisition and the African slave trade."[9] Du Bois's articles from Germany, like those of Thyra Edwards, manifested another "premature" insight of Black Antifascism, namely that the world war to come was germinating from much longer histories of Western racial capitalism and demanded a coordinated response from the Black diaspora. These were to become the contours of the US "Double Victory" campaign.

Like the International African Friends of Ethiopia (IAFE) campaign in London, the Double Victory campaign in the US was a living force of independent Black self-organizing meant to suture elements of the Anticolonial, Pan-African and Communist movements of the 1930s into a usable new framework for action and analysis. The "Double Victory" slogan carried with it internationalist lessons from the war for Africans in the diaspora. Witnessing Franco's use of Moorish troops to fight a Fascist war had laid bare for African Americans like Hughes the colonial architecture that had both created World War II and propped up the war itself. Italy's brutal colonization and internment of Ethiopians and Libyans on the Axis side of the war found complement on the Allied side, as France and England both deployed African and Asian colonial subjects to die for countries to which they did not belong. This insight of "double jeopardy" and double exclusion for colonized subjects gave birth to two of the most important theories to emerge from the Black Antifascist tradition during World War II.

Frantz Fanon's comprehension of the structures of colonialism in *The Wretched of the Earth* was prompted by his enlisting in the French Army as a colonial subject of Martinique during World War II and earning a Croix de Guerre medal for a country that refused to recognize his citizenship or humanity. Fanon's argument that colonialism produced an inflexible hierarchy of racial subordination—"two different species"—carried within it the mortal truths borne out by World War II's joint destruction of non-white races, whether in the internment camps or the colonial armies. As Fanon put it in the famous chapter "Concerning Violence," in *Wretched of the Earth*, what is Fascism "if not colonialism when rooted in a traditionally colonialist country"?[10] Likewise, Aimé Césaire's powerful and groundbreaking *Discourse on Colonialism* drew its most essential insights on Fascism in part from Césaire's experience of living in Martinique under the Fascist Vichy regime, illuminating in a flash the relationship between the colonial project and Europe's new Fascist order.

The US "Double Victory" campaign might be considered the African American application of these insights to the special conditions of American white supremacy, military and police brutality, second-class citizenship, and Jim Crow. Put another way, "Double Victory" was a means of globalizing and naming a theory of Anti-Black Fascism and raising it to a level of world historical importance. As with the theories of Césaire and Fanon, it lifted up the contradiction of Black people's enduring continuous violence in multiple forms and risking life and limb for a nation that still segregated its citizenry, its military, and its blood supplies. In short, "Double V" asserted that America's Anti-Black Fascism produced the Black subject as an internal enemy in what scholar John Dower once called a "war without mercy."[11] In turn, "Double V" was an organized *counterinsurgency* of militancy, fighting spirit, and commitment to armed struggle born from the experiences of Black veterans of the Abraham Lincoln Brigade, Anticolonial rebels in Africa, and newly armed American troops, whose experience of wearing a uniform and carrying a gun would help train their sights on Fascism domestically and internationally. Black Antifascism, in short, would take on the character of a guerilla war fought both without and within the ranks of a global Jim Crowed army.

Significantly, it was the Black press—progenitor of the "Double Victory" campaign—that provided a martial prologue to it. In September

1940, a full fifteen months before US entry into World War II, the *Chicago Defender* carried a fictitious, satirical news story titled, "Blitz over Georgia." Under the headline "Blitz in U.S.: Race in Revolt," the story began thus: "Heavily guarded, Adolf Hitler was moving northward from here Sunday after a small expeditionary force which made a surprise landing here Saturday night by air and sea had completely wiped out approximately 2,500 Negro troops in a tragic one-sided massacre which is perhaps without parallel in the history of the world."[12] Black troops were slaughtered, the story continued, while "armed only with picks and shovels." The story promised the massacre would cause "widespread revolt among Negroes." A terrified Congress, meanwhile, had taken refuge in "Wayunder, Alassippi," an act of "treason" reflecting Western racial capitalism's appeasements to Fascism and complicity with its rise: "It's the same old story of aristocratic fifth columns that was seen unfolded in Norway, England, and France. White landlords, businessmen, and politicians sold out the South and opened the gates to Hitler."[13] The *Defender*'s allegory may have been inspired by another dystopian Black Antifascist fictional work, William Thomas Smith's "The Black Stockings," serialized in the *Baltimore Afro-American* in 1937. The series depicts an Aryan presidential candidate's fantasy to deport all African Americans.[14] The "Black Stockings" designation resonates in two satirical directions at once, both to Mussolini's "Black Shirts" in Italy and to the "Black Legion," a proto-Fascist group that emerged in the US Midwest in 1931, descended from a Ku Klux Klan spinoff, the Black Guards.

Like Margaret Burroughs's "A Negro Mother Looks at War," these dystopian, "War of the Worlds"–style allegories identified Western ruling-class domination, slavery, and white supremacy as the deeply planted roots of Fascism. That Black Americans were "premature" victims of world war lay embedded in this history: "picks and shovels" had *never* been adequate defense against white terror, from the plantation of the Old South to army training bases in the heart of Dixie. Strongly hinted at in "Blitz over Georgia" were the lynch-like conditions that prevailed in the lives of Black soldiers prematurely condemned to die.

When Langston Hughes quipped that he'd never met a Black soldier inducted into the army who did not say, "I hope they don't send me down South,"[15] he was indexing the historical memory of Houston's Camp Logan Riots and the postwar lynchings of World War I–era Black veterans. "Alassippi," in the *Defender* allegory, also invoked the home state (Mississippi) of both Dixiecrat racist senator Theodore Bilbo and House member John Elliott Rankin. Bilbo was aptly and frequently compared to Hitler in the pages of the Black press after a 1938 speech on the Senate floor in which he had praised Nazi eugenics: "The Germans appreciate the importance of race values. They understand that racial improvement is the greatest asset that any country can have. . . . They know, as few other nations have realized, that the impoverishment of race values contributes more to the impairment and destruction of a civilization than any other agency."[16] In the same year, Bilbo introduced legislation to send all Black Americans back to Africa. Rankin, meanwhile, had also expressed sentiments worthy of Hitler. "The Negro is not the equal of the White man, and he never will be. It is impossible to reverse the laws of nature and lift the Negro through tens of thousands of years of civilization, education, and development, regenerate him, purge him of his weaknesses and his instincts, and endow him with Caucasian strength, traits, and characteristics, and make him the peer of the white man."[17]

The *Defender*'s dystopian allegory of wartime atrocities flipped the script of American nationalism and treason by demonstrating that US democracy was allied to rather than contesting Fascist ideology: the 2,500 Black troops slaughtered by Hitler had not even to leave home to die. "Double V" logic held up the segregated military apparatus as a mirror to America's history of slavery, eugenics, and racial violence. This point was driven home in "Blitz over Georgia," with reference to imprisoned African American conscientious objectors to the war (like the future UN diplomat Ralph Bunche and sociologist St. Clair Drake), said to be held in "concentration camps."[18] Indeed, because they were at the front lines of Double Victory contradictions, as scholar Vaughn Rasberry has noted—much like the Black and Moorish soldiers during the Spanish Civil War—African American soldiers during World War II became a recurring focal point and interpretive site for the meaning of Black Antifascism.

The Communist Harry Haywood is a case in point. After fighting with the Abraham Lincoln Brigade, Haywood returned home, only to see the Spanish capital, Madrid, fall to Fascist forces on March 28, 1939. In his autobiography, *Black Bolshevik: Autobiography of an Afro-American Communist,* Haywood assessed the moment as a consummation of Western imperial indifference to the threat of Fascism. In addition to Italy's and Germany's support of the Fascist Franco regime, France, the US, and England all remained officially or unofficially neutral in Spain's civil war. "Republican Spain," wrote Haywood in turn, "was clearly a victim of the Western imperialists' policy of appeasement. The fascist victory in Spain was another step toward World War II."[19] But brigade veteran Haywood would not give up the Antifascist fight. After the US entered the war, he enlisted as a merchant marine at San Pedro, California, in June 1943. Haywood explained the decision as a tribute to the militancy of the National Maritime Union (NMU)—founded as a Congress of Industrial Organization (CIO) union in 1937—which represented the merchant marines. The NMU was a hotbed of Black Antifascist militancy from within the ranks of the US military. As Haywood recounts, the union was "in the leadership of the antifascist movement both at home and abroad."[20] It actively supported two major Black legislative initiatives during the war: an antilynching bill and a permanent Fair Employment Practices Commission (FEPC). The former had first been proposed, with the support of the NAACP, in 1918. The campaign for legislation ramped up after the beginning of the war, fueled by the links made between lynching and Fascism by Black organizers like Du Bois, as discussed in chapter 1. The campaign for a permanent FEPC had been led by A. Philip Randolph, with the aim of forcing the federal government to legislate against racial discrimination in employment. Randolph's threat of a march on Washington in 1941 persuaded Roosevelt to support the FEPC legislation. For those on the Black left and in the trade union movement, the FEPC and antilynching fights represented an effort to save the Black working class and Black radicals from the fates of their colonial and Jewish counterparts in Africa and Europe. Both Mussolini and Hitler, after all, had ridden to power by attacking not only racial minorities but also trade unions and Communists.

In fact, the NMU had developed its wartime domestic politics directly from its Antifascist organizing during the 1930s. After Italy's invasion of Ethiopia, the multiracial NMU refused to sail ships to Italy. Many NMU members fought in the Abraham Lincoln Brigade during the Spanish Civil War. Founders of the NMU included two African Americans: Josh Lawrence and Ferdinand Smith, both of whom were on the national board of the union. The Jamaican-born Smith, like Haywood a Communist, pushed for the passage of an antidiscrimination platform into the union and rose to the level of secretary treasurer. Smith was active in the National Negro Congress (NNC), which had emerged directly out of the Communist Party's Popular Front commitment to fighting Fascism. In 1948, Smith was expelled from the NMU in a purge of Communist leadership and was deported by the federal government under the 1940 Smith Act. Smith's deportation was part of a state-sponsored campaign in the 1940s to expel and imprison Black radicals with overt histories of fighting Fascism.

Haywood's merchant marines sailed with racially integrated crews and included the first Black commander in chief of a US vessel, Captain Hugh Malzac, who commanded the *Booker T. Washington*, known as "the liberty ship." Haywood sailed on the interracial *Uruguay*, making port in Bombay and Cape Town, South Africa, where crew members openly defied apartheid social restrictions. Other merchant marines whose Antifascist politics were inflected during the war included Ralph Ellison and Woody Guthrie, who left behind a song of his service, "Talking Merchant Marine."

These examples of labor militancy and volunteerism, from Spain to the US to South Africa, demonstrate how Black Antifascism remade the figure of the Black soldier in its image. The Black international war against Fascism in Spain could be translated into fighting racism on the domestic front. As Vaughn Rasberry has brilliantly noted, "In the Second World War, the Negro soldier symbolized a struggle against 'totalitarianism' on multiple fronts: Fascism and Nazism in Europe; Jim Crow segregation in the United States; and European colonialism in Africa and Asia."[21] This battle was made manifest in the constant violence and brutality faced by the 1.2 million African American soldiers who served in the US military during World War II. On March 28, 1941, Felix Hall, a nineteen-year-old Black soldier, was found lynched from a tree at Georgia's Fort Benning. Hall, a native of Montgomery, Alabama, had enlisted in the Twenty-Fourth Infantry Regiment, one of the first all-Black army regiments in the post–Civil War era. NAACP head Walter White wrote to President Roosevelt and Secretary of War Henry L. Stimson, demanding an investigation. The inquiry that followed did not find anyone responsible for Hall's lynching.[22] On June 27, 1942, Black military policeman Charles J. Reco was shot four times and clubbed by police in Beaumont, Texas, after he was accused of sticking his knees into the "whites-only" section of a city bus. One year later, on June 15, 1943, white rioters in Beaumont attacked Black neighborhoods based on a rumor that a Black man had raped a white woman. About four thousand whites destroyed more than one hundred homes in segregated Black neighborhoods. The Black population had soared in Beaumont with Black migrants who had come to work in the local Pennsylvania Shipyard.

The Beaumont Riot—another American "holocaust"—was one of numerous wartime racial riots against Black workers and soldiers, amplifying the Double Victory analysis that the conditions of war themselves were Fascist for African Americans. In addition to the violence in Beaumont, white workers at the Alabama Dry Dock Shipping Company rioted and threw two Black workers into a river on May 25, 1943, after twelve Black workers were promoted to the position of welder.[23] In Detroit, in June 1943, more than one hundred thousand whites gathered in the Belle Island area of the city and attacked Blacks over resentments over job hiring and promotion, and rumors of Black violence against whites. At least twenty-five African Americans were killed, seventeen at the hands of police. But it was the Harlem Riot of 1943 that most directly mirrored the Double Victory conditions of war: a white cop shot and killed a Black soldier, Robert Bandy, who was attempting to intervene in a case of police brutality against a Black woman. This time, Black rioters turned the guns around, burning and destroying white-owned properties. The state, in turn, doubled down on wartime militarization, deploying US Army troops to put down the rebellion.

As was often the case, poet Langston Hughes captured the Black Antifascist imagination in his distillation of these events in his poem "Beaumont to Detroit: 1943":

> Looky here, America
> What you done done—
> Let things drift
> Until the riots come.
>
> Now your policemen
> Let your mobs run free.
> I reckon you don't care
> Nothing about me.
>
> You tell me that hitler
> Is a mighty bad man.
> I guess he took lessons
> From the ku klux klan.
>
> You tell me mussolini's
> Got an evil heart.
> Well, it mus-a been in Beaumont
> That he had his start—
>
> Cause everything that hitler
> And mussolini do,
> Negroes get the same
> Treatment from you.

You jim crowed me
Before hitler rose to power—
And you're STILL jim crowing me
Right now, this very hour.

Yet you say we're fighting
For democracy.
Then why don't democracy
Include me?

I ask you this question
Cause I want to know
How long I got to fight
BOTH HITLER—AND JIM CROW.[24]

Hughes's poem burned like wildfire through Black communities, published in New York's *People's Voice*—a progressive wartime newspaper—and circulated through the Associated Negro Press, the country's first African American news service, begun by Claude Barnett. Hughes also wrote, in June 1943, in defense of young Mexican and Black victims of a race riot by white sailors in Los Angeles, dubbed by the mainstream press the "Zoot Suit Riots." As Hughes noted in his column for the *Chicago Defender*, the rioting was triggered when the city of Los Angeles and the federal War Production Board outlawed the wearing of fashionable wide-lapeled garments by Black and Brown youth as a waste of wartime material. Hughes's column blamed the riots on racist hysteria, whipped up "no doubt, by the undercover agents of Hitler,"[25] a wink and nod to Double V accusations that the real wartime subversion of democracy in the US was state-sponsored racism. Finally, Hughes insinuated another layer of Double V Antifascism into his analysis, linking the attack on zoot suiters to the 1941 internment of Japanese Americans. "From the saffron-skinned Japanese-American citizens of Los Angeles to brown-skinned Mexican-American citizens," wrote Hughes, "is only a step."[26]

DOUBLE V ANTIFASCISM AND WORLD WAR II

A consummating Double V conjuncture, merging the plight of Black soldiers with mass protest against white supremacy, was the Port Chicago Mutiny of 1944. On July 17, 1944, a gigantic explosion killed 320 men, two-thirds of them African American, while they were off-loading naval ships at the Port Chicago naval magazine in Port Chicago, California. After the explosion, white officers were given leave, while Black enlisted men were forced to pick through the wreckage of bodies. Two hundred African American soldiers protested. Fifty were eventually charged with court-martial offenses for refusing to return to work. All fifty were found guilty and sentenced from eight to fifteen years of hard labor in federal prison at the Terminal Island Disciplinary Barracks in San Pedro. All the men were dishonorably discharged. At their hearing, according to scholar Erika Doss:

> Navy officials justified this lack of training on racist terms. African American military personnel, they argued, were incapable of learning and were essentially expendable: "Because of the level of intelligence and education of the enlisted personnel, it was impracticable to train them by any method other than by actual demonstration. Many of the men were incapable of reading and understanding the most simple directions." The inquiry concluded that no one was to fault for the explosion—neither the untrained enlisted men handling dangerous materials nor the officers in charge. Navy officials asked Congress to award each victim's family a benefit of $5,000 for their wartime service but when Mississippi congressman John Rankin learned that most of the victims were African American, he demanded that the amount be reduced to $3,000.[27]

The Port Chicago episode transported and updated the conditions that had produced the Black Antifascist uprising: white supremacist denigration of Black life; assumptions of biological inferiority; and a colonial and racial capitalist logic that cast Black people as the most egregious victims of Fascist practice throughout the world. The violence done to Black soldiers' lives by American militarization and the racist indifference to Black life of pro-Nazi politicians made the Port Chicago Mutiny a key event in the intensifying organization of Black Antifascism's war at home. From "Blitz over Georgia" to Port Chicago, the death at home of hundreds of Black soldiers enlisted to fight Fascism abroad revealed the threat to be as real and as lethal as imagined.

The Black Antifascist Cultural Front

The 1935 "Popular Front" campaign of the Comintern endeavored to draw African Americans into Communism's orbit by linking the fight against racism at home to the fight against Fascism abroad. It was thus one "seed" of Double Victory Antifascism. Another was the Popular Front's emphasis on Black art and culture as a fighting force against Fascism. In 1936, the NNC endeavored to open a "Negro People's Front," meant to raise up the special contributions of Black artists and writers to American culture.[28] Led by figures such as Paul Robeson, the campaign drew momentum during the Spanish Civil War and in response to the Italian invasion of Ethiopia. In a 1939 interview for the Theatre Arts Committee, Robeson described the African American spirituals and folk songs he performed on the Spanish battle front as both antecedents and living testimonies to the heroic struggles against Fascism across the world:

> When I sing, "let my people go," I can feel sympathetic vibrations from my audience, whatever its nationality. It is no longer just a Negro song—it is a symbol of those seeking freedom from the dungeons of fascism in Europe to-day . . .
>
> This keeping close to the feelings and desires of my audience has a lot to do with shaping my attitude toward the struggle of the peoples of the world. It has made me an anti-fascist, whether the struggle is in Spain, Germany or here.[29]

Robeson's contention that Black art carried within it the kernel of an Antifascist political aesthetic helped launch what might be called the cultural arm of the Black Antifascist Tradition. Fighting for Black culture, many artists decided, was fighting against Fascism. Most of the major Black artists and writers of the 1930s and 1940s held explicitly

Antifascist political points of view. These included novelists Richard Wright, Ralph Ellison, Ann Petry, and Langston Hughes; writer and artist Margaret Burroughs; editorial cartoonists Jackie Ormes and Ollie Harrington; as well as a cadre of lesser-known supporting artists who helped constitute the Black Antifascist Cultural Front. These artists generated not only new cultural work in the name of Antifascism but also new venues, locations, and sites for its production, helping to create new mass spaces for the consumption and distribution of Black art.

For example, in May 1935, just months before the Italian invasion of Ethiopia, Robeson declared, in an article in the London *News Chronicle*, "I believe that negro culture merits an honourable place amongst the cultures of the world."[30] The article, titled "I Want Negro Culture," cited African traditions of music and dance as an impetus for an independent Black culture that could break from European mastery and tradition and develop its own venues and cultural institutions. From 1935 to the end of World War II, Robeson pioneered performances in Black theater as *Othello* and as a leading recording artist of Black folk music, spirituals, and ballads. In 1937, after the outbreak of war in Spain, Robeson made explicit that the fight for a new Black culture was directly tied to the fight against Fascism. Speaking at a rally sponsored by the National Joint Committee for Spanish Relief in aid of the Spanish Refugee Children in London, Robeson expounded:

> Every artist, every scientist, must decide NOW where he stands. He has no alternative . . . Fascism fights to destroy the culture which society has created . . .
>
> . . . The artist must take sides. He must elect to fight for freedom or slavery. I have made my choice. I had no alternative. The history of the capitalist era is characterized by the degradation of my people: despoiled of their lands, their culture destroyed, they are in every country, save one, denied equal protection of the law, and deprived of their rightful place in the respect of their fellows.[31]

THE BLACK ANTIFASCIST TRADTION

Robeson's manifesto anticipates the argument later made by Frantz Fanon that the national culture of oppressed and colonized peoples "must lie at the very heart of the liberation struggle these countries are waging."[32] For Robeson, the protection and dissemination of Black art and culture were part and parcel of the international struggle against Fascism and the fight for racial justice at home—the twin planks of Double V.

The scope and duration of Robeson's argument can be registered by the response of the *Chicago Defender* to his performance in *Othello* some seven years later. As if in direct response to his call, in an editorial titled "Paul Robeson and Our Cultural Front," the paper enjoined:

> Our fight for democracy and full participation in the war effort is on the economic, political, and cultural fronts. Each of these fields is dominated by powerful financial groups who see more profits in the division of peoples along lines of race, creed, color and nationality than they are in national unity . . . Everywhere we must seek to make a breach in these walls of segregation. The fight on the cultural front is one of the most important.[33]

The *Defender*'s call for a "cultural front" echoed the call by the 1936 NNC for defense of "culture and cultural workers,"[34] and the cry put forward by African American painter and cultural worker Margaret Burroughs in a 1941 speech opening the South Side Community Art Center, Chicago's first all-Black cultural institution: "Now, in this critical war time period, we have our own plans for defense; a plan in defense of culture."[35] If creating Black art was tantamount to fighting Fascism, defending it was a necessary front line in the war. Though primarily a visual artist, Burroughs contributed her own Antifascist narrative to the "defense of culture" in her 1944 short story "Private Jeff Johnson," a brief parable about a Black soldier training for war, which analogizes Jim Crow and German Fascism. The story appeared in the journal *Negro Story*, which, between 1944 and 1946, became a pregnant site for Black Antifascist cultural expression.[36] In 1944, the magazine reprinted Chicago journalist and poet Frank Marshall Davis's "For All Common

People," written partly in response to the 1943 Detroit riot. The poem was a virtual call to Black Antifascist arms:

> Let the common people smash all foes of the common people;
> Let the people fade fascism to a sour memory,
> Let the people snort goodbye to empire;
> Prepare soundproof cells for the hating rabble rousers,
> Plant the greedy in the earth they covet,
> Chase the munitions makers to the poor house,
> Spade soft soil over the warlords,
> Sterilize the minds of all Hitlers from Berlin to Birmingham . . . [37]

Davis's effort to analogize Berlin and Birmingham transmuted Black suffering under Jim Crow into the suffering of those everywhere living under Fascism. Poet Grace Tompkins used the same alchemic logic in her 1944 *Negro Story* entry, excerpted from her book *The Birth Pangs of a New Order*. Following the lines used as epigraph to this chapter on the "smell of death" at Buchenwald and in Georgia, Tompkins made a Fascist universal of the singular experience of Black lynching:

> Just one man died
> Not thousands as at Buchenwald
> But each man dies but one death
> It is an individual matter
> And all the others
> Touch him not at al [*sic*]
> When his turn comes for dying
> Mass murder is appalling, yes,
> But each death of the whole is one
> The total makes the mass.[38]

Davis and Tompkins were joined arm in arm in a Black Antifascist poetry insurgency prepared by Langston Hughes's relentless and proliferating body of work dating to the Spanish Civil War. In addition to his Antifascist Spanish war poems and "Beaumont to Detroit" cited earlier, Hughes toured Black communities after his travel to Spain, lecturing on the theme "A Negro Poet Looks at A Troubled World," effectively using his platform as a Black artist, like Robeson, to build the Black Antifascist cultural front. Even so generally nonpolemical a poet as Gwendolyn Brooks wrote several poems during the war that linked the conditions of Black soldiers before and after battle to the prospects under Anti-Black Fascism. In her 1945 poem "The Progress," Brooks queries the fragile psychological state of Black soldiers returning from war while "inward grows a soberness, an awe,/A fear, a deepening hollow through the cold./For even if we come out standing up/How shall we smile, congratulate?"[39] As scholar Vaughn Rasberry notes, Brooks's poem hollows out the jingoistic fanfare of victory into a form of racial PTSD: "Shaken by the traumas of war, Negro soldiers who could not remain in Europe are compelled to reenter a social order less hospitable than Nazi Germany."[40] The poem subtly captures what Hughes himself more brazenly offered, as a jackbooted finale to the war, in his poem "Will V-Day Be Me-Day Too?" Written to his "Fellow Americans" by a "Tan-skinned Yank/Driving a tank," the soldier poet asks, about the end of war:

> When I take off my uniform,
> Will I be safe from harm—
> Or will you do me
> As the Germans did the Jews?
> When I've helped this world to save,
> Shall I still be color's slave?
> Or will Victory change
> Your antiquated views?
> You can't say I didn't fight
> To smash the Fascists' might.
> You can't say I wasn't with you
> in each battle.
> As a soldier, and a friend.
> When this war comes to an end,
> Will you herd me in a Jim Crow car
> Like cattle?[41]

DOUBLE V ANTIFASCISM AND WORLD WAR II   91

Like Gwendolyn Brooks, the novelist, journalist, and short story writer Ann Petry used her art to forward Black Antifascist themes. Petry's 1950 essay "The Novel as Social Criticism" provides a framework by which to read her wartime fiction. "Being a product of the twentieth century (Hitler, atomic energy, Hiroshima, Mussolini, Buchenwald, USSR)," she writes, "I find it difficult to subscribe to the idea that art exists for art's sake. It seems to me like all truly great art is propaganda."[42] Petry's 1944 short story "In Darkness and Confusion" and her 1946 novel *The Street* enunciate her propagandistic critiques of both domestic and international Fascism. In the former, the racist treatment of a young Black soldier and one-time migrant and sharecropper leads to a riot in Harlem. Petry's story was inspired by the same 1943 Harlem Riot whose rebels, as commemorated by Langston Hughes, "have long known the evils of local fascist practices—although in the past we have not called Jim Crow fascist by name."[43] The Fascist subtext of Petry's story surfaced in a more pronounced manner in *The Street*, written during the war and first published in 1946. In the novel, wartime mother and domestic worker Lutie Johnson is nearly sexually assaulted by a leering white overlord. Lutie responds by tossing black ink in his face while sardonically referring to his "master race" status in her life.[44] Lutie's controlled act of rage and rebellion recalls Thyra Edwards's admonition from Spain that "Fascism degrades women."

Petry's novel was a literary response to a landmark of African American fiction, Richard Wright's 1940 novel *Native Son*. *Native Son* tells the story of eighteen-year-old lumpenproletariat Bigger Thomas, growing up on Chicago's South Side in post-Depression conditions. In his essay "How Bigger Was Born," Wright explained that Bigger's alienation and economic desperation were so severe that he might become a force of "either Communism or Fascism."[45] Early in the novel, Bigger considers his envy of martial societies, which provide an order lacking in his fragmented and chaotic social reality. Here, Wright indexes the marginal appeal of extreme racial nationalism to Black communities during the 1930s and 1940s—such as the "Ethiopian Pacific Movement," cultivated by Jamaican-born Robert Jordan, which attempted to recruit African Americans to a program through which thousands of Africans would live under benevolent Japanese rule as a "champion" of the darker races. Wright's long unpublished novel *The Man Who Lived Underground*, based on a 1941 short story written immediately after *Native Son* but not published until 2021, again shifts the Fascist analytic: the book's working-class Black protagonist, Fred Daniels, is driven into a literal and metaphorical underground of the city after being falsely accused of murdering a white couple. Wright makes the refuge a symbol of both "underground" resistance to Fascism on the European front (the Netherlands, France, the Warsaw Ghetto) and of a hideaway for suspected "fifth column" traitors to the US war effort. Fred inhabits a no-man's land comprehensible only within an appreciation of what might be called a Black Antifascist aesthetic.[46]

The massively repressive police apparatus in both *Native Son* and *The Man Who Lived Underground* also includes techniques of torture and execution that conjure a surveillance mechanism proximate to a Fascist state. Here, Wright gestures both to the totalizing character of policing in Black communities (Langston Hughes reported that New York was "flooded" with police to contain Antifascist rallies for Ethiopia) as well as the deep, ongoing surveillance and stigmatization of Black Antifascists as traitors, especially during the war. As noted earlier, in 1942, Thyra Edwards received a letter from the federal government, asking, "Are you or have you ever been a member of the Communist Party?"[47] Edwards was targeted as part of a campaign to harass and intimidate veterans of the Antifascist war against Spain, as were James Yates and others. Earlier that year, on June 22, FBI director J. Edgar Hoover, under the code name RACON (for "Racial Conditions"), had ordered FBI field offices to survey "the extent of agitation among Negroes which may be an outgrowth of any effort on the part of the Axis powers (Germany, Italy) or the Communist Party."[48] In addition to Edwards and Yates, Langston Hughes, W. E. B. Du Bois, Richard Wright, and many others in the Black Antifascist Tradition would end up with their names and dossiers in FBI files.

So, too, would two of the most important visual artists of the Black Antifascist Tradition: Jackie Ormes and Ollie Harrington. Both were

DOUBLE V ANTIFASCISM AND WORLD WAR II 93

pioneers in the genre of the newspaper editorial cartoon, which became an optic complement to the Antifascist newspaper messaging of writers like Langston Hughes. Ormes was the primary editorial cartoonist for the *Chicago Defender* during Hughes's tenure as a columnist. In 1937, she launched the comic strip "Torchy Brown" in "Dixie to Harlem" in the *Pittsburgh Courier*, the first cartoon strip to feature an African American woman. In 1945, she debuted the strip "Candy" in the *Chicago Defender*. According to her biographer Nancy Goldstein, Ormes circulated in a Communist Party milieu in Chicago, befriending, among others, Margaret Burroughs. On October 6, 1945, after the war's end, she published in the *Pittsburgh Courier* a single-panel strip from her "Patty-Jo 'n' Ginger" series about an African American mother and daughter. The strip shows the young Patty-Jo in front of a dressing panel labeled with the words "Solidarity Confinement. Jap Prison Camp. Nazzi Horror Sell." Patty-Jo is complaining to her mother about "an ol' Mrs. Blowhard . . . All I said was maybe the neighbors won't LET her Sammy grow up to be a drummer in Basie's band," another postwar postmortem—a la Hughes's "Will V-Day"—on the dark racial hangover facing Black Americans after the war.[49] Ormes's depiction of a Black child's potential "dreams deferred" by American Fascism portends a radically unstable Black future.

Ollie Harrington, the child of a Jewish Hungarian mother and African American father, was deployed as a correspondent to France and Germany by the *Pittsburgh Courier*. His 1942 cartoon "Sikeston, Missouri and Germany" was a visual comparison of Cleo Wright, brutally lynched in Sikeston, Missouri, to a Jewish woman executed by the Nazis. The cartoon appeared in the progressive *People's Voice* newspaper, where Thyra Edwards also briefly worked during the war. As if in synergistic response to Harrington's cartoon, poet Benjamin Bardner published a poem, "Remembering Sikeston, Mo," in the *Defender*, demonstrating how artists turned the Black press into a vigilant Antifascist watchdog. A friend of Paul Robeson and Richard Wright, Harrington worked for Communist New York City councilman Ben Davis. Afterward, hounded by the FBI for his radical political sympathies, Harrington fled the US for Paris and later lived in East Germany, from

1961 to 1995. Harrington's political cartoons, as scholar Brian Dolinar has detailed,[50] can only be understood in the context of his wartime Antifascism: in a 1973 interview, looking back at the period, Harrington said, "I personally feel that my art must be involved, and the most profound involvement must be with the black liberation struggle."[51]

The special attacks by RACON targeting Black radicals during World War II underscore the particular threat that Black Antifascism represented to a US state seeking to purge the memory of the fight against Spanish Fascism in the name of shoring up anticommunism at home and sanctifying US power for the coming cold war. RACON also anticipated the better-known COINTELPRO campaign of the 1960s, which similarly targeted Black radicals bold enough to declare the US a Fascist state.

An "Ethiopian Utopia": Double V Antifascism and War's End

In May 1943, Langston Hughes published back-to-back *Chicago Defender* columns titled "America after the War" and "The World after the War." In the former, Hughes postulated that at war's end, "America is going to be a paradise. We are fighting for democracy, and democracy is what we intend to have."[52] Poll taxes and grandfather clauses would be gone, as would Jim Crow. "Hitlerian race theories," wrote Hughes, "will all be wiped off the books of American democracy." In "The World after the War," Hughes speculated about an end to world colonization: India would be free of the British Empire and China would control its own destiny, while Latin America "will no longer be suspicious and afraid of the great Yankee Colossus to the North . . . No longer will the mixed-bloods, the Indians and the Negroes of South America fear the Jim Crow customs of the United States."[53] Hughes ended both columns with the same refrain—"Am I dreaming?"[54]

Hughes's twinned utopian and satirical vision of the postwar world was laid out along the two tracks of Double Victory: defeat racism at home, defeat Fascism abroad. In the late stages of the war, these tracks merged into an itinerant internationalist version of Black Antifascism that sought to build from the ashes of World War II a decolonizing

Third Space. That vision harked back to, recapitulated, and pulled forward its founding international ideological tenets: Anticolonialism, Pan-Africanism, and Communism. In short, it sought to transform the internationalism of the diasporic Black fight against Fascism that had begun in the 1930s into a formula for the liberation of the Black planet.

For example, in 1944, in London, George Padmore officially disbanded the International African Service Bureau (IASB), formed after the Italian invasion of Ethiopia. Together, Padmore and IASB Antifascist veterans Jomo Kenyatta and T. Ras Makonnen founded anew the Pan-African Federation. The effort was to revive and make explicit a Pan-African movement that had been both subordinated to and informed by the struggle against Fascism. Both the IASB and International Friends of Ethiopia were anticolonial organizations in the guise of fighting Fascism. They had also demonstrated the need and opportunity for Black international leadership in the formation of a postwar world order. Thus, one year later, in October 1945, in Manchester, England, the new federation sponsored the fifth Pan-African Congress, with the intention of building from wartime organizing an even more radically ambitious assault on racial capitalism.

Fittingly, it was W. E. B. Du Bois, cofounder of the Pan-African Movement and of its original 1900 London conference, who articulated this vision at Manchester, a symbolic tying together of both the American and international aspirations for "Double Victory." Du Bois officially launched the six-day event, as the newly elected president of the Pan-African Congress, with a keynote address retracing the organization's history. For the more than three hundred participants, he remembered calling together the first Pan-African Congress in Paris in 1919 to coincide with the Treaty of Versailles talks that ended World War I. Du Bois's proposed plan to the Versailles delegates had put African decolonization at the center of the postwar world. As reported at the time by the *Chicago Tribune*, Du Bois noted, the plan called for an "Ethiopian Utopia, to be fashioned out of the German colonies." Specifically, it described an "internationalized Africa, to have as its basis the former German colonies," while returning Portuguese- and Belgian-landed territories to the colonial subjects. In this way, the Treaty of Versailles might recognize "the wishes of the intelligent Negroes of the colonies themselves, the Negroes of the United States and of South America and the West Indies, the Negro Governments of Abyssinia, Liberia, and Equatorial Africa and Basutoland, Swaziland, Sierra Leone, Gold Coast, Gambia and Bechuanaland and in the Union of Africa."[55]

Du Bois's "Ethiopian Utopia" of 1919 and its proposed reversal of the colonial world order was made imaginable and legible to attendees at Manchester by a ten-year international struggle of Black Antifascism. As Du Bois had written just a year earlier, "The Second World War . . . found the colonial question really unsettled and was precipitated by the determination of Italy to enter upon an imperial career in Africa. On the part of Germany there was a distinct and increasing pressure for the return of her colonies and for even larger colonial expansion. Thus the problem of colonies has been certainly a main cause of two world wars and unless it is frankly faced and its settlement begun, it may easily cause a third."[56]

Du Bois's analysis of a possible Third World War dovetailed with the warnings of Hughes, Ormes, and other Double V veterans that World War II had represented a crossroads between a perennial instantiation of a Fascist world order or its as yet undetermined alternative. For much of 1944 and 1945, Black Antifascists sounded this alarm at every turn: the Pan-African Federation organized an All Colonial People's Conference in London to counter the formative deliberations taking place in San Francisco at Dunbarton Oaks, where planning meetings for the United Nations Organization were being held. For Black Antifascists, the emerging UN was a crucial development that threatened either to repeat the errors of history, or, in Du Bois's words, to "frankly face" them. Those errors were the appeasements to racial capitalism of colonization, imperialism, and racism that had produced the Fascist world order in the first place. Here, Du Bois was again most lucid in his analysis. According to the proposals at Dunbarton Oaks, the UN, he wrote, would be constituted of "an indeterminate number of free nations, mostly white folk and comprising about one thousand million people . . . Some of these nations, however, are so under the economic domination of great powers that they will hardly be able to take an independent stand . . . There will be six hundred million colored and black folk inhabiting colonies owned by white nations, who have no rights that white people are bound to respect."[57] In sum, the colonized world as living death camp.

Du Bois's analysis of the UN's prospective new world order, written at the age of seventy-seven, stemmed from a lifetime of analysis of Fascist threats, nurtured by his long-developing Pan-African, anticolonial, and, increasingly, Communist-influenced perspective on the world. It was also hailed into being by the freight train of a cold war order, coming hard down the same utopian tracks Double Victory had laid out, threatening to smash everything that Black Antifascism had stood for. Within a short time, Du Bois and the broad cadre of radicals tempered and steeled by war would face a new Fascist threat—and would conceive of the United Nations as a new weapon to fight it.

— CHAPTER 4 —

LEGAL ANTIFASCISM
The "We Charge Genocide" Campaign, 1946–1956

Your petitioners will prove that the crime of which we complain
is in fact genocide within the terms and meanings of the United
Nations convention providing for this prevention and punishment
of this crime. We shall submit evidence, tragically voluminous,
of "acts committed with intent to destroy, in whole or in part, a
national, ethnical, racial or religious group as such"—in this case the
15,0000,000 Negro people of the United States.
—**Civil Rights Congress**, "We Charge Genocide: The
Crime of Government Against the Negro People," a petition
submitted to the United Nations, December 1951[1]

BLACK ANTIFASCISM'S POPULAR RISE during World War II drew the microscopic scrutiny of democratic capitalist states attuned to its insurrectionary potential. The Fascist impulse to racialize, stigmatize, hierarchize, quarantine, and eliminate Black people vacillated between colonizing countries like Germany, Spain, and Italy and putatively liberal democracies worried about internal rebellions against their hegemonic place in the postwar order. The perceived threat of the Double Victory campaign in the US, for example, helped engender what scholar Charisse Burden-Stelly has described as a "Black/Red Scare."[2] In the emerging cold war US state, Black Antifascism became a primary target of a sprawling disciplinary apparatus meant to solidify racial capitalist hegemony over and against world Communism. As a result, Black Antifascism would be forced to engage the state more directly on its own terms. As governments, courts, judiciaries, international governing bodies, and police were deployed to control challenges to white-supremacist, ruling-class power, Black Antifascism developed its own legal and extralegal strategies for keeping its movement and its members alive, in struggle, and out of jail.

This massive political drama is the main plot line of one of the most riveting and compelling narratives in the Black Antifascist Tradition, the We Charge Genocide movement of 1946–1956. A groundbreaking social movement within the US Black Antifascist Tradition, the We Charge Genocide campaign looked both backward and forward, synthesizing currents of the tradition from its inception and predicting with uncanny prescience the future terrain of Black struggle against Fascism. Formally organized by the Civil Rights Congress (CRC), a broad left network with roots in the Communist Party, We Charge Genocide was at once a legal campaign to racialize and criminalize Fascism, an international diplomatic strike challenging and deploying new global institutions of political power, and a theoretical reorganization of the role and rule of law in racial capitalist societies. These were the elements of what this chapter will call *Legal Antifascism*. As we documented in our introduction, US race law was a significant influence on the development of European Fascism. Legal Antifascism in the US developed from an understanding of this conjuncture. It sought to undermine US liberal legality's long history of violence, coercion, and inequality against Black citizens as a potential prototype and mechanism for Fascism within US borders. Key to this campaign was an attempt to use newly developing international law as a bulwark against America's massively discriminatory legal history. From 1946 to 1956, the We Charge Genocide campaign was the leading edge of US Legal Antifascism, using the courts, international bodies, and the media to protect the Black right to live in the face of savage legal inequalities. Perhaps the most famous civil rights campaign most Americans have never heard of, We Charge Genocide has also survived into our political present as one of the most powerful legacies of the Black Antifascist Tradition.

Though it formally launched at the end of World War II, the We Charge Genocide movement and the campaign for Legal Antifascism was best predicted and anticipated by events of the 1930s. The Communist Party's creation of the International Labor Defense (ILD) legal team to challenge false allegations of rape against the Scottsboro Boys marked a turning point in the Black Antifascist Tradition. The ILD's defense was predicated not just on refuting the charges against the nine Black young men and boys but also on incriminating the US state for deploying race law to strangle the lives and life expectancies of African Americans. In particular, the ILD identified lynching, lynch law, police brutality, and racist courts—for instance, all-white juries—as the primary tools in the state's monopoly on violence against its Black citizenry. The head of the ILD team was Black attorney William Patterson, whose father was from St. Lucia. Patterson was born in the San Francisco Bay Area and graduated from Hastings Law School at UC Berkeley, eventually becoming a partner in the Black law firm of Dyatt, Hall, and Patterson in New York City. By 1926, Patterson had joined the Communist Party, and in 1932, he served on the ILD team to defend Communist Party member Angelo Herndon, arrested in Atlanta for organizing Black and White industrial workers. That same year, Patterson joined the Scottsboro Boys' defense team. In 1934, Patterson traveled to Germany, where Hitler had one year earlier become chancellor. There, he reported finding "hundreds of Jewish friends of mine hiding or already entrapped and imprisoned in concentration camps."[3]

Patterson's travel to Germany was a logical extension of his work defending the Scottsboro Boys. The ILD made clear that it considered the Scottsboro frame-up an example of legal Anti-Black Fascism. Reporting on the Scottsboro case in its newspaper, *Labor Defender*, the ILD put its defense of the Scottsboro Boys and the persecution of political prisoners in Germany side by side in its pages. "Help the Prisoners in Hitler's Dungeons," read the headline of one 1933 report, set between articles on the fate of the Scottsboro Boys. The article cited Hitler's outlawing of Rote Hilfe (Red Aid)—the legal organizational parallel to the ILD in Germany. The paper also included a sidebar titled "International Labor Defense Fights," enumerating the organization's causes. These included the fight for Negro rights and "self-defense in their struggle for self-determination" and the fight against "all forms of police brutality, terror and persecution," including "lynching, Jim-Crowism," "legal murders," and "Fascist terror."[4] Patterson himself provided the legal analysis of "Fascist terror." In a 1933 article for *Labor Defender*, Patterson argued that it was the system of US jurisprudence and racial capitalism, not the Scottsboro Boys, that was on trial in Alabama. His article appeared on the second anniversary of the boys' arrest; after an initial conviction of eight defendants and the mistrial of the ninth, the Supreme Court had responded to appeals from the ILD by declaring their right to a second trial. Noting that the Thirteenth, Fourteenth, and Fifteenth amendments, guaranteeing Black freedom, legal equality, citizenship and voting rights, had been passed during Reconstruction's expansion of Black freedoms, Patterson argued that the Scottsboro "frameup" was a legal lynching that caught both white and Black workers in the noose: "The government at Washington, we are told, holds the states responsible for carrying out the Constitution. . . . If those who rule in Alabama can deny Negroes the rights guaranteed to them by the Constitution of the United States, Alabama's ruling class stands above the Constitution—or else the Constitution was never meant to apply to the oppressed people of a nation."[5] The prerogative denial of rights to Black people would also put white legal rights in jeopardy by making them culpable in a system of oppression and exploitation "because the rulers tell them 'white supremacy must be maintained.'"[6]

Patterson's simultaneous attention to the role of law in the repression of African Americans and the Nazi persecution of Jews was shaped by important legal and political currents. Mussolini's rise to power in Italy had been enabled by revision of its penal code in 1930, which made political opposition to the state (and, eventually, being Jewish) a crime.[7] The so-called Rocco penal code was to become a partial model for the Nazi Nuremberg Race Laws of 1935, which criminalized race, religion,

LEGAL ANTIFASCISM

and ethnicity and rewrote the legal code to affix Nazi rule. By 1937, after its invasion of Ethiopia, the Italian state was, in turn, following the German example by equating Blacks and Jews as inferior races. As Patterson knew, both Fascist regimes had been influenced by US Jim Crow race laws. As noted earlier, the Italian magazine *La Difesa della Razza* codified Italian state raciology by asserting that Italians were decidedly "Aryan," "Hebrews" were decidedly not, and Negroes, particularly US Negroes, were congenitally inferior.[8] Both the Rocco and Nuremberg penal codes were influenced by legal framings that had also caught Patterson in a political web: in 1918, the US Congress had created the Overman Committee to investigate "Bolshevik elements" in the US who might constitute a special threat to the US military campaign in World War I. Patterson had already been arrested for opposing the war even before becoming a Bolshevik. The Overman Committee and the creation of the Bureau of Investigation (later the FBI) were the first manifestations of what would become the "Red Scare." In 1919, the "Red Scare" merged with the "Black scare" when thousands of African Americans across the US were attacked by white racist mobs in what James Weldon Johnson dubbed the "Red Summer." None of these murderers was brought to justice. Under attack, in particular, were Black soldiers returning from World War I and Black radicals seen as a threat to the postwar domestic order in the US. Jamaican poet Claude McKay, radicalized by the Russian Revolution and the Red Summer, captured this dynamic in his brilliant poem "If We Must Die," defending the lives of Black workers under siege across the US and earning his own place as a "premature Black Antifascist." In another poem from 1922, "To the White Fiends," McKay explicitly threatened to take up arms against what the ILD dubbed "Fascist terror":

> Think you I am not fiend and savage too?
> Think you I could not arm me with a gun
> And shoot down ten of you for every one
> Of my black brothers murdered, burnt by you?[9]

104 THE BLACK ANTIFASCIST TRADTION

Throughout the 1920s, the US state ramped up its legal repression and surveillance of Black Bolsheviks like McKay. In 1930, four years after Patterson had joined the Communist Party, fervent anticommunist Hamilton Fish spearheaded the Fish Committee to investigate Communist influence and organizations in the United States. From 1934 to 1937, these tasks fell to the so-called McCormack-Dickstein Committee, otherwise known as the Special Committee on Un-American Activities Authorized to Investigate Nazi Propaganda and Certain Other Propaganda Activities. In 1938, that committee became the House Special Committee on Un-American Activities chaired by Texas congressman Martin Dies. The Dies Committee became the prototype for the House Un-American Activities Committee in 1945, famously chaired by Senator Joseph McCarthy.

What did all this mean to William Patterson and Black Antifascists? Much, it turns out. The Dies Committee immediately targeted as "subversive" the National Negro Congress (NNC) and its leader, Alphaeus Hunton. As noted earlier, the NNC had been central to advancing the US campaign against Mussolini's invasion of Ethiopia. It had also served as part of the Communist Party's efforts to link the attacks on Black Americans at home to the fight against Fascism overseas. Claudia Jones, a Trinidadian émigré who would eventually sign her name to the "We Charge Genocide" petition, cited this conjuncture when explaining why she joined the Communist Party in the 1930s: "I was impressed by the Communist speakers," she wrote, " who explained this brutal crime against young Negro Boys [the Scottsboro Nine]; and who related the Scottsboro Case to the struggle of the Ethiopian people against fascism and against Mussolini's invasion."[10]

For Patterson, Jones, Hunton, and others in the Black Antifascist Tradition, the state's new legislative codes repressing political dissent made African Americans the canaries in the coal mine of an anti-Black legal order. The fight against Fascism as a political force either external to the US (Spain, Italy, or Germany) or as an adjunct to American racism (the Double Victory campaign) took on a special urgency whereby one's *legal* standing in the US was quite literally a matter of life and death. It was this fundamental political, philosophical, and economic dilemma that became the rational kernel of the We Charge Genocide movement. Its many legal coordinates deserve careful marking and telling.

In June 1940, a coalition of Black, Jewish, and white radicals formed a new organization called the National Federation for Constitutional Liberties (NFCL). Modeled on the Communist Party's Popular Front strategy of the 1930s to weld cross-class alliance in the war against racial capitalism, it included Detroit minister Owen A. Knox as chairman; Black Antifascist Tradition veteran and former NNC president Max Yergan as vice chairman; New York political fellow traveler Vito Marcantonio; writer and journalist Carey McWilliams; radical attorneys Alfred K. Stern and Morris Watson; and former Roosevelt administration economist George Marshall. Using a Popular Front rhetoric meant to mainstream Antifascist sentiment in the service of "democratic rights guaranteed by the Constitution and the laws of the United States," the federation called for the FBI to "put an end to its Gestapo activities," abolition of the poll tax, passing of federal antilynching law, and an end to government persecution of the "alien and foreign born."[11] The latter was a reference to the Alien Registration Act (popularly known as the Smith Act), voted into law by Congress the very same month and a major impetus for the creation of the NFCL. The Alien Registration Act was the most sweeping repressive measure yet passed in the wake of the creation of the Dies Committee. It criminalized all "subversive activities," including membership in the Communist Party; required all non-US citizens to register with the US government, and broadly expanded state powers of deportation to include persons seeking to organize and become members of a group considered a threat to the US state.[12]

The 1940 conjuncture of the Smith Act and formation of the NFCL indicated the legal and judicial terrain upon which Legal Antifascism would unfold. This was evident in one of the NFCL's first major publications, the *Anti-Fascist Civil Rights Declaration for 1944*. In it, the federation called for a permanent Fair Employment Practices Committee (FEPC), to eliminate job discrimination in industry; equality within a still Jim Crowed military; legislation against antisemitism and what the federation called "incitement" of racial hatred; a ban on discrimination in employment and in housing; and the abolition of Jim Crow. One year earlier, the federation had gathered more than 1,200 signatures demanding the elimination of the Dies Committee, calling it an impediment to winning the war.[13] The petition was the mass organizing arm to the federation's first book, *Investigate Martin Dies!*, published in 1942. The book accused Dies of soft-pedaling investigations of pro-Nazi propagandists in the United States, such as William Dudley Pelley; failing to investigate homegrown white supremacist groups like the Ku Klux Klan; and using anticommunism as a shield for both: "Dies, like Goebbels, uses the demagogy of 'anti-communism' to obscure his efforts to weaken and destroy the anti-Axis, antifascist unity of the American people."[14]

Like the Double Victory campaign, the NFCL attempted to flip the script on the US discourse on democracy: Fascism, it argued, was the threat of a *legal* counterrevolution over and against the ideal of substantive judicial equality under the law. Thus, in its political work, the federation toggled between acting as pro bono legal consultant to the masses—for example, publishing a book on New York's antidiscrimination laws and "how to use them"—while agitating for recognition of what it perceived as an imminent, legalistic Fascism bearing down from the state, courts, and judiciary. In 1941, it published a book on anticommunist witch hunts in the US government, and, in 1945, another book titled, *They Still Carry On! Native Fascists: How to Spot Them*, a play on the Red Scare's hysterical Communist-phobia.[15]

As in the broader fight against racial capitalism, Black Antifascism also insisted on being internationalist. Just as Double Victory and Pan-African Antifascism had constructed a global fight against Fascist foes, Legal Antifascism insisted on universalizing civil rights along lines of race, class, and nation. It was for this reason that Black Antifascists gravitated immediately to the proposed United Nations. As early as 1942, W. E. B. Du Bois had called the newly signed "Declaration by the United Nations" a moment for international attention to the plight of the colonies, which were, with the exception of India, notably excluded from the original statement.[16] Du Bois also attended the San Francisco planning conference for the UN at Dunbarton Oaks, in 1945, as an invited observer for the NAACP. Du Bois, who was to play a key role in the We Charge Genocide movement, regarded the formation of the UN as a critical opportunity to globalize the aims of Pan-Africanism, Anti-colonialism, and Black Antifascism. For example, Du Bois regarded the adoption of Section 73 of the UN Charter on "non-self-governing territories" to be a paternalistic platitude that failed to recognize colonial self-determination or to give colonized nations a seat at the UN table.[17] The NAACP was also dismayed when the US, led by Eleanor Roosevelt as chair of the UN Commission on Human Rights, acted in 1945 to insert a "domestic jurisdiction" clause into the UN Charter that would prevent the UN investigation of US crimes such as lynching and other violations of African American civil rights.[18] As Carol Anderson has noted, Roosevelt in essence assured "that the sacred troika of lynching, Southern Justice, and Jim Crow schools would remain untouched, even with an international treaty to safeguard human rights."[19]

In 1947, in a frustrated response, Du Bois published his own "Statement on Race and Colonies," calling on the UN to create an international colonial commission, "on which colonial people shall have representation."[20] Du Bois adroitly used the category of race to conjoin the appeals of African Americans within the US to those of colonized subjects. "The United Nations recognizing democracy as the only just way of life for all people make it a first statute of international law that at the earliest practical moment no nation nor group shall be deprived of effective voice in its own government."[21] In the same year, the NAACP, with Du Bois serving as director of research for the project, presented a petition to the UN.[22] Titled "An Appeal to the World!" the document catalogued extensive evidence of Black discrimination in jobs, voting, schooling and social life. Three sections of the document focused on the "legal status" or "legal rights" of the Negro. Its concluding section, written by Howard University professor Rayford Logan, urged the UN to allow the petition to be undertaken by the General Assembly as part of the commitment to human rights and the rights of minorities as stated in its charter. The petition attempted to leverage a January 1947 resolution condemning the treatment of Indian laborers in the Union of South Africa as "contrary to the Charter" of the United Nations.[23] In total, the NAACP petition argued for the application of UN human rights law on minority populations to Black Americans as a realizable path to legal inclusivity.

The NAACP petition had been motivated in part by a petition brought to the UN the previous year by the NNC. On June 6, 1946, the NNC submitted "A Petition to the United Nations on Behalf of 13 Million Oppressed Negro Citizens of the United States" to UN representatives at Hunter College. The congress deviated from the NAACP's more liberal analysis of prospects for Black life, contending that by betraying African American support for the fight against Fascism overseas, the US had revealed its own indigenous Fascist strain:

> Barred from most industrial and business employment on the spurious grounds of "race," bound to the soil in semi-feudal serfdom on the cotton plantations of the Deep South, forced to live in overcrowded slum ghettoes in our great cities, denied any education for millions of our children, lynched and terrorized, kept from effective use of the ballot in many states, segregated like pariahs, the more than 13,000,000 Negro Americans still suffer an oppression which is revolting to all the canons of civilized society.[24]

The NNC petition also charged that white supremacist politicians, including US secretary of state James Byrne, from South Carolina, and Dixiecrat senator Theodore Bilbo of Mississippi, "subscribe(s) to the same policies of anti-Negro oppression as did the late Herr Hitler." The document, in turn, characterized the UN as a "Parliament of Man" meant to "crush the fascist monster," appealing for relief for African Americans via its founding principles of "respect for human rights and for fundamental freedoms without distinction as to race, sex, language, or religion."[25]

The NNC petition proceeded to flood the UN with statistics assembled by Communist writer (and friend of Du Bois) Herbert Aptheker, emphasizing economic hardships, noting that more than one million

African Americans labored as domestic workers and more than half of African Americans occupied two of the lowest-paying positions in the US economy. Thus, the petition's special appeal to the Economic and Social Council of the UN was to conduct research into the conditions of "Negro life" and to make recommendations so that "higher standards" of human rights could be achieved. It also urged on the creation of an international bill of rights that would advance the "protection of minorities."[26]

The NNC's aspiration to recast the UN as an Antifascist tribunal underscored its continuities with prewar Pan-African and Marxist Antifascisms, which had viewed Western imperialism and colonialism as the seedbeds of a Fascist futurity. Yet, the petition was to be the NNC's last hurrah. In April 1946, after months of internal turmoil, the organization was merged with the NFCL and the ILD to form a new entity, the Civil Rights Congress (CRC). The merger, guided by the hand of the Communist Party, was intended to create a sturdier, better resourced, and more coalitional organization that could both withstand persisting state repression and more loudly declaim the fight against creeping state Fascism. The CRC was intended to combine the Legal Antifascist tactics honed by the ILD, NFCL, and NNC with mass organizing strategies to draw in the widest realm of public support. In so doing, it intended to create the first mass Black Antifascist organization in the United States.

This double direction was clear at the CRC's launch: more than six hundred individual sponsors attended its inaugural convention in Detroit. Prominent founding members represented a broad range of the US left. In addition to ILD veteran William Patterson, they included attorney George Marshall from the NFCL; Communist attorney Aubrey Grossman, named as the CRC's first executive secretary; and trailblazing Black journalist and author Louis Burnham, one-time director of the pioneering Southern Negro Youth Conference. A veteran of protests against the Scottsboro Boys case and Italy's invasion of Ethiopia, Burnham had already collaborated with Marshall, having sent him a report as head of the NFCL about the case of Willie McGee, a Black man wrongly accused of rape in Louisiana in 1945. In addition, the new national board of the CRC included prominent feminist organizer Elizabeth Gurley Flynn and trailblazing African American journalist Charlotta Bass, editor of the progressive, Los Angeles-based Black newspaper the *California Eagle*.

As scholar Gerald Horne has noted in his history of the CRC, the group sought to combine cutting-edge legal strategies with mass organizing. Toward these goals, the CRC built a network of lawyers across the US, available to take up mainly two kinds of cases: those of political dissidents being repressed for radical views, like members of the Communist Party; and those of African Americans charged with politically loaded crimes, like rape. It also built an alliance with the National Lawyers Guild, launched in 1937 as a radical alternative to the American Bar Association, which had often complied with repressive state legislation. This legal army of attorneys often worked for the CRC for minimal money, raised through grassroots means (for example, the sale and distribution of pamphlets highlighting ongoing CRC cases), or provided pro bono legal advice. At the same time, the CRC opened official local organizing chapters around the country. These chapters held meetings and rallies in conjunction with CRC legal campaigns, conducted fundraising efforts, and distributed CRC literature, including, eventually, the "We Charge Genocide" petition. All told, according to Horne, CRC membership may have approached ten thousand people.[27]

The ecumenical, confederated range of voices joining the CRC chorus was in direct emulation of the Communist Party's Popular Front strategy against wartime Fascism, with a narrower remit: namely, to become a legal battering ram to challenge the US state monopoly on judicial and political violence. This conception lay at the heart of what became the CRC's most important legacy to the Black Antifascist Tradition, the We Charge Genocide campaign. Its roots, too, lay in several tributaries of the tradition. The first and most important was the broad-based movement against lynching documented in chapter 1. In 1948, the CRC launched a "Lobby to End Lynching" campaign on Capitol Hill in support of the Wagner-Case bill against lynching. The CRC's

LEGAL ANTIFASCISM

support for the bill hinged on opposition to ongoing lynchings across the country, including a rise after the end of World War II with the return home of Black soldiers. Yet, the "Lobby to End Lynching" campaign was also meant to draw attention to what the CRC called "legal lynchings" of Black men—treated in courts with the same inhumanity and inequality as on the streets—and to draw parallels between forms of legal and extralegal violence.

The opening salvo of the CRC's public work was the case of Willie McGee. A Mississippi laborer arrested and charged in November 1945 with the rape of a white woman, McGee was executed by the state in 1951 after three separate trials. In each instance, McGee was convicted and received the death penalty. The CRC defense won its appeal after the first trial, arguing that a raging lynch mob outside the courtroom necessitated a second trial. CRC won a second appeal on the grounds that Blacks had been excluded from the petit and grand juries that had indicted McGee. Along the way toward McGee's eventual execution, CRC raised the issue of the disproportionate use of the death penalty against African Americans, a violation of the Eighth Amendment prohibition against cruel and unusual punishment, and noted that McGee's confession had been beaten out of him, in violation of his constitutional rights. In an effort to build something like a broad front against Anti-Black Fascism, the CRC attracted and incorporated wide support for McGee into its legal and public relations campaign: a young New York attorney named Bella Abzug helped to defend him; Communist Party member and writer Jessica Mitford, under the name Decca Treuhaft, a veteran of the Joint Anti-Fascist Refugee Committee, worked for the CRC on McGee's public campaign; Nobel Prize laureate William Faulkner made a statement of public support; and Albert Einstein publicly pleaded McGee's innocence.

Alongside their defense of McGee, the CRC was also defending seven African American men charged with raping a white woman in Martinsville, Virginia, the "Martinsville Seven." In their defense, the CRC pointed out that their confessions had been obtained without legal counsel, under duress of a lynch mob assembled after their arrest, and their cases had been tried before all-white and all-male juries. When the state and US Supreme Court refused to hear appeals of their original conviction, the Martinsville Seven all died in the electric chair in February 1951, in the largest mass execution for rape in US history. (It should be noted that, on August 31, 2021, Virginia governor Ralph Northam pardoned all seven convictions.)[28]

In the weekly bulletin that publicized its work, the CRC attempted to connect the McGee and Martinsville cases to creeping US Fascism. It compared their executions to "Hitler's attacks upon the Jewish people." It cited US Supreme Court Chief Justice Robert H. Jackson's condemnation of the "German mistreatment of the Germans" at the Nuremberg trials, substituting the words "ruling circle's mistreatment of Black Americans," in a "scathing condemnation of Nazism to the American scene."[29] They also analogized the state's annihilatory racial violence to the war against Koreans overseas, comparing the electric chair used to execute McGee and the Martinsville Seven to the 32,000 tons of napalm bombs dropped by the US during the Korean War.[30] The elements of the CRC's definitional understanding of the threat of Anti-Black Fascism were taking shape: state sovereignty over Black life based on violence both domestic and international; a conjunction of legal and extralegal juridicial processes used to railroad African Americans; a legal logic that ran parallel to examples from Nazi Germany; a conception of due process in which the legal definitions of race were deployed to maintain immovable hierarchies of power, like Jim Crow, analogizable to Fascisms in Italy, Germany and the colonies.

These global dimensions of Anti-Black Fascism were imperative to the CRC's decision to itself appeal to the UN as a site for building its allegation of genocide. On December 9, 1948, the year William Patterson assumed CRC leadership as national secretary, the UN General Assembly adopted the Convention on the Prevention and Punishment of the Crime of Genocide. Building on Polish lawyer Raphael Lemkin's prior definition of the term, Article II of the UN convention defined genocide as "any of the following acts committed with intent to destroy, *in whole or in part*, a national, ethnical or religious group as such":

(a) Killing members of the group

(b) Causing serious bodily or mental harm to members of the group

(c) Deliberately inflicting on the group conditions of life calculated to bring about the physical destruction in whole or in part

(d) Imposing measures intended to prevent births within the group

(e) Forcibly transferring children of the group to another group

Article III of the UN Convention provided that "The following acts shall be punishable":

(a) Genocide

(b) Conspiracy to commit genocide

(c) Direct and public incitement to genocide

(d) Attempt to commit genocide

(e) Complicity in genocide[31]

The UN's definition of genocide provided the CRC with a legitimating framing for an historical and theoretical analysis of Anti-Black Fascism. The definition of genocide as killing "in part or in whole" members of a group dovetailed with the orientation in the NNC's 1946 petition on behalf of the "13 Million" Negroes of the United States, documenting the loss of life, health, and legal rights specific to Black life. Influenced by the Communist Party's analysis of national liberation struggles around the world, the CRC had already begun to describe African Americans as an "oppressed national minority," with its own historical, social and political characteristics. One of those characteristics, the CRC argued, was vulnerability to what it called "premature death" at the hands of its own state apparatus. These ideas were, in turn, woven into the "We Charge Genocide" petition to the UN General Assembly. The petition's first section, called an opening statement, served as both an amicus brief on behalf of African American people and as a prosecutorial charge of genocide based on the new UN convention. It formally charged the US government with "mass murder of its own nationals, with institutionalized oppression and persistent slaughter of the Negro people in the United States on the basis of 'race.'" It elaborated thus, drawing language directly from the new UN definition of genocide:

We shall submit evidence proving "killing members of the group," in violation of Article II of the Convention. We cite killings at night by masked men, killings always on the basis of "race," killings by the Ku Klux Klan, that organization which is chartered by several states as a semi-official arm of government and even granted the tax exemptions of a benevolent society.[32]

Several elements of the CRC's strategy are important signposts on the road of the Black Antifascist Tradition. First, the killing of members of the group "based on race" indexed anti-Black violence and racism as particular characteristics of American Fascism. Second, the petition's insistence on legal and extralegal violence as a continuum refused to grant political autonomy to the state. Rather, "genocide" was a collaboration between the branches of government and mass mobilization on the street. The CRC term for this collaboration was "conspiracy," a deliberate inversion of political meaning. The 1940 Smith Act included a "conspiracy provision" targeting subversive political coordination—like membership in the Communist Party. In the "We Charge Genocide" petition, the government itself was deemed a conspiracy against Black life. Finally, the petition used the term "incitement," drawn directly from the UN definition of genocide, leveled against the state, the media, and ruling political organizations:

We shall offer evidence that this genocide in not plotted in the dark but incited over the radio into the ears of millions, urged in the glare of public forums by Senators and Governors. It is offered as an article of faith by powerful political organizations, such as the Dixiecrats, and defended by influential newspapers, all in violation of the United Nations charter and the Convention forbidding genocide. Neither Hitler nor Goebbels wrote obscurantist racial incitements more voluminously or viciously than do their American counterparts, nor did such incitements circulate in Nazi mails any more freely than they do in the mails of the United States.[33]

LEGAL ANTIFASCISM

As the petition noted, "incitement" toward genocide was a punishable crime under Article III of the UN convention. Yet, the petition's analogy of American Anti-Black Fascism and German Nazi rule did not end at allegations of incitement. It also argued that genocide against African Americans was a *precondition* for wars and wartime atrocities—like the US bombing of Hiroshima—that would be Fascist in character:

> We solemnly declare that continuance of this American crime against the Negro people of the United States will strengthen those reactionary American forces driving towards World War III as certainly as the unrebuked Nazi genocide against the Jewish people strengthened Hitler in his successful drive to World War II. It is not without significance that it was President Truman who spoke of the possibility of using the atom bomb on the colored peoples of Asia, that it is American statesmen who prate constantly of "Asiatic hordes."[34]

By drawing US atomic war into its purview, the CRC updated earlier Black Antifascist Tradition analysis to calibrate and resist the US ascent to power during and after World War II. At the heart of this analysis was a fresh legal interpretation of racial capitalism. In one of the longest sections of the opening statement, "We Charge Genocide" offered an historical materialist account of the long duration of American genocide. The petition described the conditions of African Americans in the nineteenth-century South as a "Black Belt," where they were hard-birthed into Fascist conditions: "Much of the law of those states in the Black Belt," they noted, "is directed towards guaranteeing an American peasantry without political or human rights available to work the land without pay sufficient for proper livelihood."[35]

The description in "We Charge Genocide" of slavery and its aftermath as a prolonged period of rightslessness—absent voting rights, mobility rights, marital rights, citizenship rights—was for the CRC both the past and prologue to the making of an Anti-Black Fascism that it called "Genocide for Profit":

The intricate superstructure of "law and order" and extra-legal terror enforces an oppression that guarantees profit. This was true of that genocide, perhaps the most bloody ever perpetrated, which for two hundred and fifty years enforced chattel slavery upon the American Negro. Then as now it increased in bloodiness with the militancy of the Negro people as they struggled to achieve democracy for themselves. It was particularly bloody under slavery because the Negro people never ceased fighting for their freedom.[36]

The comprehension in "We Charge Genocide" of law as superstructure invoked the Marxist conception of bourgeois law as "determined in [its] form and content by the relations of production"[37]—an insight that had driven 1930s Black Antifascism to link racial capitalism, imperialism, and Fascism. Its insistence that Anti-Black Fascism was also a *counterrevolution* against Black freedom struggle would become a core argument of Black Antifascists in the 1960s and 1970s, as we shall see. In making this argument, the CRC drew directly from the work of the petition's coauthor W. E. B. Du Bois. In his magisterial 1935 book *Black Reconstruction*, Du Bois termed slavery and the backlash after the collapse of Reconstruction a "counterrevolution of property" that opened the door for domestic and foreign US racial violence. In a subsection of the opening statement titled "Reconstruction," the CRC made the same argument. After the end of Reconstruction, "terror was unleashed" against African Americans, with more than 1,955 recorded lynchings. "Side by side," the petition's authors wrote, "went terror unleashed abroad, as American imperialism entered the international arena by subjugating the Filipino, Puerto Rican, and Cuban peoples and reduced many Latin-American countries to economic and political vassalage."[38]

The CRC's synthesis of genocide, imperialism, and war was critical to its claim for the UN as a bulwark against global Fascism. Throughout the petition, it noted that the UN and especially the Convention on the Prevention and Punishment of the Crime of Genocide were direct responses to the global threat of Nazism: "The Convention, to a marked degree," they noted, "is a result of the Nuremberg trials of the Nazi war

LEGAL ANTIFASCISM

criminals at the end of World War II."[39] This argument was central to the petition's assertion that "We Charge Genocide" was to be an American answer to the Nuremberg trials. To this end, the Congress argued that, since the UN Charter had been ratified by Congress, UN law "superseded" US law in adjudicating charges and crimes of genocide. US law, they argued, had put African Americans in a political chokehold, portending premature death: "The United States Government has made no move, recommendation, or act to pass the domestic legislation 'to give effect to the provisions of the present convention' to which it is solemnly obligated under international law. It has failed even to pass a Fair Employment Practice Act, or a Federal anti-lynching law, or even to enforce laws technically in being which could be used to eliminate genocide."[40] This claim was buttressed by an appendix chronicling congressional acts that either failed to take up legislation to protect and defend African Americans or passed legislation that would restrict those freedoms.

The CRC also used as a methodology what Critical Race Theory (CRT) would later term "legal counternarrative." Part III of the petition's text, titled "The Evidence," was an exhaustive catalog of legal and extralegal executions of African Americans meant to fulfill Article II (a) of the UN convention, "Killing Members of the Group." The evidence focused on three types of deaths: lynchings, police shootings, and state executions of Black prisoners. This evidence was sourced from "Negro yearbooks, the Negro press or the labor press. The vast majority of such crimes are never recorded. This widespread failure to record crimes against the Negro people is in itself an index to genocide."[41] Two appendices to the 1951 book supported these claims: the first, a list of "violence and illegal acts" in the state of Georgia between 1940 and 1950; and the second, a study of cases in which rape law and punishment were differentially applied to African Americans and whites in the state of Louisiana. The CRC's "counternarrative" of evidence was meant to create no less than a legal historiography of Anti-Black Fascism. The examples proceeded chronologically, beginning with the June 6, 1945, shooting by police of twenty-two-year-old World War II veteran Denice Harris, and ending with the November 11, 1950, report in the African American *Pittsburgh Courier* of Negro troops from the Twenty-Fourth Infantry in Korea on trial for court-martial. Channeling the spirit of Double V Antifascism, the petition demonstrated that those years represented a *domestic* war against Black life. "We Charge Genocide" framed the service of African American soldiers and their subsequent betrayal by the state as a special form of legal double jeopardy, consonant with the Double Victory campaign. At the same time, World War II remained integral to the CRC's definition of Anti-Black Fascism, especially as it related to the treatment of political dissidents Black, white, and other. This became especially critical to the CRC's work around the 1940 Smith Act.

On July 20, 1948, a conspiracy indictment was handed down by the Southern District of New York Grand Jury, charging twelve members of the National Committee of the Communist Party with violating Sections 10, 11, and 13 of Title 18 of the US code commonly known as the Smith Act. The grand jury charged that the twelve had "conspired" to "organize as the Communist Party" to "teach and advocate" for the overthrow of the United States by "force and violence." All were convicted, eleven sentenced to five years in prison, and one to three years. On June 4, 1951, the Supreme Court upheld all twelve sentences. Thirteen days later, seventeen more members of the Communist Party were arrested on similar charges. Eventually, all were convicted. Of these nineteen total Smith Act indictments, nine were of African Americans. The CRC promptly extended its "We Charge Genocide" analysis to the Smith Act verdicts. "Today," they wrote, "our country has allied itself with that unhappy group of nations who are either fascist or well on the way to fascism."[42] In so doing, the CRC elaborated its analysis of what Charisse Burden-Stelly calls the "Black Scare/Red Scare." As they wrote, the CRC "[had] always considered the defense of the Communist Party the first line of defense of all the people. It is under the smokescreen of anti-Communism that the rights of labor are being destroyed. It is anti-Communism that is used to justify Genocide against the Negro people, racism, anti-Semitism, and attacks on the foreign-born."[43] The CRC made a similar point to analogize its work against legal lynchings to US wars overseas. In its May 1951 bulletin, the CRC mobilized the memory of its work in defense of Willie McGee: "Willie McGee's murder," the CRC wrote, "is as much a way to contain Communism as is the murder of the 'gooks' in Korea, the 'chinks' in China, or as the bi-partisan support of the remnants of fascism on a world scale. . . . The lessons of anti-Semitism in Germany have not yet been learned in America. That is why Willie McGee is dead."[44]

The CRC's focus on state violence against African Americans and Communists was part of its larger strategy of turning back on the US state the material threat of "force and violence." In its September 1951 bulletin, the CRC asserted, "Acts of force and violence do occur and have occurred in the U.S. and have gone unpunished—the criminals still at large. Crimes of violence against labor, 300 years of genocide against the Negro people and other national groups have filled many pages in our national history."[45] In a book promoted by the CRC, *Stand Up to Freedom! The Negro People vs. the Smith Act*, author Lloyd Brown charged the US with a version of juridicial genocide. The Smith Act, he wrote, "is a deadly menace to every effort of the Negro people to win for themselves first-class citizenship and equal rights."[46] The book also pointed out that the Smith Act's author, Representative Howard Smith of Virginia, was opposed to antilynching law and anti-poll tax law, and he represented "the white ruling-class of Virginia which legally lynched the Martinsville Seven." Brown also noted, as had CRC lawyers on numerous occasions, that the Smith Act was passed under the Alien Registration Act of 1940 and was effectively a sedition law. Brown ended by citing the appeal to the US Supreme Court by attorneys Earl Dickerson and Richard Westbrook to overturn the Smith Act verdicts: "The inevitable effect of the decision is to undermine, if not destroy, effective protest with respect to government practice and policies inimical to the Welfare of Negroes."[47]

The CRC also defended the Smith Act defendants with a guerilla strategy critical to its campaign of Legal Antifascism. It published pamphlets with titles like "Half a Million Bullets or the Smith Act Fight," evoking the armed insurrectionary tactics of the Spanish Civil War, and reminding readers that several Smith Act defendants had served in the Abraham Lincoln Brigade in Spain. It published political cartoons portraying the Smith Act as a goonish conspiracy of Wall Street, the Klan, and the police. Its local chapters organized mass street marches in protest of the Smith indictments. It held reading groups in neighborhoods around "We Charge Genocide." It published the location of the country home of the sitting Smith Act trial judge, New York Circuit Judge Harold Medina, and listed his social club memberships. It published the names, workplaces, and occupations of grand jury members, dubbing them "Wall Street financiers and Park Avenue Playboys," and took note of the absence from the grand jury of Negroes, workers, and other minorities. "Does this represent the democratic system," the CRC asked, "or thought control?" Finally, it printed a small booklet titled "Deadly Parallel," comparing victims of anticommunist hysteria to the arrested Black civil rights protesters in the South and Jews in the Warsaw Ghetto. The booklets were sold for five cents apiece to raise defense funds and to pay CRC attorneys' fees.

The use of marches, meetings, pamphlets, and fliers to advocate for the Smith Act defendants was the legal equivalent of a CRC picket line against Fascism. The CRC's insistence that Black life was the first target of and first line of defense against Fascism was meant to indict the logic of Anti-Black Fascism: the Negro was the American Jew under the Nazis, the bellwether group for the potentiality of a permanent Fascist order for all. By marching under the banners of civil rights and the United Nations, the CRC hoped to make of Black life a universal condition for the portension—and prevention—of a Fascist future, a theme that would persist well past the CRC's own demise.

Not surprisingly, the militant mass and logistical organizing of the We Charge Genocide movement was met with vicious legal repression. Paul Robeson and William Patterson formally presented the "We Charge Genocide" petition to the UN in two separate venues, on December 17, 1951: Robeson delivered the petition to the UN headquarters in New York City, and Patterson delivered it to the UN secretariat general at a meeting in Paris. Afterward, the US attempted to confiscate

Patterson's passport, and he fled to Budapest, Hungary. Patterson was in and out of jail between 1948 and 1952 for refusing to hand over to the federal government the enrollment records of the CRC, technically a violation of the Smith Act and McCarran Internal Security Act, the latter passed by Congress in 1950. Robeson was eventually called before the House Un-American Activities Committee, where he thundered against the committee and refused to name names. Famously, co-author W. E. B. Du Bois was prevented from accompanying Patterson to Paris to deliver the "We Charge Genocide" petition, as he had been stripped of his passport in 1951 and brought to trial as an "agent of a foreign enemy" for his work in support of the Stockholm Petition, which called for the elimination of atomic weapons; Du Bois was eventually acquitted. Meanwhile, CRC attorney George Crockett was given a four-month contempt sentence by Judge Medina for attacking the judge and the jury system in the Smith Act trial. The CRC also was subject to direct state surveillance that had begun during the war as part of the FBI's "RACON" program to investigate "racial conditions" in the United States, including infiltration of the ranks of the congress. In 1950, David Brown was exposed by the Los Angeles chapter of the CRC as a paid FBI informant. He was expelled, but not before seriously disrupting the chapter's work. In 1954, the state turned to the same tactic it had used to help destroy Marcus Garvey's Universal Negro Improvement Association; namely, financial intimidation and harassment: the IRS began an audit of the CRC, demanding that Patterson turn over all receipts of the organization. When he claimed not to have them, he was charged with contempt and served ninety days in Danbury Prison. In 1956, faced with narrowing finances, depleted legal resources to defend itself, and waning political support from a public terrified by cold war rhetoric and ideology, the CRC disbanded. In 1962, Attorney General Robert Kennedy finally dropped an internal investigation against the CRC, which had been fueled by four paid federal informants who testified against Patterson. Even in its demise, Kennedy insisted that the CRC was a "Communist Front." As the CRC would have predicted, the blacklist was becoming very Black.[48]

Significantly, the "We Charge Genocide" petition also faced torrential opposition from liberal organizations like the NAACP, which coordinated with the State Department to discredit the petition as Communist propaganda. NAACP head Walter White denounced the petition as a too negative depiction of the United States. African American NAACP member Edith Sampson was given formal support by the State Department to travel the world to denounce the "We Charge Genocide" petition and to defend the US record on race. In Finland, she bragged that the KKK had "disappeared" from America.[49] Internal to the UN, State Department maneuvering and pressure prevented the petition from going before the General Assembly. Meanwhile, the US refused to become a signatory to the UN Convention on the Prevention and Punishment of Genocide, for fear that it would expose US Jim Crow laws to formal censure. In the 1950s, the introduction, by racist Southern senators, of the Bricker Amendment, a collection of proposed amendments that would limit presidential power to enter into treaties and conventions,[50] challenged the Eisenhower administration, again, to take a stand and sign the UN Convention on Genocide. It refused. In fact, the US would not sign the convention until 1988, some thirty-seven years after "We Charge Genocide" implored it to do so. As scholar Carol Anderson notes, "The [Eisenhower] administration's sacrifice of the Covenants and Genocide Convention, the loss of real American involvement in the development of international human rights protocols, and the pervasive notion that there was something un-American and foreign, if not totally communistic, about human rights converged to severely constrict the agenda for real black equality."[51]

These machinations further justified to the CRC and supporters of the "We Charge Genocide" petition its characterization of a homegrown American Fascism run wild. The specter of a state committed to using the law, the police, the courts, the military, and the press to destroy an *Antifascist* movement in the United States, like the CRC, was perceived as a doubling down against Black Americans. At the same time, as in the Double Victory campaign, the We Charge Genocide movement made Black Antifascism a permanent force to be reckoned with by the state apparatus. During the time of the campaign, the state expanded its judicial oversight, disciplinary mechanisms, surveillance techniques, spying tactics, and arrest and deportation means, all in the name of defeating Black Antifascism. Not just William Patterson but also George Marshall, George Crockett, Benjamin Davis, and numerous other CRC organizers would spend time in jail for the crime of opposing Fascism native and foreign, as would the Smith Act defendants who were veterans of the fight against Fascism in Spain and Ethiopia. Claudia Jones, a signatory to "We Charge Genocide" and a Communist, would be deported from the United States in 1955, not before pronouncing on the state of US Fascism: "Instead of prosecuting the Ku Klux Klan, the anti-Semites, and the reactionaries, the government is arresting anti-fascists."[52] The state's destruction of the CRC also demonstrated the difficulty of Black Antifascists' fighting the law on its own terms—indeed, the fact that Patterson and so many other Black lawyers were *jailed* by the state for fighting Fascism ironically proved the Antifascists' point: the legal system under racial capitalism would never bend toward real justice.

But, as we shall see in subsequent chapters, the We Charge Genocide campaign and its actors also fertilized the soil of the Black Antifascist Tradition in ways that would sustain its growth in perpetuity. The war against US Anti-Black Fascism had generated a political current in Black American politics that would not die. The CRC's strategy of Legal Antifascism would pave the way for subsequent court challenges to de facto and de jure forms of racial violence against African Americans, from segregation to what the CRC called *police brutality*. It also reframed the American justice system as culpable in the monopolization and distribution of state-sanctioned violence. The central conception— that Black life mattered in the face of what We Charge Genocide called "premature death"—would remain a powerful and reverberating echo into a newly shaped Black Antifascist movement in the postwar period.

Into the 1960s, We Charge Genocide and Patterson continued to shape a new generation of Black Antifascists, a generation whose strategy shifted from Legal Antifascism to what we call *Black Power*

Antifascism in the following chapter. During a 1967 speech outside the UN headquarters in New York City, Stokely Carmichael (later Kwame Ture), a major architect and organizer of the Black Power era, referenced We Charge Genocide throughout his speech, proclaiming,

> When we look at the America which brought slaves here once in ships named Jesus, we charge genocide. When we look at the America which seized land from Mexico and practically destroyed the American Indians—we charge genocide. When we look at all the acts of racist exploitation which this nation has committed, whether in the name of manifest destiny or anti-Communism, we charge genocide . . . There is an almost endless list of these other Americas, but they all add up to the same thing: this nation was built on genocide and it continues to wage genocide. It wages genocide in many forms—military, political, economic and cultural—against the colored peoples of our earth. This nation has been not only anti-revolutionary but anti-poor, anti–wretched of the earth.[53]

Carmichael helped foreground the CRC's hallmark campaign and Antifascist analytical lens within the very fabric of Black Power, an analysis that would carry over in the work of other Black Power luminaries that we discuss in the next chapter.

— CHAPTER 5 —
BLACK POWER ANTIFASCISM

FASCISM IS AMERICA
ALL POWER TO THE PEOPLE!
> —**Raymond "Masai" Hewitt**, minister of education for the
> Southern California chapter of the Black Panther Party, 1969[1]

FROM **JULY 18 TO JULY 21, 1969,** the Black Panther Party (BPP) hosted the United Front Against Fascism (UFAF) conference in Oakland, California. With more than five thousand participants, the "who's who" of the New Left was in attendance, including the Progressive Labor-Worker Student Alliance (PL-WSA); Students for a Democratic Society (SDS); the Young Patriots Organization (YPO); the Asian American Political Alliance (AAPA); the Red Guard Party; the Young Lords; Los Siete; the Third World Liberation Front (TWLF); Communist Party USA (CPUSA); the Peace and Freedom Party; the Southern Christian Leadership Conference (SCLC); Women for Peace; and more. As Bobby Seale, cofounder of the BPP, told the *Liberation News Service,* the UFAF conference was

> . . . not called just to save the Black Panther Party. It's called so that we can save the people and save the organizations. Because if the pig power structure is allowed to get away with what they are trying to do to the Black Panther Party, they'll do the same to any organization, any union, any church, any group of people who are using their basic democratic rights as a weapon against oppression.[2]

THE BLACK ANTIFASCIST TRADTION

Although the conference marked a major shift within the BPP's strategy and political ideology, it has widely been underexamined by Black Power scholars and those on the left. Aptly positioned as the vanguard of the racial and social justice organizations of the 1960s and founded in the epicenter of 1960s youth-led radicalism—the San Francisco Bay Area—the BPP called upon those on the spectrum of leftist, Third-Worldist, pro-labor, and anticapitalist organizing to convene in Oakland to take up the charge of actualizing a coalitional model to combat what they deemed as the greatest threat to working-class people in the US and abroad—Fascism.

The BPP was met with immense federal surveillance, infiltration, disruption, and violence via J. Edgar Hoover's notorious FBI counterintelligence program (COINTELPRO). BPP chapter members across the country were targeted by law enforcement, as the organization had been deemed by Hoover "the greatest threat to the internal security of the United States." There were numerous deadly shootouts between the state and BPP members. Dozens of Panthers across the nation were accused of unsubstantiated crimes, and many were driven underground or into exile to avoid incarceration. This highly orchestrated state repression was largely in response to the BPP's audacious platform, which sought to (1) challenge police brutality and systemic racism head-on via armed self-defense and struggle; (2) reimagine Black communities through self-determination and survival programs (akin to mutual aid); and (3) raise the consciousness of the lumpenproletariat through political education and Third World studies (later to be refashioned as ethnic studies).[3]

Similar to the BPP, many of the leftist organizations represented at the UFAF conference also encountered forms of state repression. The students from San Francisco State College (later San Francisco State University) who comprised the TWLF were brutalized by campus and local police during their student-led strike.[4] The white Chicagoans from the YPO were derided as "hillbillies" and targeted by the notoriously violent and torture-inflicting Chicago Police Department.[5] The Young Lords were infiltrated by undercover law enforcement agents and state-sponsored informants.[6] Labor groups had long endured an

BLACK POWER ANTIFASCISM   127

antagonistic relationship with the state, corporations, and the overall capitalist class, which was marked by decades of violent union busting.[7] And the Communists had been largely forced underground in the two decades prior, in response to McCarthyism, "Black Scare/Red Scare" rhetoric, policy, and surveillance initiated by the House Un-American Activities Committee (HUAC)—which Paul Robeson, when he was called before them, brazenly denounced as "neo-fascist."

The BPP had an astute understanding that the state—specifically, the law, courts, law enforcement, and elected political leaders—was working to repress not only their organization but also those they were in solidarity with on a range of social and political issues. Drawing on their Marxist-Leninist-Maoist (MLM) political framework, the BPP was keenly aware that the nation's privatized corporations and wealth holders—the capitalist class—were ardent supporters of the state and deeply invested in Anti-Black Fascism, as Fascism legalized and perpetuated the same exploitative and authoritarian systems that businesses needed to extract maximum surplus value. Moreover, the analyses of Huey P. Newton, the BPP's leader and theoretician—and those of many of the Third World, Anticolonial, and Black radicals the BPP was influenced by, like Frantz Fanon, Robert F. Williams and William Patterson—all understood the racialized violence and authoritarianism of the US to be part and parcel of the Anti-Black Fascist project and legacy of colonization.[8] While the BPP had undergone many ideological and strategic shifts during a short span of time (1966–1969), by 1969, the organization had identified that the best way to counter the authoritarian-style repression that they, and others on the left, were experiencing was through Antifascist politics and organizing strategies.

This chapter, situated within the height of the Black Power era, interrogates how Black Power organizations and activists, mainly the BPP and Robert F. Williams, coalesced emergent ideologies around Black Power with Antifascist politics and strategies, cementing what we call Black Power Antifascism. As of the mid-1960s, Robert F. Williams began writing about "American fascism" in his widely disseminated newsletter, *The Crusader*, and, by 1969, critiques of everyday acts of Fascism were a regular occurrence in the *Black Panther*, the newspaper of the BPP. These two publications helped reintroduce discussions on American Fascism, or what we call Anti-Black Fascism, to the Black masses, providing political education—a language and an analytical tool—as a means to understand and frame many of the racist and systemic inequities Black folks were experiencing in the late 1960s, from slumlords and redlining to police brutality and mass incarceration, as fascism. At the center of this chapter is the UFAF conference and Huey P. Newton's theorizing on intercommunalism, a new iteration of writings to the Black Antifascist Tradition. The UFAF convening not only resulted in a new coalitional model, Intercommunal Committees to Combat Fascism (ICCF), but also proved to be a moment of reckoning as it related to the gender politics of many of the organizations that were in attendance. Women members of the BPP and the AAPA used the space to scathingly rebuke the chauvinism and patriarchy of their respective organizations, noting that patriarchy in itself was part of the Fascist apparatus. The conference served as a moment for both internal and external Antifascist organizing. This chapter concludes by tracing the fall of Black Power Antifascism, linking it to the BPP's shift toward electoral politics, the emergence of Black anarchisms, and the state's success in the imprisoning, incarcerating, killing, and exiling of many Black Power–era activists.

The Crusading Black Antifascist: Robert F. Williams

As captured in Williams's unpublished autobiography, *While God Lay Sleeping*, and Timothy Tyson's biography, *Radio Free Dixie*, Robert F. Williams was most influenced at a young age by his grandmother, Ellen Williams. The matriarch was born into slavery, resisted the violent backlash of Reconstruction, and married a fellow rabble-rouser, Sikes Williams, who campaigned for the North Carolina Republican Party and published *The People's Voice* during the Reconstruction era. Ellen instilled in her children and grandchildren a social and political consciousness and passion for history, and she reminded them to be proud of their Blackness in spite of the omnipresence of anti-Black violence

BLACK POWER ANTIFASCISM 129

in deeply segregated Monroe, North Carolina. Robert F. Williams and his siblings would sit at their grandmother's feet, listening as she read the newspaper aloud. She would often highlight geopolitical and racial conflicts that were occurring, sprinkling in her own analysis. Robert F. Williams recalled his grandmother's many accounts throughout the 1930s on the rise of Hitler and the rapidly shifting social and political grounds in Germany. As Tyson notes, "Hitler's genocide against the Jews became the central metaphor for evil . . . and the clear necessity of stopping Hitler by any means necessary endured for him [Robert F. Williams] as an unanswerable challenge to pacifism." Grandmother Williams grew deeply concerned with the state of affairs in Germany, particularly the antidemocratic and white natalist and nationalist elements of Fascism, as she saw similar politics and rhetoric being espoused by white leaders across the American South. At the age of fourteen, Robert F. Williams began delivering newspapers. He gained the moniker "the newsman" from a group of railroad workers who sat outside of a local store, listening to Williams read and analyze the news, just as his grandmother had done.

Ellen Williams's reading and politicizing to her grandchildren was certainly a practice of the Black oral tradition, but beyond that she helped foster in her grandson a great appreciation for the written word, international news, and racial politics, all of which would be major components of his activism and legacy. She had also inadvertently introduced her grandson to Fascism, and her analysis helped him draw connections between what was happening in Germany to what *had been* happening in the South. Decades later, Robert F. Williams would use the term *American fascism* in multiple issues of the international newsletter, *The Crusader*, which he co-authored and published with his wife, Mabel Williams. His grandmother, on her deathbed, fearing that the social conditions would only worsen for her family and all Black folks inhabiting the South, gave Robert F. Williams her late husband's rifle. Sikes Williams had used that rifle to ward off white supremacists and protect two generations of their family. The rifle became symbolic of Robert F. Williams's future.

130   THE BLACK ANTIFASCIST TRADTION

The periodization and distinctions between the Civil Rights and Black Power movements have long been a source of debate among scholars of those eras. Within the early historiography of both movements, there was a push to cast the Civil Rights Movement as deeply rooted in "peace and nonviolence," while Black Power became synonymous with guns and militancy. The life and legacy of Robert F. Williams disrupts that historical narrative, as does the work of scholars like Charles Cobb, Charles Payne, and Akinyele Umoja. Williams serves as a bridge between the two movements. His birth into Black radical organizing happened in the late 1950s, when he became president of the Monroe, North Carolina, chapter of the NAACP, placing him firmly within the periodization of the Civil Rights Movement. However, he was not necessarily of the prevailing tradition embraced by his contemporaries, like the Reverend Dr. Martin Luther King Jr., Bayard Rustin, Rosa Parks, and others associated with the leading Civil Rights organizations of the time (for example, the NAACP and Southern Christian Leadership Conference [SCLC]). Williams's formal organizing occurred after his participation in years of armed self-defense, including helping to fight off a racist white mob during the 1943 Detroit race riot. Williams was also a former marine, so he had received formal combat training and was not new to armed struggle.

In 1955, Williams had been discharged from the marines after lamenting the racial discrimination he experienced from commanding officers. He soon returned home to Monroe and, in that same year, joined the local branch of the NAACP in Union County.[9] By this time, the NAACP had begun mounting major campaigns, including the Montgomery Bus Boycott, and had secured a major win with the passage of the landmark Supreme Court decision, *Brown v. Board of Education*. In contrast, the Union County chapter was on the cusp of dissolution as its membership dwindled. Williams was elected president of the nascent chapter and recruited sixty members, most from the local pool hall, within a year. The Union County chapter stood out from others across the South not only because it was among the first interracial chapters, with several white pacifist members, but also because it

BLACK POWER ANTIFASCISM 131

was overwhelmingly composed of working-class people (many of whom were also veterans), a stark difference from the many NAACP chapters that were led by clergy and middle-class Black folks.

Early on, the chapter made some initial headway in helping to desegregate the county. In 1957, the chapter led a successful campaign to integrate the local public library. Simultaneously, they launched a crusade to desegregate the local swimming pool, after several Black children had drowned in unsupervised swimming holes. This would be one of their most audacious campaigns. The chapter's first direct actions were several peaceful acts of civil disobedience, stand-ins at the pool, where they were almost immediately confronted by the KKK. Even after the stand-ins, the KKK would follow Black members back to their community, continuing their reign of terror (firing shots, forming a motorcade, holding Black civilians at gunpoint, and more). After several legal cases in which the KKK and other white racist perpetrators were allowed to terrorize and kill Black civilians in Monroe with impunity, Williams and other local NAACP members, including the pacifists, determined that it was essential to "meet violence with violence, lynching with lynching."[10] They understood that there was no justice to be found in the law or the courts.

In response, the Union County members began arming themselves with rifles, and Williams launched a Black chapter of the National Rifle Association (NRA) that was later renamed the Black Armed Guard. The group would serve as a model for other Black gun clubs, like the Deacons for Defense, and inspire the gun-toting leaders of the Black Panther Party.[11] Union County's campaign to desegregate the local swimming pool quickly escalated when NAACP members showed up with their rifles, ultimately leading to a standoff between the chapter, local law enforcement, and several thousand white civilians. While state police were eventually able to disperse the white mob, had Williams and chapter members not been carrying their rifles, it is doubtful that they would have escaped the mob alive. Williams's endorsement of armed self-defense drew the ire of the national NAACP leadership, specifically Roy Wilkins, executive secretary and later executive director of the organization. In 1959, Wilkins suspended Williams from the NAACP. Williams's attempt to appeal the decision to the broader NAACP governing body forced the organization to reckon with the question of armed resistance and self-defense in the fight for civil rights. Reverend Dr. Martin Luther King Jr. directly addressed the question, and Williams's position, in his July 1959 speech at the fiftieth annual NAACP convention, stating:

> For the Negro to privately or publicly call for retaliatory violence as a strategy during this period would be the gravest tragedy that could befall us . . . Violence is also impractical as a method because it would only serve to increase the fears of the white South, and thereby increase the resistance. It must also be stressed that there are more and more white persons of goodwill who are willing to be our allies in this struggle, and certainly we need them if we are to win. But the minute we call for violence as a method, that support would almost completely disappear. So even if we cannot go to the point of accepting non-violence as a philosophy of life, we must admit that it is the best strategy for the present situation.[12]

The "Great Debate," as it would come to be known within the mainstream, resulted in the NAACP national leadership overwhelmingly maintaining a platform of nonviolence, a stance that Williams and others viewed as an attempt to kowtow to influential Northern white "allies."[13] Amid the national uproar surrounding the Union County chapter, the local membership maintained that Williams's position on armed resistance was righteous and needed to combat the Anti-Black Fascism they experienced in Monroe. This unflinching loyalty to Williams resulted in his wife, Mabel Williams, being tapped to serve as interim president during his suspension. Looking to stay politically engaged, Robert F. Williams used his time away from the chapter to create a newsletter. Williams recounts, "I went home and concentrated all of my efforts into developing a newsletter that would in accurate and no uncertain terms inform both Negroes and whites of Afro-American liberation struggles taking place in the United States and about the particular struggle we were constantly fighting in Monroe."[14] The first issue of *The Crusader* was published on June 26, 1959.

The monthly newsletter did just that—it amplified Black struggles and provided a much needed counternarrative to mainstream analyses of movement work. The newsletter was published well into the 1980s, and early issues showcased Williams's sharpening internationalist and Antifascist political lens. During the cold war, Williams used his newsletter to dispel myths about the Cuban Revolution, drawing connections between the struggles of Afro-Cubans and the struggles of Black folks in the South. Williams would also go on to visit Cuba and regularly express being in solidarity with Fidel Castro and the Cuban revolutionaries. Consequently, Williams again drew the ire of the national NAACP office, this time for maintaining sympathies with an American imperial foe. He was castigated and compared to another vilified Black Antifascist, Paul Robeson. Williams published the letters he received from NAACP national leaders, as well as his responses to them, in issues of *The Crusader.*

In 1961, Robert and Mabel Williams were forced into exile, fleeing the FBI and presumed incarceration after being slapped with bogus kidnapping charges—a blatant attempt to repress Williams and the Union County NAACP chapter. They first settled in Cuba, where, with the support of Fidel Castro, Williams established a broadcast station, Radio Free Dixie. The couple continued to refine and grow *The Crusader,* with Mabel often serving as the publication's illustrator and regular columnist. Robert F. Williams also wrote his magnum opus, *Negroes with Guns,* during their early years in exile.[15] In the book, Williams noted that exile opened him up to a much larger battlefield. Living in Cuba brought with it a deeper understanding of US imperialism, Black internationalism, and a reverence for the liberation struggles that were occurring across Latin America, Africa, and Asia. In 1963, the Williams family continued their exile in China with the full support of Chinese Communist leader Mao Zedong. While Williams was certainly more of a Black Nationalist during this period—he was elected president of the Black Nationalist group the Revolutionary Action Movement (RAM)—Maoism played a major role in his political imagination, particularly its anti-imperialist and class analysis. As Robin D. G. Kelley and Betsy Esch charge, Black radicals, particularly those who would be integral leaders and ideologues within the Black Power Movement, "came to see China as the beacon of Third World revolution and Mao Zedong as the guidepost."[16] Judy Tzu-Chun Wu describes this arguably romanticized view of Mao and China as a "radical orientalism."[17]

The influence of Maoism would extend further into the Black Power Movement, as Marxist-Leninist-Maoism (MLM) would serve as a prevailing philosophy among many organizations, including RAM and the League of Revolutionary Struggle (LRS). While clunky in naming and philosophy, at its core, MLM stresses the following: (1) the proletariat masses should be among the vanguard of society; (2) in order to understand the current class conditions, historical materialism must be at the center, thus outlining the necessity of the emergence of communism in lieu of capitalism, the former of which was regarded as a more just economic and social system; and (3) a commitment to a united front (with emphasis on unity across the Third World) to advance anticolonial, anti-imperial, and Antifascist movements. Moreover, Mao and China took an overtly Antifascist position, not only condemning the Fascist rulers of Germany and Italy, but also actively fighting Japan's Fascist rulers, who sought to engulf China into its empire during the Second Sino-Japanese War (1937–1945).[18] Thus, it is of no surprise that, during Williams's time in China, he began to write more explicitly about the role of Fascism, connecting the experiences of the Chinese to those of Black Americans.

As early as 1962, Williams began writing about Fascism in *The Crusader*. A February 1963 article entitled "Creeping Fascism" details the adoption of a "right to work" law in Wyoming. Williams decried the legislation, deeming it anti-union and part of a concerted national effort to minimize the power of workers—a collaboration between the state, private businesses, and corporations. Although short, the article alludes to the pro–racial capitalism and power consolidation elements of

Fascism. Fascism is the more insidious evolution of capitalism, or, as J. T. Murphy surmised, Fascism is "capitalism in its most desperate, violent form . . . a product of the crisis of capitalism," and represents the state's attempt to save capitalism through authoritarianism and repression.[19] Williams and his Black Power contemporaries foregrounded a class analysis around Fascism (one that centered the Black working-class), as they keenly understood how anti-Blackness was inextricably linked to the success of capitalism and saw anti–working class rhetoric and policy as direct products of Fascism during the era.

In a May issue of *The Crusader* from that same year, Anne B. Lim, a Chinese Canadian illustrator and supporter of the newsletter, had one of her illustrations published on the cover page. The dynamic artwork, entitled "White Man's Kingdom!," highlights the many elements, systems, and figures integral to Anti-Black Fascism. The piece is multifaceted. In the top left corner is a swastika with the American flag and "Brotherhood" written directly beneath, drawing overt connections to Nazi Germany and the Aryan Brotherhood. The presumed figures leading the "American Brotherhood" are the "Three Wise Monkeys" (see no evil, hear no evil, and speak no evil), Robert Kennedy, John F. Kennedy, and J. Edgar Hoover, who were depicted as sitting on a pedestal, surrounded by guns, bullets, money, and pieces of paper representing legislation. Lim is drawing on key elements of Fascism, highlighting in particular the role of the law and law enforcement in perpetuating a dual application of the law or, as is explicitly written in the image, "Justice for

White Man's Kingdom by Anne B. Lim, circa 1963, The Robert F. Williams Papers, Bentley Historical Library, University of Michigan and The Freedom Archives.

The Crusader Editorial Letter by Robert F. Williams, circa 1982, The Robert F. Williams Papers, Bentley Historical Library, University of Michigan and The Freedom Archives.

Whites Only." In the lower tiers of the image, Black people are drawn with balls and chains attached to their appendages, representing the bondage of racism, Jim Crow, and discrimination—legacies of slavery and Anti-Black Fascism. To highlight the role of religion in Fascism, Lim portrays several Black people kneeling in a subservient praying position. Crucifixes also adorn John F. Kennedy and the KKK figure. Lin is illuminating the intersection of Fascism and Christianity (Christofascism), particularly the influence of fundamentalists, evangelicals, and Catholics who have weaponized the law to institute repressive social policies that disproportionately impact Black and Indigenous people, people of color, women, and LGBTQIA-identifying people. The image is a tour de force in its capturing of the many facets and intersections of Anti-Black Fascism.

By 1964, Fascism and Antifascism had become salient topics and themes throughout *The Crusader* in longer-form articles, published speeches, illustrations, and poems. Williams and the publication's contributors deduced that:

(1) Fascism and racism were inextricably linked.
(2) American fascism was both omnipotent and omnipresent, and embedded throughout key institutions (the courts), systems (schools), and culture (Christianity), and shrouded by the veneer of "American democracy."[20]
(3) US imperialism, particularly the war in Vietnam, was part of the expansion of American fascism.[21]

(4) Black radicals and organizations resisting Fascism were being railroaded in the "kangaroo court system."[22]

(5) The relationship between the state and Black people was one of subjugation, genocide, terrorism, and incarceration; in sum, Anti-Black Fascism.

(6) There was little difference between law enforcement and the white mob.

(7) Rebuffing Anti-Black Fascism would require Black people to wage a bloody and violent revolution.[23]

Williams's writings and analysis of Anti-Black Fascism would prove pivotal to the next generation of Black radicals that would deepen the Black Antifascist Tradition throughout the Black Power Movement.

The Makings of Black Oakland Radicalism

Negroes with Guns had the "single most important intellectual influence on Huey P. Newton," and this was most evident in the BPP's militant orientation, incorporation of armed self-defense into the organization's ten-point platform, and Newton's later theorizing on intercommunalism.[24] The visceral and legislative reaction to the sight of BPP members openly carrying shotguns and rifles was swift. In 1967, BPP members marched to the California State Capitol to protest the Mulford Act—restrictive gun control legislation that was created in direct response to BPP members engaging in lawful open carry. The law's passage was widely viewed as an attempt to repress a major strategy of the Black Power Movement—armed self-defense. But Williams's influence on Newton and the BPP didn't end with the guns; his weaving together of Third-Worldism and Antifascism would be a central feature of the UFAF conference.

Many early members of the BPP, including founders Newton and Seale, had roots in the American South, and their families had taken part in the Great Migration westward, often as a form of resistance to the "mob rule" and Fascism that Ida B. Wells-Barnett laid out in *Southern Horrors*.[25] As Donna Murch captures in *Living for the City*, Oakland became largely a city of migrants, both domestic and those from

138   **THE BLACK ANTIFASCIST TRADTION**

"another shore."[26] Oakland exploded in the postwar era, quickly becoming the epicenter of radicalism and movement-building because of these newcomers' "underlying anxieties, frustrations, and material circumstances."[27] For Black folks, Oakland represented the farthest west that Black people could go in the contiguous United States to escape Jim Crow segregation, racial terror, and the legacies of antebellum slavery. If they couldn't carve out a piece of freedom and their own "California Dream" in the seemingly more progressive West, it would be difficult to do it elsewhere, including in the Northeastern and Midwestern cities that had longer histories of racial exclusion.[28] Similarly, Oakland and San Francisco represented a site of resistance for many East Asian immigrants and their Asian American children—and, later, for South Asian and Pacific Islander immigrants—who fled their homelands, often due to the influences of colonialism, imperialism, and authoritarian regimes. The concentration of several universities and colleges (including the University of California, Berkeley; then San Francisco State College; Merritt College; and others), as well as dynamic racial enclaves and cultural sites (West Berkeley Shellmounds, Glide Memorial Church, Marcus Books, the Fillmore District, and many more) also greatly contributed to Oakland's radicalism and that of the Bay Area more broadly. Black Oakland was an embodiment of the Black Panther; its people had been geographically pushed back as far as they could go, and, instead of trying to flee, it was time to pounce![29]

Arriving at Antifascism: The Evolution of BPP Rhetoric and Ideology

There has been a host of dynamic books published in the last thirty years on the BPP, including a number of autobiographies, biographies, and scholarly interventions, that animate the BPP's history, survival programs, gender politics, solidarity work, engagement with electoral politics, and even cultural production. However, few have deeply interrogated the BPP's Antifascist politics and organizing strategy and most overlook the UFAF conference and the creation of NCCFs/ICCFs entirely.[30] Sean Malloy's *Out of Oakland: Black Panther Party Internationalism during the Cold War* does a good job of detailing how the BPP was steeped in anticolonial and anti-imperial writings and ideologies that would go on to form the foundation of their internationalist politic and commitment to Third World solidarity.[31]

Reading was a central component of member onboarding, as the organization maintained a rigorous political reading list that included the works of many ardent Antifascists who are discussed in earlier chapters, including Frantz Fanon, C. L. R. James, and Albert Memmi. Elaine Brown, former chairwoman of the BPP, recalls in her autobiography, *A Taste of Power,* how members sold copies of Mao's *Little Red Book* to UC Berkeley students as a fundraiser and were commanded to memorize quotations as a sort of political mantra and affirmation.[32] The BPP, particularly the Oakland and surrounding Bay Area chapters, sought to put into practice the Third Worldist theories and writings that they were engaging, often by elevating in their newspaper the anticolonial and anti-imperialist struggles across what was then referred to as the Third World, and by using speeches and other public forums to directly connect the struggles of African Americans to struggles in Africa, Latin America, and Asia. Many members would also travel and spend a significant amount of time in countries across the Third World to provide support, amplify struggles, and share knowledge(s) of Antifascist resistance.[33]

Furthermore, the BPP was of the Bandung imaginary: they believed that African and Asian people (including their descendants across the diasporas) should work to develop Afro-Asian solidarity via cooperative economics and a united front against the West/Global North.[34] At the local level, this manifested in the form of the BPP collaborating with the San Francisco-based Asian American radical organization, the Red Guard Party, for political education courses and rallies.[35] The BPP would also play a crucial role in the Third World Liberation Front (TWLF), a student group at San Francisco State College that organized the longest student strike in American history, demanding—and winning—the first College of Ethnic Studies. Third Worldism helped the BPP understand that the repression, systemic racism, and militarism they were experiencing at the hands of the state was connected to many of the wars and struggles occurring in places like Cuba, Vietnam,

THE BLACK ANTIFASCIST TRADTION

Ghana, South Africa, and Palestine, among other Third World nations led by colonial and imperial regimes. As Bobby Seale succinctly put it, Anti-Black Fascism was "domestic imperialism." In Seale's 1969 speech, given during his tour across Scandinavia, he captured the BPP's stance on Third World solidarity and the urgency for all marginalized people to develop an Antifascist politic and strategy. Additionally, Seale began to draw connections between the burgeoning and racialized prison-industrial complex (PIC) and the genocidal features of Fascism:

> We could go on and on and on. But it's high time that the people of the world unite. It's high time that the people of the world make a reality of what the Black Panther Party tried to put forth when we were there last March, when we in fact stated (and we have always practiced) the following: that we will not fight racism with more racism; we'll fight racism with solidarity . . . And we'll fight imperialism, right here in America with the same. Domestic imperialism, meaning fascism, has made its appearance here in America. No, there aren't 6 million of us going to the gas chambers, YET. But there are millions of us in prisons. But why should we wait 'til 6 million go to the gas chamber . . . The running dogs of the fascist power structure tend to commit genocide against the poor, oppressed masses of the people in America. And we can't stand for it because our idea is to be free from oppression that we've been subjected to for hundreds of years by the fascist ruling class in America.[36]

Huey Newton would be integral to helping imagine a new reality that would counter the "fascist ruling class" that Seale identified. During his incarceration from 1968 to 1970, Newton had charted a course to shift the BPP's ideology toward Antifascism. Ideologically, the BPP had aligned itself with MLM, Third Worldism (internationalism), Socialism, and Black Nationalism during the organization's infancy; however, the later years of the organization were most influenced by revolutionary intercommunalism, Newton's philosophical brainchild and response to Anti-Black Fascism. At its core, revolutionary intercommunalism stood as a rejection of the BPP's earlier Black Nationalist framework, as Newton and others understood the contradictions of seeking liberation through the creation of a new nation-state. He surmised that nation-states often (d)evolved into empires, necessitating the division of land and resources, while simultaneously calling for the creation of governmental structures that would exert a "certain control over their destiny and their territory" and ultimately create circumstances under which nation-states would feel compelled to fortify borders and/or quarrel over resources (war).[37] In short, Black Nationalism, even in its most revolutionary and internationalist iteration, was arguably an extension of the "master's tools" and would not result in true liberation. In a 1970 speech delivered at Boston College, Newton summed up this political evolution in a nutshell:

> We found that in order to be Internationalists we had to be also Nationalists, or at least acknowledge nationhood. Internationalism, if I understand the word, means the interrelationship among a group of nations. But since no nation exists, and since the United States is in fact an empire, it is impossible for us to be Internationalists. These transformations and phenomena require us to call ourselves "intercommunalists" because nations have been transformed into communities of the world. The Black Panther Party now disclaims internationalism and supports intercommunalism.[38]

Through the lens of revolutionary intercommunalism, Newton reimagined the world as a "dispersed collection of communities," where each community functioned as a "small unit with a comprehensive collection of institutions that exist to serve a small group of people."[39] *Reactionary* intercommunalism represented the then (and current) state of the world, in which the "small communities" were shaped by racial capitalism, globalization, imperialism, colonialism, and, ultimately, Fascism. Moreover, the small community was controlled by an even smaller group of people (governing and nongoverning Fascist elites) that often chose to use the community's resources and technology to control its people and other small communities. *Revolutionary* intercommunalism called for these small communities to work together, sharing resources, knowledge(s), technologies, and wealth to solve the world's problems and create a just society. Newton imagined a sort of "global village" and advocated for the abolition of borders.[40] Revolutionary intercommunalism in many ways represented a new phase of Communism, stressing the integration of principles rooted in dialectical materialism in the process—a recognition of real-world material conditions and the understanding that contradictions were part of human social and political existence that should not be avoided. Because of these contradictions, transformation would be a *constant* within revolutionary intercommunalism, as transformation mitigated domination. Newton surmised that under revolutionary intercommunalism, antagonistic contradictions (conflicts often rooted in money and capital) would be less frequent, and nonantagonistic contradictions (conflicts rooted in social and cultural issues) would lead to interpermeation, resulting in a more mutually beneficial society. This society and its governance would stand in stark contrast to Anti-Black Fascism. This shift toward viewing Black Power through the lens of Anti-Black Fascism/Black Antifascism was also evident in the BPP's shift in rhetoric. As one example, the moniker for police, "pigs," evolved to "Fascist pigs." With a new ideology in place, the remaining pieces to actualizing revolutionary intercommunalism and Antifascism were more targeted rhetoric, the creation of a united front, internal structure, and strategy for moving forward.

The UFAF Conference, NCCFS/ICCFs, and Dispelling Fascism among the Ranks

In 1968, the US political landscape was marked by the assassinations of the Reverend Dr. Martin Luther King Jr. and Robert Kennedy, the election of right-wing president Richard Nixon, and student antiwar protests across the country. Kathleen Cleaver, then communications secretary of the BPP, called the concerted effort to assassinate Black leaders and civil rights advocates "political murder." Coupled with the brutal, state-sanctioned attacks on students, the US was entering a phase when the entire country, not just Black people, was being subjected to

BLACK POWER ANTIFASCISM 143

a police state and witnessing the more overt rise of Fascism.[41] During the first half of 1969, state repression of the BPP escalated. Multiple BPP chapter offices were raided by law enforcement, often erupting into deadly shootouts between local police and rank-and-file BPP members. This trend continued through the end of 1969 into the early 1970s, with one of the most notorious raids involving the murders of Chairman Fred Hampton, leader of the Chicago chapter, and BPP member Mark Clark. Prior to his death, Hampton had proclaimed, "School is not important. Work is not important. Nothing is more important than stopping Fascism, because Fascism will stop us all." A number of BPP leaders and members, including Newton, Ericka Huggins, and Eldridge Cleaver, were incarcerated or forced into exile, often in response to unsubstantiated criminal charges. Their experiences would help serve as the foundation for the nascent political prisoner and prison abolition movements. For the BPP, these major events, on top of high unemployment, predatory and discriminatory housing, inaccessible and racist health care, food insecurity, and a host of other systemic issues disproportionately impacting Black people and those on the margins, were demonstrative of Anti-Black Fascism at work, stifling the lives of and killing Black people. In calling for the creation of a united front against Fascism, the BPP aimed to develop a multiracial working-class movement that could resist and combat Fascism by implementing various phases of revolutionary intercommunalism.

The July 1969 conference was organized in the spirit of Georgi Dimitrov's 1938 book, *The United Front: The Struggle Against Fascism and War*, and his call for "unity of the working class against Fascism." Dimitrov, in 1938 the general secretary of the Comintern, vividly described Fascism and how it worked, noting that it would "assume different forms in different countries," ascend among struggle, appeal to the masses' "most urgent needs," inflame prejudice, manifest in foreign policy as extreme hatred of other nations, and ultimately be governed and enacted by the puppeteering of the state by finance capital.[42] In response to the Fascist uprising across Europe in the early half of the twentieth century, Dimitrov and the Comintern called for the following:

The first thing that must be done, the thing which to begin, is to form a united front, to establish unity of action of the workers in every factory, in every district, in every region, in every country, all over the world. Unity of action of the proletariat on a national and international scale is the mighty weapon which renders the working class capable not only of successful defense but also of successful counter-attack against fascism, against the class enemy.[43]

The BPP's United Front Against Fascism convening was based largely on Dimitrov's definition of Fascism and his call for a unified international working-class Antifascist movement. However, as Christopher Vials and Bill Mullen aptly point out, the BPP diverged from Dimitrov's class-reductionist analysis in their belief that "racial genocide form[ed] the ultimate horizon of fascist politics," which drew a direct connection to the CRC and William Patterson's "We Charge Genocide" campaign.[44]

The UFAF conference began on July 18, 1969. An estimated five thousand members across many radical leftist organizations were in attendance. Registration cost four dollars, and the BPP's Oakland headquarters served as the coordinating offices for the event, with conference sessions taking place at the Oakland Auditorium and Lil' Bobby Hutton Memorial Park (DeFremery Park). The program was led by Seale and David Hilliard, then the BPP chief of staff. At the outset, Seale called for no disruptions from attendees—a tall order, as corralling five thousand people with varying viewpoints across the spectrum of the left was difficult and arguably impossible, considering the conference's limitations and outcomes. Members from the Progressive Labor/Worker Student Alliance were ejected from the conference by BPP security for disruptions, only to return the following day and again get into disputes with BPP members and conference organizers, this time for leafleting during sessions.[45] Above all, however, the most resounding and necessary disruptions to the conference came from the many women in attendance.

The leadership of the BPP, like that of other radical leftist organizations of the time, was composed of men who maintained deeply sexist and patriarchal gender politics. The inclusion on the BPP's reading list of *Soul on Ice*, the memoir of convicted rapist and BPP Minister of Information Eldridge Cleaver, encapsulates some of the organization's early gender politics and relations. In an about-face, during the lead-up to the UFAF conference, Cleaver released a letter calling on male BPP members to "purge our ranks and our hearts, and our minds, and our understanding of any chauvinism," a shift from his earlier sexist rhetoric.[46] While the BPP relied heavily on women to perform rank-and-file duties (distributing newspapers, organizing rallies, completing secretarial tasks, coordinating the "survival" programs, and much more), women's issues, especially those related to intra-group sexual assault and violence, were largely ignored by the leadership. Few women were elevated to leadership roles, even though it was widely understood that women ran the BPP, particularly its most successful survival programs.[47] Additionally, many women members were also incarcerated, shot at, and surveilled by the state alongside their male counterparts. Black women were equal-opportunity targets under Anti-Black Fascism. Their gender did not safeguard them from the state; in fact, it made them even more vulnerable to gender-based violence under Anti-Black Fascism. Woman BPP members, including Ericka Huggins and Afeni Shakur, often wrote about the intersection of mothering and activism, reflecting on the experiences of BPP women who were forced to give birth to their children in exile or in prison, were shot while caring for their children, or were forced to leave their children with relatives who could provide them with greater safety and stability. These issues were often shared by women in poems and articles published in the *Black Panther*, but seldom were they taken up by BPP leadership as legitimate concerns. Many women viewed the UFAF conference as an optimal space to address and dispel the sexism that was rampant across the New Left.

In predictable fashion, the women's panel was added to the program in the final hours of the conference organizing, then postponed, as earlier speakers carried on longer than their allotted time. This signaled to the women in attendance that, once again, their concerns, specifically the issue of "male supremacy and chauvinism," were not being taken seriously, and that they were merely an afterthought. These issues came to a head in three separate speeches, given by Roberta Alexander (BPP), Penny Nakatsu (AAPA), and Ericka Huggins (BPP). Elaine Brown read the speech written by Ericka Huggins, who was incarcerated at Niantic State Prison at the time. Huggins succinctly declared, "We need no backsliders . . . chauvinists to cause division in our ranks," in her statement of support for a united front against "capitalism, imperialism, class divisions, racism, and fascism."[48] Alexander's speech directly addressed male chauvinism and supremacy, noting the subordination of the women's panel and the earlier disruptions by women attendees in response to over-long speeches by men. She stated, "We talk about divisions among the people and how the ruling class uses those divisions to weaken the people and to weaken the people's struggle. We are now faced with a rising tide of fascism in this country . . . And we must recognize the enemy when we see it. This is also very important because if we don't know what the enemy is then we're in bad shape."[49] The enemy that Alexander was referring to was patriarchy, which she articulated as being a product of "capitalist society," where women are confined to a particular role. Alexander illustrated how the BPP's gender politics were very much influenced by the same Fascist society that they claimed to be united against. Fascism is a patriarchal, capitalist, and natalist project, all of which call for the explicit control and exploitation of the bodies of women and birthing people, often for the sake of reproducing future labor forces. For Black women, this is all too familiar. For

BLACK POWER ANTIFASCISM

147

generations, Black women were forced and coerced into motherhood by their enslavers to bolster future profits. Women working within the BPP sought real liberation along the lines of race, class, gender, and sexuality. Simply put, a race-first or race-only stance was *neither* Antifascist *nor* revolutionary.

Nakatsu's speech followed Alexander's. She, too, raised the issue of male supremacy and chauvinism and detailed how women were integral in the fight against Fascism, sharing, "As an Asian woman . . . I can speak well and long of the heroic women who have died combating racism and imperialism."[50] Nakatsu used her time to amplify several examples of Fascism in the US and in Asia, including the internment of Japanese Americans, which she directly connected to the German concentration camps, proclaiming, "I come from a generation of children born in concentration camps."[51] Nakatsu's speech was powerful for two reasons. First, because she chose to stand in solidarity with the Black women that had come to the stage to challenge their male counterparts' sexism. In sharing the struggles of Asian and Asian American women, Nakatsu affirmed Huggins's and Alexander's earlier statements that women were integral to revolutionary work and were indeed dying and being incarcerated in their fight against Fascism. While the gender politics in some Asian American left organizations were contentious at times, women certainly had greater opportunities to be in positions of leadership, even helping found groups, like the AAPA (Vicki Wong, cofounder), and serving as key editors and writers for seminal Asian American movement publications, like *Aion* (co-edited by Janice Mirkitani) and *Gidra*. Nakatsu's speech was also brilliant in that it showed another manifestation of American Fascism, one that explicitly impacted Asians and Asian Americans. Nakatsu also connected the internment camps to Nazi concentration camps, noting that the incarceration of Jews happened around the same time that Japanese people across the US were incarcerated. She questioned how the US could have possibly been against Fascism when it was employing Fascism at home to fight Fascism abroad? Furthermore, Nakatsu's speech also drew subtle connections between the concentration camps she was forced to grow up in and the burgeoning prison-industrial complex, including the unjustified incarceration of many political prisoners.

The women's speeches and struggles were integral to helping address the gender politics of the BPP and the New Left, creating more egalitarian organizing spaces for women members and further grounding the attending organizations in an Antifascist politic that included an analysis of how patriarchy and gender-based violence were linked to Fascism.[52] Beyond the issues of sexism and male chauvinism, women continued to lead the major political discourse within the UFAF conference space, and they were at the center of discussions concerning the National Committees to Combat Fascism (NCCFs). While attendees discussed a number of tactics to address Fascism on its many fronts, the most concrete strategy to emerge from the conference was that of the NCCFs. These committees were imagined as hyperlocal, multiracial BPP chapters that would focus primarily on survival programs and community-led policing. The NCCFs were later renamed Intercommunal Committees to Combat Fascism (ICCFs), to further align with Newton's philosophy on intercommunalism. The ICCFs functioned as a nationwide network, with about twenty committees sprouting up in Berkeley, Oakland, Salt Lake City, Las Vegas, Sunflower (Mississippi), Austin (Texas), and Erie (Pennsylvania) by 1970.[53] Most committees took direction from the BPP, although they had the autonomy to evolve as necessary to meet the needs of their communities.

Serving the People and Radical Care as Antifascism

Survival programs existed prior to the UFAF conference, most notably the BPP's free breakfast for schoolchildren program. The creation of the ICCFs allowed organizers to focus exclusively on community programs that amounted to acts more commonly discussed as mutual aid and radical community care work. Seldom is mutual aid discussed as a form of Antifascism, often because care work isn't read as being radical or revolutionary. But, for the BPP and the ICCFs, providing the services, resources, and tools that Black communities needed to survive day to day in the absence of government support was revolutionary and Antifascist.

The BPP understood that under Anti-Black Fascism, the government showed little regard for the humanity and livelihood of non-white and working-class people. The BPP and the ICCFs worked to fill the gaps left by centuries of Anti-Black Fascist legislation and policy that had created and perpetuated racialized social inequalities. Black people deserved access to dignified and safe health care, food, transportation, employment, education, public safety resources, and so much more.

Mutual aid is often hyperlocal work that involves reimagining and transforming systems and institutions to serve a community's liberation. When Berkeley ICCF members recognized that many Black folks across the city were living in dilapidated buildings with poor plumbing, owned by do-nothing slumlords, members were trained in how to provide basic plumbing maintenance services and dispatched across the community. They called themselves "the People's Plumbers." Similarly, Bobby Seale made it a point to prioritize health care, calling on BPP and ICCF chapters to establish free health-care facilities.[54] He charged the committees and chapters with providing early sickle-cell anemia testing for people of African descent, as they had a much higher risk of the genetic disorder yet were largely left untested and untreated. Articles in the *Black Panther* described the sickle-cell anemia public health crisis and medical inequality along racial lines, as a type of medical Fascism and "black genocide."[55] In 1971, Dr. Tolbert Small, a white physician, worked alongside the Berkeley ICCF to start the Bobby Seale Free Clinic (later renamed the George Jackson Free Clinic). Dr. Small trained ICCF and BPP members to provide sickle-cell and gonorrhea testing, initiate wellness checks for babies, offer health education, and deliver a host of other services free of charge to Black people in Berkeley and the broader Bay Area.[56] The ICCFs also provided poison-control classes, free childcare, film and entertainment programming, and communal living spaces for members.[57] Many women within the BPP also pivoted to intercommunal and mutual aid work. Ericka Huggins went on to direct the BPP's longest-standing survival program, the Oakland Community School (OCS). OCS functioned as a community-based nonprofit liberation school that fused political education, place-based

150   **THE BLACK ANTIFASCIST TRADTION**

learning, Freierian pedagogy, mindfulness, and self-defense education for students four to twelve years of age.[58]

The mutual aid work of the BPP and the ICCFs can best be understood by drawing on the work of abolitionist activist and educator Mariame Kaba. Mutual aid is rooted in solidarity, deep interpersonal relationships, and often a shared politic. It "rejects hierarchy and authoritarianism," resting at the intersection of community service and care, political education, and radical activism.[59] Overall, the mutual aid work of the late 1960s, as championed by the BPP and ICCFs, as well as the more contemporary mutual aid work undertaken by organizations like the Anti-Police Terror Project, Funky Town Fridge, For the People Detroit, National Bail Out, and a host of others, is inherently Antifascist work that fundamentally challenges state repression, divestment, and oppressive systems of power by completely reimagining society's possibilities through solidarity and radical community care. Mutual aid requires activists and organizers to circumvent traditional capitalist structures, negotiating community and collective routes to fundraise and gain access to facilities, organizing spaces, and the tools and resources necessary for the work at hand. Moreover, legal defense and bail funds, another form of mutual aid, have been instrumental in helping free some of history's most brazen Black Antifascists, including Newton, from incarceration, as well as contemporary #blacklivesmatter and Antifa protesters and organizers. It could be said that mutual aid work has helped sustain the Black Antifascist Tradition.

Beyond mutual aid, the Berkeley ICCF was instrumental in helping to advance police reform, sowing the seeds of current police abolition work by launching a campaign for community control of the Berkeley Police Department. After the ICCF collected enough signatures in support of the initiative, it was placed on the ballot in April 1970.[60] This was just one of several campaigns in which ICCFs worked to reimagine policing, even calling for police abolition, with the hope of creating a new, community-led policing structure. The BPP also sought to leverage electoral politics to change policing from the "inside out." Bobby Seale's 1973 Oakland mayoral campaign was one of the final ICCF projects.

The Berkeley chapter was especially impactful during the campaign, helping to rally white voters and bolster support for the BPP leader. But, as the BPP and ICCFs moved into the 1970s, chapters dissolved as fissures widened across the BPP. The steady exiling and incarceration of members further dismantled the once vibrant organization to the point that only its newspaper and the OCS maintained operation.

The Seeds of Abolition and Anarchy

Black Power Antifascism inspired Black people to understand their relationship to the US as one rooted in Anti-Black Fascism and called upon Black people to resist Fascism through (1) armed self-defense; (2) a commitment to radical world-building and transformation via Newton's intercommunalism; (3) cooperative investment in mutual aid and radical care work; and (4) a resolve that leaned toward abolition. The BPP and the ICCFs aspired to radically reimagine society as the intercommunal fractals that Newton had envisioned; however, the approach that Newton and Seale took to the organization's vision and leadership was at times critiqued internally as being less abolitionist and radical, but more reformist. The focus on survival programs, for instance, was met with opposition from Eldridge Cleaver, who claimed that the programs were reformist, not revolutionary. Rank-and-file members also grew disillusioned with the BPP's focus on political education. Cleaver bluntly summed up this growing sentiment, stating, "This shit has been examined and analyzed for decades and generations from every angle. My opinion is that most of what happens in this country does not need to be analyzed any further."[61] By the early 1970s, the BPP had split into two major factions—Newton and Seale's intercommunal camp and another that took up Cleaver's analysis, calling for a Black Antifascist strategy that prioritized armed struggle, "the urban guerilla concept," and anarchy.

— CHAPTER 6 —
4A BLACK ANTIFASCISM
On Anarchy, Autonomy, Antagonism, and Abolition

The hypocrisy of American fascism forces it to conceal its attack on political offenders by the legal fiction of conspiracy laws and highly sophisticated frame-ups. The masses must be taught to understand the true function of prisons. Why do they exist in such numbers? What is the real underlying economic motive of crime and the official definition of types of offenders or victims? The people must learn that when one "offends" the totalitarian state, it is patently not an offense against the people of that state, but an assault upon the privilege of the privileged few.

—**George Jackson**, *Blood in My Eye*[1]

N OCTOBER 1970, Angela Davis was arrested on charges of conspiracy, kidnapping, and murder. She was accused of providing firearms to a seventeen-year-old Black youth, Jonathan Jackson, who had stormed the Marin County courtroom in Northern California, demanding the release of the Soledad Brothers, two months earlier. George Jackson (Jonathan Jackson's older brother), Fleeta Drumgo, and John Clutchette, collectively known as the Soledad Brothers, were incarcerated at Soledad State Prison and accused of murdering a prison guard. Their case had gained national attention with the publication of George Jackson's *Soledad Brother* and the amplification of their stories by Davis, Newton, and various other Black Power–era activists. George Jackson had become a sort of "dragon philosopher" and Black Power luminary while serving an indeterminate prison sentence for his involvement in a 1961 armed robbery.[2] Building upon the work of earlier political prisoners like Martin Sostre, discussed below, Jackson spent his time in one of California's oldest prisons studying the works of Communist and Pan-Africanist leaders and philosophers. He went on to write two books, *Soledad Brother* and *Blood in My Eye*, while incarcerated. Both works highlighted the inhumane conditions incarcerated people were (and continue to be) subjected to, particularly solitary confinement and unjust sentencing. George Jackson argued that the Black experience in the US was a continuum of captivity and bondage, a life under constant police surveillance and violence, with the distant illusion of democracy never fully in reach: in other words, Anti-Black Fascism. He boldly claimed that prisons were being used to repress Black movements and prophesied that they would continue to be weaponized (in the form of mass incarceration) to enact the anti-Black tendencies of American Fascism.

As Dan Berger argues in *Captive Nation*, in the early 1970s, Black Power moved from the streets to the prisons. Political prisoners like George Jackson, Angela Davis, Martin Sostre, Lorenzo Kom'Boa Ervin, Assata Shakur, Mumia Abu-Jamal, and Ashanti Alston, among others, became integral to helping evolve the philosophy and organizing strategy of the movement to its most radical stage. Newton, often revered as the theoretician of the Black Power movement, maintained that George Jackson "had genius" and was a "true believer" and embodiment of "revolutionary suicide," a term that Newton would use as the title of his 1973 autobiography.[3] The term also encapsulated the unflinching spirit of many political prisoners, who developed a keen understanding and critique of Anti-Black Fascism while in bondage. They determined that Anti-Black Fascism must be met with revolutionary action, often in the form of anarchy, autonomy, antagonism, and abolition. Should those modes of resistance fail, death—revolutionary suicide—was regarded as a righteous outcome.

The campaigns to free political prisoners not only brought awareness of the individuals and rebellions (for example, the Attica Prison uprising) but also drew attention to the overall criminal justice system and what Michelle Alexander would later aptly describe as the "new

4A BLACK ANTIFASCISM   155

Jim Crow" and mass incarceration. As more activists and leaders were swept into prisons, many on trumped-up charges, the Black Power Movement evolved from one rooted in self-defense, self-determination, and mutual aid work to an increasingly antagonistic, anarchistic, and violent movement. Political prisoners understood and experienced the dual application of the law that we outlined earlier, identifying the law and prisons as bedrocks of Anti-Black Fascism—"a key component of the state's coercive apparatus, the overriding function of which is to ensure social control."[4] George Jackson dedicated much of the latter half of *Blood in My Eye* to discussing the evolution of Fascism in America. Davis critiqued the "built-in racism of the judicial system" and its deep ties to corporate interest in *If They Come in the Morning,* calling on white workers to interrogate how they, too, were being impacted by the proliferation of Fascism.[5] Many within this iteration of Black Power determined that it was no longer enough to call for reform, leverage traditional electoral politics or Legal Antifascism, or even serve and defend the people. Emergent groups like the Black Liberation Army (BLA) worked to create an "armed front" willing to wage "revolutionary violence"—not as reactionaries but as antagonists engaged in a "legitimate form of political policy" against the Fascist American state.[6]

Beyond advancing the theorizing on American Fascism, the writings of political prisoners also generated wholly new understandings of Black life and organizing. Lorenzo Kom'Boa Ervin's *Anarchism and the Black Revolution* called upon Black people to embrace anarchy as a philosophy as well as autonomous zones, "armed expropriation of government financial resources," and other tactics that necessitated a complete disregard of the state. It is then of no surprise that Black radicalism of the 1970s became marked by anarchist tactics like the kidnappings of judges and other high-profile officials, bank robberies, the hijacking of planes, several prison breaks, the creation of autonomous zones and communal living communities such as MOVE (modeled after a subset of anarchism called primitivism or anarcho-primitivism), and other acts that were certainly a pivot from the direct actions of just a few years earlier.

156   **THE BLACK ANTIFASCIST TRADTION**

This chapter traces how the theorizing of Anti-Black Fascism and Black Antifascism evolved during the 1970s, primarily via the writings of Black political prisoners. In critiquing the emergent shift towards "fascist-corporativism," and directly connecting the rise in mass incarceration to the repression of Black Power organizations, political prisoners helped usher in a period in which Black activists embraced what we call *4A Black Antifascism*: anarchy, autonomy, antagonism, and abolition.

Political Prisoner Intellectuals on Fascism

In a letter of support demanding the release of Angela Davis, James Baldwin wrote, "The enormous revolution in Black consciousness which has occurred in your generation, my dear sister, means the beginning or the end of America. Some of us, white and Black, know how great a price has already been paid to bring into existence a new consciousness, a new people, an unprecedented nation."[7] Baldwin accurately captured the work of Davis and her Black Power comrades. Black Power, and all of its politics and strategies, certainly reshaped the social and political landscape of the mid-1960s into the 1970s. As a consequence—in a typical Anti-Black Fascist response to her audacious activism—Davis found herself among a growing collection of activists targeted by the state and incarcerated in some of the nation's most brutal and inhumane prisons, largely on charges stemming from their political affiliations. Political prisoners produced an entire genre of Black Antifascist writings (mostly books and pamphlets) that were written to reshape and propel the movement, with the revenue from some authors' book sales reinvested in Black Power organizations.[8] Their writings, both political and intellectual in substance, became a primary mode (for some, their only mode) of resistance and movement-building, pushing the bounds of Black consciousness even further by shaping the "political priorities of those on the outside."[9] For them, it was no question that the Black experience in the United States had been forged in Fascism—that wasn't up for debate. Their works took a new direction, gesturing toward the rising confluence of conservatism, white evangelical Christianity, far-right groups and movements, and neoliberalism, a kindred match that would shape the future of Anti-Black Fascism for the next fifty years.

In his early writings, George Jackson had defined Fascism as "a police state wherein the political ascendency is tied into and protects the interests of the upper class—characterized by militarism, racism . . . and concedes further that criminals and crime arise from material, economic, socio political causes."[10] By 1971, with the publication of *Blood in My Eye*, Jackson's analysis of Fascism had deepened. He argued that the next phase of Fascism emerging within the US would be a response to the rapidly shifting economic and political landscape of the 1970s and would ultimately serve as a repudiation of major civil rights advancements. Jackson began using the term "fascism-corporativism" to describe the impact that the rise of neoliberalism and conservatism had in reshaping Fascism in the immediate post–civil rights era. That same year, Louis Powell Jr., soon to be Supreme Court associate justice, issued an inflammatory memorandum, entitled "Attack on American Free Enterprise System" (more commonly known as the "Powell Memorandum") to Eugene Sydnor Jr., then chairman of the Education Committee of the US Chamber of Commerce. Powell decried the state of American society, particularly the youth- and student-led social movements of the 1960s (such as the Black Power, Asian American, Chicano, American Indian, antiwar, disability rights, and environmental conservation movements) that advanced the "dignity of minority personhood and the preservation of the earth itself."[11] Powell argued that recent civil rights laws, progress made by labor unions, environmentalist policy and sentiments, the emergence of the New Left, and tightened regulation were all viciously aiding an assault on American capitalism and corporations. In an effort to reassert a pro-capitalist agenda, Powell called upon his fellow conservatives to infiltrate and surveil colleges and universities as a means to disrupt the popularity of anticapitalist politics and liberal pundits. He advocated that more conservative faculty be hired to review textbooks that may have cast conservative and pro-business values negatively. Powell deemed it a high priority for corporations and conservatives to leverage the courts, similar to the way labor unions and nonprofits did, to challenge civil rights, environmental, and any "anti-business" laws. Finally, and most audacious, he called for a full shift in government that aligned with the notion of "corporate personhood."[12] Powell saw businesses as a "minority" in need of defense from "the challenges put to them by actual people," thinly veiling his ultimate ambition—to bolster corporate privatization and profit margins, while undoing the social gains made less than a generation prior that helped actual minoritized people. As a Supreme Court associate justice, Powell helped actualize some of his vision—a vision that would inform conservative politics for generations to come, primarily through the economic policies of presidents Richard Nixon, Gerald Ford, Ronald Reagan, and, later, Donald Trump. Beyond Republican administrations, Powell's memorandum continues to be heralded as the blueprint for conservative and far-right movements, with the overturning of *Roe v. Wade* and the recent "school choice" and "anti-CRT" movements all part of Powell's greater legacy.

While George Jackson did not live long enough to see the fruits of Powell's vision, Jackson's use of "fascism-corporativism" fittingly captured the blurring, and ultimately the convergence, of state and corporate interests for which Powell advocated. Angela Davis echoed this assessment of 1970s Anti-Black Fascism in a statement to the University of California Board of Regents, where she named the "Nixons, Agnews, and Reagans" as "capitalist yes-men who have stolen the wealth of the world from the people by exploitation and oppression."[13] Furthermore, the convergence of state and corporate interests was at the crux of Benito Mussolini's vision of Fascism in Italy, as he had notoriously proclaimed, "Fascism should more properly be called corporatism because it is the merger of state and corporate power."[14] Both Davis and Jackson understood that the latest stage of capitalism—neoliberalism—would have major implications across racial lines.

Early in the decade, the US economy began showing signs of shock and strain, much of it brought on by a steady pivot toward neoliberalism and its hallmark agenda of deregulation, privatization, tax reductions for corporations and high-income earners, and greater concern for shareholder profit margins. These policies helped usher in high unemployment, deindustrialization, and sharp inflation throughout the decade, spilling over into the 1980s (and beyond). Jackson deduced that much of the early defining and theorizing on Fascism within Black radical spaces had focused mainly on the nationalist and white supremacist characteristics of the system and not enough on understanding Fascism as an "economic rearrangement."[15] He identified two major economic shifts that drew the country closer toward Fascism. The first was the rise of neoliberalism or "corporativism" that he witnessed in the years immediately leading up to the 1970s. The second shift had occurred more than a century earlier and can best be summed up as monopoly capitalism and the consolidation of political power. Following the Civil War, the myriad of plantations, small businesses, and factories were largely replaced by corporations that were propelled by the Industrial Revolution and the exploitation of the working class, in particular Black workers. Those same corporations used their wealth and status to influence not only economic markets but also social and political affairs at the federal, state, and local levels. Nearly every US president since Reconstruction has worked to uphold and/or bolster this system of monopoly capitalism. Furthermore, this major economic shift had coincided with the expansion of law enforcement and the modernization of the criminal justice system, both of which were integral to the repression of Black people and the simultaneous protection of corporations and their capital, serving as tools to exercise authoritarian-style rule, should resistance to forms of monopoly capitalism emerge. Jackson posited that this early consolidation of business and political power marked the early stage of Anti-Black Fascism in the US. His work ultimately rejects the notion that the US has been a "bourgeois democracy," asserting instead that monopoly capital and the coalescence of power between the state and corporations does not allow for *any* form of democracy, not even bourgeois democracy. Under this consolidated system of power, Fascism can exist, and arguably thrive, with or without a far-right nationalist political party, as the survival of capitalism will be dependent upon maintaining a rigid racialized and classed social order that must constantly be maintained through state-sanctioned violence, terror, and the law. It is here that Jackson's theorizing on Anti-Black Fascism intersects with Cedric Robinson's racial capitalism. To put it plainly, there is no capitalism without Anti-Black violence and exploitation, and there is no Fascism without capitalism. Fascism and capitalism are highly racialized and interdependent systems.

While many were drawn to Jackson's theorizing on Fascism, his fellow political prisoner intellectual, Angela Davis, held slightly diverging views. The two often sent letters through their shared lawyer, John Thorne, debating the merits, conditions, phases, and outcomes of Fascism. At the time, Davis did not believe the US was in a state of Fascism.[16] She maintained that "fascist tactics have been employed against Black people, Black communities, for centuries" and that the country was barreling down a path toward "South African-style fascism" under the Nixon administration's "law and order" and neoliberal agenda. As a distinction from Jackson, she offered that the US had not reached a mature state of Fascism.[17] In contrast, Jackson deemed Fascism to be in its "most advanced form" in the US.[18] What Davis and Jackson did agree upon is that Fascism is anti-movement and insists on the "complete destruction of all revolutionary consciousness"; it is for that reason that their writings were so integral to the Black Power Movement and the overall Black Antifascist Tradition.[19] For these political prisoner intellectuals, the existence of Anti-Black Fascism was not dependent upon comparative analyses of European Fascism. Davis and Jackson helped reconceptualize the meaning of Fascism by placing the Black experience at the center and shrewdly naming the rise of the far right and neoliberalism in the 1970s as a major turning point. Moreover, in their writing from prison, Davis and Jackson's perspective reflected a keen understanding of one of Fascism's most brutal outcomes, second only to death itself.[20]

The writings of political prisoner intellectuals provided a stark contrast to mainstream Black politics of the time. During the 1970s, a wave of first Black mayors was elected across the nation, most of them in urban cities and along the Rust Belt. Even Black Panther Party leader

4A BLACK ANTIFASCISM   161

Bobby Seale unsuccessfully ran for mayor of Oakland in 1973. Contrary to Black Power radicalism, many of the elected Black mayors embraced pro-capitalist and conservative agendas, aiding the repression of Black activists in the very communities that many of them had come from.[21] In *White Reconstruction: Domestic Warfare and the Logics of Genocide,* Dylan Rodriguez illustrates how this cohort of Black mayors and diversity among police departments emerged as response to the civil rights era and reflected an embrace of multicultural/diversity/inclusion frameworks within American politics. Yet, these frameworks of multiculturalism and diversity worked against Black Power organizations and activists. Rodriguez casts the adoption of multiculturalism as an extension of white supremacy, terming it "multiculturalist white supremacy," asserting,

> The notion of multiculturalist white supremacy indexes how the logics, protocols, compulsory normativities, and gendered racial violence of hegemonic institutions—and of the anti-Black, racial-colonial social formation generally—become increasingly capacious, flexible, and promiscuously inclusive as the monopoly-based systems of racial dominance (for example, apartheid Jim Crow and other versions of "classical" white supremacy) are abolished and displaced in the name of (liberal, teleological, national-to-global) racial progress.[22]

In an effort to preserve the system of Fascism-corporativism, "diverse" politicians offered a superficial veneer of racial representation. They stood as an abrupt disruption to the stronghold of white male political leadership across both major political parties. Race aside, many of the Black mayors were, at best, moderates. They kowtowed to business and corporate interests. Tom Bradley's tenure as mayor of Los Angeles (1973–1993) was indicative of this phenomenon. At the outset, Bradley was decried as a "Black Power militant" by his opposition, but Bradley was far from it. He had been a police officer in the city since the 1940s. His campaign was propelled by a multiracial coalition, not solely Black voters, and, similar to President Barack Obama, Bradley worked to

162 THE BLACK ANTIFASCIST TRADTION

distance himself from explicitly Black issues, engaging them only when absolutely necessary (for example, the 1992 Rodney King uprising) or beneficial. Bradley made major concessions to big business and corporations. One of Bradley's first projects, the 1974 redevelopment plan, reflected his pro-capitalist agenda. Notably, the plan resulted in the unprecedented growth of the Los Angeles financial district and Bunker Hill neighborhood. The two areas would completely reshape the city's skyline, as numerous skyscrapers were erected for corporate and commercial use, all while Black and Brown neighborhoods remained grossly underinvested in by the city. Toward the end of his tenure as mayor, Bradley became mired in a number of controversies, including a major financial conflict of interest after he accepted a payment of $42,000 for advising two banks that also had done business with the city.[23] Bradley and other Black mayors of the period found political success by maintaining the economic status quo—the Fascism-corporativism that Jackson had cautioned against. Bradley and his contemporaries represented a type of surface-level racial progress, yet their ascendence was largely made possible because of their acceptance of Fascism-corporativism and sidelining of racial politics, especially Black Power. As Keeanga Yamahtta-Taylor put it, Bradley and his ilk were no more than "Black faces in high places."[24]

Black Anarchy

As Black mayors stepped into power, at the grassroots the Black Power Movement's prevailing organization, the Black Panther Party (BPP), was on a visible decline. Following the United Front Against Fascism (UFAF) conference, many BPP members became disillusioned with the vision and leadership from the organization's governing body, arguing that the central committee was too reformist, patriarchal, and hierarchical. The leaders were seen as out of touch with the rank and file, as many members, particularly those on the east coast, believed that the organization's push toward electoral politics (such as Bobby Seale's mayoral bid) and mutual aid work via the ICCFs was simply not enough to combat Nixon's "law and order" agenda, Fascism-corporativism, and the emergent right-wing movement. Even more concerning, many members were rightly troubled by the FBI's infiltration of the BPP, following several high-profile shoot-outs, assassinations, and other subversive acts under COINTELPRO. From 1969 to 1972, there was a steady shuttering of BPP chapters across the country, with the organization soon consolidating its efforts around Oakland. The decline of the BPP allowed for the emergence of new organizations, ideologies, and Black Antifascist tactics that would completely reshape Black Power in the 1970s. The Black Liberation Army's (BLA) anarchist approach was one of the most influential.

No Black Power figure captures the shift from the BPP's political organizing framework to Black Anarchy quite like Assata Shakur. Shakur started as a BPP member in Oakland, eventually moving back to New York, where she continued her work with the BPP, organizing rallies and coordinating Harlem's free breakfast program and other mutual aid work. In 1969, Shakur was among the group of East Coast Panthers that broke off from the BPP, dissatisfied with the organization's focus on mutual aid and electoral politics instead of armed resistance and revolutionary violence, which Shakur and her comrades ardently believed were necessary. The BLA, of which Shakur was a core member, emerged from this moment of despondence with the BPP. Inspired by the revolutionary movements in Algeria and Vietnam, the BLA sought to engage in forms of agitation guerilla warfare, as popularized by the National Liberation Front (NLF), or Viet Cong. Between 1971 and 1973, Shakur was named as a conspirator and/or accomplice in several incidents across the Tri-State region and Southeast, including bank robberies, assault and attempted murder of several law enforcement agents, and possession of firearms, hand grenades, and other munitions. Shakur was never convicted of any of these crimes. In May 1973, Shakur was traveling on the New Jersey Turnpike with two other BLA comrades, Zayd Shakur and Sundiata Acoli. They were pulled over by a state trooper, and an alleged shootout ensued, resulting in Zayd Shakur's death and the death of a state trooper, while Assata Shakur and Sundiata Acoli were captured. Assata Shakur would remain in prison until her escape in 1979.

Throughout her autobiography, Shakur wrote extensively about her time in prison, vividly describing the harassment, substandard care, and violence she endured during each trooper shift change. It was not uncommon for the troopers tasked with guarding Shakur to share their own political beliefs as a means of psychological harassment. She found that many of the guards held an affinity for Hitler and Fascism. Troopers would greet each other with "Nazi-style" salutes; they donned uniforms patterned after German and South African police uniforms; and Shakur vividly recalled being subjected to extensive diatribes from troopers professing fidelity to Hitler. One trooper brazenly shared, "If Hitler had won, the world wouldn't be in the mess it is in today . . . " and other sentiments that valorized European Fascism, while demonizing "niggers like me."[25] Shakur, like other BPP members, openly called police "Fascist pigs," the phrase popularized in BPP chants. But chants and even writings felt like empty rhetoric to Shakur. Being incarcerated and guarded by New Jersey state troopers who were openly Nazi sympathizers brought to life the Black Antifascist rhetoric she had long been steeped in.

As a formative member of the BLA, Shakur adopted the underground organization's philosophy and strategy of anarchism. Although often conflated ideologically, anarchy and Antifascism are quite different, albeit linked at times through political overlap.[26] Antifascism is a reactive response to Fascism, and those who organize under the banner of Antifascism are committed to dismantling Fascist regimes with the goal of creating a more democratic, equitable, and just political system. However, all Antifascists do not maintain a singular political viewpoint, and a number of political perspectives could be represented within an Antifascist movement or coalition, including Communist, Socialist, anarchist, liberal, and so on. Antifascists are united in their commitment to dismantle Fascism, not necessarily in their vision for the future. Anarchists are opposed to government and the state. Anarchists believe in the abolition of authority and institutions in the hope of being able to create a new world, free of tyranny. Black Power activists understood anarchy as both a political philosophy and organizing strategy that *must* be coupled with Antifascism. The BLA defined Anarchism as follows:

4A BLACK ANTIFASCISM 165

The philosophy of total freedom without any governmental structure, or state. [Anarchy] negates the necessity of the dictatorship of the proletariat to re-educate and organize the masses and protect the gains of the revolution as a transitory stage in the development towards true Communism where the state will wither away.[27]

The BLA discerned that any US government, whether run by white men or Black men, would ultimately result in the maintenance of the Anti-Black Fascist status quo. Echoing Jackson and Davis, the BLA believed, "Most people do not see the real relationship between the development of western law and the development of western capitalism; therefore, these people cannot deal with the reality of injustice being an integral part of the prevailing system."[28] And they arguably arrived at similar conclusions as Afropessimists Jared Sexton, Christina Sharpe, Frank Wilderson III, and Saidiya Hartman; namely, that society is incapable of being reformed because it is wholly dependent upon anti-Blackness—specifically, the relegation of the Black experience to one of a perpetual social death. Within the BLA, reformism was deemed "unprincipled collaboration with [the] enemy," and the law was derided as being inherently Anti-Black.[29] Like Wells-Barnett and other Black Antifascist luminaries discussed in earlier chapters, the BLA knew that the law was far from impartial and functioned to protect capital. Thus, it was only through anarchy (the complete disregard of and opposition to government and its institutions) and revolutionary violence that the BLA believed they would be able to advance the abolition of existing systems of power and, by extension, Anti-Black Fascism.

Because they were committed to direct action toward dismantling the state, the BLA took a proactive rather than reactive approach to Antifascism. The development of an armed front, or "urban guerilla front," became imperative to combating the increasing violence of state repression and was ultimately seen as the primary means to ensure the state's demise. This armed front was not meant to supplant existing Black Power Antifascist organizing but to bolster the movement overall, through a more tactical military approach. The decentralized organization had members and networks across the nation, with much of their membership located and incidents occurring in New York and New Jersey. From 1970 to 1981, BLA members coordinated a number of armed actions on government and private property, including several prison breaks, bombings, and bank robberies (or "expropriation of funds").[30] Although they were deemed criminals by the federal government, the BLA framed their disregard of the law as "revolutionary violence" and "legitimate forms of political policy."[31] Their anarchist tactics were coordinated to liberate political prisoners (prison escapes and plane hijackings), finance future actions and directly attack American capital (bank robberies), and, overall, weaken the US government and "drive the capitalist system further into crisis."[32]

Chronicling the BLA's anarchist approach to Black Antifascism provides a necessary intervention in both academic scholarship and organizing spaces that have long framed anarchy as a white organizing tradition, often highlighting Italian and Italian American anarchists, such as Nicola Sacco, Bartomoleo Vanzetti, and Alfredo Bonanno, or even the efforts of white far-right anarchists Cliven and Ammon Bundy. As the BLA more broadly drew on anarchy/Anarchism largely as a strategy, several of its members—former BPP members and political prisoners, all situated on the East Coast, including Lorenzo Kom'Boa Ervin, Kwasi Balagoon, Martin Sostre, and Ashanti Alston—further theorized Black Anarchisms throughout the 1970s and into the 1980s. Their theorizing continued to echo the anticapitalist and anti-imperialist politics of their Black Antifascist predecessors. Their work also directly challenged prevailing European and white American Anarchists who failed to prioritize or discuss race and anti-Blackness. Furthermore, their work, which also advocated for gender and sexual liberation, would also help inform some of the radicalism within the concurrent gay liberation movement in New York City.

Lorenzo Kom'Boa Ervin's seminal work, *Anarchism and the Black Revolution*, chronicles this rich history of Black anarchy and has served as a foundation for recent scholarship on Black Anarchisms, primarily via the work of William C. Anderson and Zoé Samudzi, while also

4A BLACK ANTIFASCISM 167

influencing more contemporary digital Black anarcho networks like the Afrofuturist Abolitionists of the Americas. Ervin came of age during the civil rights era in Chattanooga, Tennessee. In the late 1960s, he became a member of the Student Nonviolent Coordinating Committee (SNCC) and, later, the BPP. Similar to Shakur, Ervin left the BPP in 1969 after growing disillusioned with the organization's political ideology and what he identified as a "corrupted" and "authoritarian" shift.[33] In February 1969, Ervin hijacked a plane to Cuba in an effort to evade arrest after allegedly attempting to kill a member of the KKK. He escaped to Cuba, later ending up in Berlin. He was eventually extradited and sentenced to life in prison for the hijacking. Ervin traces his formal introduction to anarchy to his time at a federal detention center in New York City, where, in September 1969, he met his mentor, Martin Sostre, a Black Puerto Rican political prisoner and former owner of the nation's first Afro-Asian bookstore.

Sostre, an unsung political prisoner activist who has been regarded as "the George Jackson of the East Coast," spent much of his time in prison studying Marxist, Antifascist, anti-imperialist, and Pan-African texts as well as constitutional law. He filed a number of lawsuits that brought attention to the inhumane conditions of prison, particularly solitary confinement. Most notably, he and another inmate sued a prison warden for the right to practice Islam. This case was pivotal in strengthening the constitutional rights of the incarcerated, particularly Black Muslims.[34] Sostre had long before arrived at anarchy as a philosophy because of his own experiences in Buffalo, New York, where he was targeted by law enforcement for holding political meetings and radical education classes at his bookstore. Early in their comradeship, Sostre instilled in Ervin that anarchy was a "non-governmental form of socialism" and that anarchists stood in opposition to both capitalism and the state. Sostre's teachings and activism inspired Ervin immensely and would serve as a guide for much of his own political work.

In an effort to help build out the "Anarchists of Color" school of thought that Sostre had once envisioned, Ervin began writing articles for various anarchist presses, ultimately culminating in the publication of his 1979 book, *Anarchism and the Black Revolution*.[35] In the work, Ervin outlined tenets of anarchy and painted anarchy and Anarchists as existing on a spectrum (he details the many types of anarchists, including individual Anarchists, mutualists, Anarchist-Syndicalists, Anarchist-Communists, and so on), and put forth a vision for a Black Anarchist future.[36] The text is deeply theoretical while also functioning as a sort of utilitarian handbook for anarchists. At its core, Ervin's work emphasized that Black Anarchism (1) centered around autonomy; (2) was antagonistic toward the state; and (3) worked toward the abolition of the state, capitalism, and Anti-Black Fascism.

On Autonomy

For Ervin, anarchy and autonomy were synonymous. Autonomy functions as an organizing strategy of anarchy that calls for the creation of independent spaces that are free from the state, from authoritarian leadership within other radical organizations, and from the overwhelming whiteness of Anarchist spaces. Autonomy also came to represent the radical imagining of political ideas and futures that were not dependent upon existing systems or even "authoritarian left propaganda."[37] Autonomy was/is organizing in "the barrios, the ghettos, the hamlets, the "quarters," hovels, college dorms, high schools, churches, prisons, and other places . . . to organize a federation of autonomous people of color and begin to practice a lost art among activists these days: community based organizing for grassroots peoples' power."[38] In praxis, Ervin would later found the Black Autonomy Federation, in 1994, to address Black issues—specifically unemployment, police brutality, and mass incarceration—through grassroots organizing and mutual aid work, and as a means of rebuffing the racism Black anarchists experienced in the majority white anarcho networks.[39]

Beyond Ervin's intersection of Black anarchist and autonomous thought, Black anarchists have also engaged in autonomy as a tactic via the creation of autonomous zones, anarchist-occupied lands or communities that have been seized from the state or a private entity with the aim of operating with absolute sovereignty. During the height of the

2020 protests in response to multiple acts of state-sanctioned violence, including the deaths of George Floyd, Breonna Taylor, and Ahmaud Arbery, activists across Seattle erected one of the most recent autonomous zones in American history.[40] The 2011 Occupy movement also relied upon the creation of autonomous or "occupied" zones as a form of sustained international protest. Autonomous zones are designed to disrupt the status quo—in particular, business and the flow of capital—and are intended to serve as safe and self-sufficient places for anarchists to live and organize on their own terms. Because autonomous zones often are rooted in the seizure of public and/or private property and blatantly disregard local ordinances, historically, autonomous zones have also been sites of lethal state-sanctioned violence.

One of the nation's most enduring autonomous zones was launched by the Black anarcho-primitivist members of the MOVE organization. Led by John Africa, the MOVE organization aligned with a sect of anarchism that did not believe in government or industrial or technological progress. Founded in 1972 and based in Philadelphia, John Africa and his followers fused elements of Christianity with Black Power militancy and anarchy. The group was pro-Black, and in their quest to return to a more natural state of living sans modern technology, industry, or even organized labor, MOVE was inherently anti-capitalist.[41] While their political protests were audacious, it was their communal living style that ultimately drew the ire of the state. The city of Philadelphia deemed the commune to be in violation of several laws and ordinances related to improper heating, noise, trash disposal, harboring of vermin and stray animals, and the harassment of neighbors, to name just a few. From 1977 to 1978 there were several major stand-offs and shootouts between city police and MOVE members. In a display of unabashed hypocrisy, the city proclaimed MOVE to be "reactionary and fascist."[42] And, in 1985, the city authorized the bombing of MOVE's commune, killing and injuring several members and their children and destroying more than sixty homes in the neighborhood. In its most radical form, autonomy often comes at hefty price, including gratuitous state-sanctioned anti-Black violence.

170 THE BLACK ANTIFASCIST TRADTION

Mutual aid—the creation of resources, programs, and institutions in the absence of and/or as a means to circumvent state authority—is also a form of autonomy. While certainly less violent and obstructive than some other forms, mutual aid has been quite radical work. From the BPP's survival programs to crowd-sourced bail funds and the training of "street medics," mutual aid work relies upon the creation of autonomous networks to sustain communities that have been underinvested in/divested from. It should be noted that even mutual aid work has met with the staunchest state repression—case in point, the recent arrest of three Atlanta organizers who were charged with charities fraud and money laundering for coordinating a bail fund for "Stop Cop City" protesters in Atlanta.[43] Autonomy has been a salient strategy and tactic within the Black Antifascist Tradition, as both the theory and praxis have allowed Black people to create their own networks, systems, and communities of refuge, thus distancing themselves from some of the most visceral and pervasive elements of Anti-Black Fascism. Nonetheless, autonomy alone has never been enough to defend communities against the ills of Anti-Black Fascism.

On Antagonism

After generations of practicing self-defense across various Black freedom movements, antagonism is arguably a natural evolution and escalation of strategy and tactic that is often coupled with autonomy. As mentioned above, the BLA staged several robberies, hijackings, prison breaks, and bombings across the country during the 1970s. The revolutionary violence touted by the BLA consisted of acts of antagonism that directly targeted the state, prisons, businesses, and/or sources of capital as a means of weakening the totality of Anti-Black Fascism. This shift toward antagonism both marks a defining delineation within the Black Power Movement and represents a key characteristic of anarchy. It was no longer enough to "shoot back" or "police the police," and "turning the other cheek" was considered a dated tactic that was all but written off by 1970s Black Anarchists. Antagonism was/is the very notion of being able to "shoot first" and approach movement work like warfare, deserving of sophisticated and tactical schemes to bludgeon one's enemy—no matter how vast.

Assata Shakur's prison escape, in 1979, which was orchestrated by BLA members including Kuwasi Balagoon, is one of several examples of the BLA's antagonism against the state. Balagoon, who had twice escaped prison, was also a former BPP member who had grown disillusioned with the organization and turned to anarchy. On October 20, 1981, Balagoon, also known as "Maroon" among comrades, worked alongside a group of white radicals to mount an "expropriation"—another form of antagonism—of a Brinks armored truck in Rockland County, New York.[44] Balagoon's call for "complete revolution" underscored the need for anarchy, autonomy, and antagonism to be leveraged in concert:

> Where we live and work, we must not only escalate discussion and study groups, we must also organize on the ground level. The landlords must be contested through rent strikes, and rather than develop strategies to pay the rent, we should develop strategies to take the buildings. We must not only recognize the squatters movement for what it is, but support and embrace it. Set up communes in abandoned buildings, sell scrap cars and aluminum cans. Turn vacant lots into gardens. When our children grow out of clothes, we should have places where we can take them, clearly marked anarchist clothing exchanges, and have no bones about looking for clothing there first. And of course, we should relearn how to preserve food; we must learn construction and ways to take back our lives, help each other move and stay in shape . . . I refuse to believe that Direct Action has been captured.[45]

Balagoon identified as a New Afrikan Anarchist, a subset of Black Anarchism that he developed by intersecting Black Anarchism with Black Nationalism. Unlike other strains of Black Anarchism (and Anarchism more broadly), Balagoon's New Afrikan Anarchism did not wholly disavow the possibility of creating a new nation—a New

Afrikan nation. While challenging "the necessity of states, nationalism, and (usually) cults of personality" are typically shared traits among Anarchists, Balagoon also took inspiration from Black Nationalist organizations, such as the Republic of New Afrika (RNA), that argued that Black people's existence was one of a "subjugated nation."[46] In 1968, the RNA and other associated Black Nationalists demanded that the US government grant independence to Black people and offer five Southeastern states (Louisiana, Mississippi, Alabama, Georgia, and South Carolina) as reparations for generations of Anti-Black Fascism.[47] These states would serve as the home for New Afrika—an independent Black nation. This new nation appealed to Balagoon, as it offered a site to radically reimagine and co-create a shared future through Black Anarchism. In his riveting essay "Anarchy Can't Fight Alone," Balagoon highlights the limitations of Communism, nationalism, and Marxism, calling for all people to seek "complete revolution" and further underscoring anarchy's ability to help facilitate such:

> Of all ideologies, anarchy is the one that addresses liberty and equalitarian relations in a realistic and ultimate fashion. It is consistent with each individual having an opportunity to live a complete and total life. With anarchy, the society as a whole not only maintains itself at an equal expense to all but progresses in a creative process unhindered by any class, caste or party. This is because the goals of anarchy don't include replacing one ruling class with another, neither in the guise of a fairer boss or as a party. This is key because this is what separates anarchist revolutionaries from Maoist, socialist and nationalist revolutionaries who from the onset do not embrace complete revolution. They cannot envision a truly free and equalitarian society and must to some extent embrace the socialization process that makes exploitation and oppression possible and prevalent in the first place.[48]

Ashanti Alston, also a BLA member and former East Coast BPP member, echoed Balagoon's insistence that, through anarchy, nationalism could evolve and root out some of its most negative and disempowering attributes, particularly sexism, authoritarianism, and queerphobia:

> So my nationalism, my Black Nationalism, evolved from thinking about Black Power as just control of our communities and institutions in our communities to seeing that there were other dynamics within this Black Power that was trapped in maybe heterosexism, or the European sense of nationalism. So, starting to look at them things critically, and Anarchism was such a big help. It just allowed me to like rethink some things and see that we needed to go beyond some of the things that were important to us at a particular time. So, it's like, I get my hands on feminist materials, and it's helpful because I have these other lenses to begin to look at things and to see this more recent past, from Panther in the streets to, you know, BLA in prison—where did we make mistakes? Why did we make mistakes? What about this hierarchy thing? To look at what went on with the Huey P. Newton situation that led to the split in the Black Panther Party, why did it happen? Did it have to happen? What's this thing about cult leadership? And are there other ways that decision makings could have happened?[49]

Alston's and Balagoon's push to evolve Black Nationalism through Black Anarchism would also help the ideology and tactics they were advocating to reach a larger audience. Balagoon's legacy has directly informed the contemporary organizing within The Malcolm X Grassroots Movement (MXGM) and Cooperation Jackson. Moreover, in navigating the BLA, Black Nationalist, and Black Anarchist spaces as an openly bisexual man—a fact that has often gone undiscussed—Balagoon, in many ways, represented the nexus between the Black radicalism of the 1970s and the queer liberation movement that was also rapidly unfolding on the east coast.[50]

Beyond the BLA, antagonism, autonomy, and anarchy also served as a key ideology and as organizing tactics for emergent Black queer and trans organizing during the late 1960s and early 1970s. Black queer theorist Cathy Cohen argues that queer politics directly challenge and antagonize "the multiple practices and vehicles of power" that render queer people invisible by putting forth a new set of "anti-normative characteristics and non-stable behavior."[51] For Black and Brown LGBTQIA+ people, liberation very much included challenging Fascism and state-sanctioned violence head-on, often while leveraging what were described as antagonistic strategies.[52] Street Transvestite Action Revolutionaries (STAR), a predominately Black and Brown transgender and gender-nonconforming organization, was founded in 1970 by Marsha P. Johnson, Sylvia Rivera, and Bubbles Rose Marie. Johnson, Rivera, and Marie formed STAR following their participation in a six-day occupation of New York University's Weinstein Hall basement, a site that had served as a space for dance parties for the nearby LGBTQIA community until university administrators and trustees shut down the dances out of concerns about "morality."[53] This was the group's first collective engagement with antagonism. A year earlier, Rivera and Johnson had been credited as major agitators within the Stonewall Rebellion, the event largely responsible for sparking the gay liberation movement.

From the outset, STAR sought to provide immediate support for homeless LGBTQ youth of color.[54] The first STAR house was an abandoned trailer truck that was later recovered by its owner. STAR later relocated to a partially burned building on the Lower East Side of New York City, where the collective worked to cobble together funds for food and other necessities (representing a mix of autonomy and mutual aid).[55] While other organizations had created communal housing previously, STAR's vision of providing housing for

Marsha P. Johnson, Sylvia Rivera, and members of Street Transvestite Action Revolutionaries at the Christopher Street Liberation Day, March 1973, Leonard Fink Collection, The LGBT Community Center National History Archive.

trans people of color and simultaneously using the space to organize demonstrations that were inherently antagonistic stood in stark contrast to the mainstream white LGBT spaces that overwhelmingly settled for inclusion, parades, homonormativity, and what Jasbir Puar has coined as *homonationalism* instead of "LGBT power."[56] STAR members were characterized at the time as a "subculture unaccepted within transvestitism and looked down at in horror" because of their radical politics, "third world looks," "cut-the-crap-tongues," and "larger-than-life presence," which set them apart from their white counterparts within the gay liberation movement.[57] However, STAR's approach to gay liberation went beyond seeking gay rights, as they sought liberation in the areas of race, class, gender, and sexuality. In STAR's manifesto and early interviews, the collective was cast by its founding members as "antagonists" who "believe[d] in picking up the gun, starting a revolution if necessary."[58] Johnson and Rivera had ties to the BPP and Young Lords, and STAR adopted similar outlooks on self-determination—one of their early STAR houses was decorated with "Free Angela Davis" and "Free All Political Prisoners" posters, and they decried the increasing incarceration of LGBTQIA+ youth.[59] In sum, the organization was steeped in and aligned with many of the ideologies and politics that came to shape Black Anarchism and Black radicalism more broadly in the 1970s. Although STAR was short lived, through 1972 the organization planned demonstrations outside prisons and coordinated mutual aid resources for homeless LGBTQIA+ youth; however, their most revolutionary work was around housing.

As mentioned above, the STAR house, which was among the first LGBTQIA+ houses to emerge during the 1970s, provided a space for LGBTQIA+ youth who were grappling with homelessness. While the history of queer houses is often conflated with the history of the New York City LGBTQIA+ Ball scene, scholars such as Frank Leon Roberts remind us that Black and Brown LGBTQIA+ houses ultimately served as a response to the many implications of Fascism-corporativism in a postindustrial New York City—which included "a spiraling decline of the city's welfare and social services net, early gentrification of urban neighborhoods through private redevelopment, decreases in funding for group homes and other social services targeting homeless youth, a sharp rise in unemployment rates among [B]lack and Latino men, and a virtual absence of funding during the Reagan era for persons newly displaced and/or homeless as result of HIV/AIDS."[60] These conditions would ultimately spur high levels of poverty and homelessness, especially among Black and Latino LGBTQIA+ people across the city.[61] The STAR house and others that emerged throughout the 1970s and 1980s served as "alternative kinship networks" that sought to recreate homes and familial bonds through cooperative means (in other words, mutual aid). In spite of STAR members' envisioning themselves as "gun-toting revolutionaries," revolutionary violence was not at the center of their antagonism. Going back to Cohen's analysis, STAR's antagonism was the collective's ability to destabilize notions of being and normativity in white LGBTQIA+ spaces while standing against Fascism.

Another example of 1970s antagonism was evidenced in the work of the George Jackson Brigade. The Pacific Northwest underground group was composed of Black and white members, many of whom were women and/or queer identifying. They named themselves after Jackson, thus not only connecting themselves to the political prisoner's philosophy on Anti-Black Fascism but also choosing to engage in his style of Antifascism, which was very much animated by armed struggle and antagonism. The group, whose history is best documented in Daniel Burton-Rose's book *Guerilla USA: The George Jackson Brigade and Anticapitalist Underground of the 1970s,* waged a three-year campaign of antagonism aimed at weakening corporate and state institutions in Seattle and the surrounding Pacific Northwest. Burton-Rose accounts the brigade with being responsible for fourteen bombings, several bank robberies or "armed expropriations," and a jailbreak. They intentionally bombed sites like prisons, a revolutionary act that also symbolized calls for the abolition of the carceral state.

On Abolition

Abolition is the most salient and visionary feature of Black Anarchism. The framework and organizing strategy have roots in slavery and, later, in the works of political prisoner intellectuals like Jackson and Davis, which would lay the foundation for the Prison Abolition movement. Abolition and its many-tentacled genealogy also serve as a major delineation between Black Anarchist thought and non-Black formations of anarchy. Drawing on Avery Gordon's work, abolition involves "critique, refusal, and rejection of that which you wish to abolish," all of which overlap with anarchy, illustrating how the two are inextricably linked.[62] While often deemed utopian and intangible outside of organizing spaces, abolition is at the crux of contemporary Black Anarchist studies and strategy. William C. Anderson's framing of Black Anarchism as not just an organizing strategy but as an understanding of Black life as being in constant opposition to the state (statelessness), whether we choose this position voluntarily or involuntarily, forces us to start from a place where we are able to seriously grapple with imagining and working to advance an abolitionist future—as there is no Black future within the state, only social death. As Anderson seamlessly ties it together, "There can be no true push to abolish anything if we do not foreground the demand for autonomy in an anti-state abolition that draws from Black anarchisms."[63]

The endpoint of abolition is not destruction but futurity. Thus, abolition must engage Afrofuturism to envision the radical potential of a Black future absent of Fascism. The digital Black Anarchist network Afrofuturist Abolitionists of the Americas takes up this charge, imagining the following:

> Out of the ashes of this apocalypse come countless Afro-futures waiting to be; wondrous, speculative universes where Black people are free and push the boundaries of what is possible. Perhaps there is a future where Black people live on floating cities after the consequences of climate change cause sea levels to rise. Or maybe we will live in atmospheric cities high above the

clouds caused by a nuclear winter. In a future where the ozone layer is gone, perhaps we will live in subterranean Afrikan villages. Or maybe we are nomadic tree-planters, terraforming the Earth after its desertification. Imagine a future where there are billions of genders, each with their own temple dedicated to them and their own community of disciples. Imagine stargazing sisterhoods, time traveling ancestors, and intergalactic maroon communities. Imagine interstellar voyages aboard the Black Star space shuttle, or perhaps a cosmic Harlem Renaissance. Imagine futures where the human has disappeared and has made way for the emergence of a new being. Anarkata asks us to dream of Black possibilities that have not yet been imagined. From the end of the world comes new ways of being, new ways of living, new visions of freedom.

But we don't have to use our imaginations to dream up those futures; the evidence of them can be seen in our struggle today. From the growing concern for the most vulnerable in our communities, to the exchange of mutual aid for our survival, to the political education of our people, and the flexible responsiveness of our movements, the formations that emerge in our communities and the small and large ways we take back autonomy and kinship with the land, water, and soil—these are all precursors to our Afro-future. Anarkata envisions Afro-futures where all Black people are free to express their bodily autonomy, where Black nonmen are honored and at the fore, where disabled Black people are accommodated and validated. We foresee horizontal futures where hierarchy is abolished, and collaboration occurs across people, localities, and networks. We foresee the abolition of prisons and the emergence of communal arbitration to settle disputes. We envision autonomous localities that govern themselves through direct democracy, critique, and consensus. We foresee futures where the people have access to their needs and are not subject to bare survivalism, exploitation, or intracommunal violence. We envision communal and liberatory education for our children. And we envision a Black masses who have the political education and leadership capacity to be autonomous. These futures are not utopias where no problems exist, but they are futures in which our adaptability to new problems are heightened by the strength and health of our communities.[64]

Black Antifascism of the 1970s, as foregrounded by political prisoner intellectuals and activists, helped cement both new tactics and strategies employed within the Black Antifascist Tradition. Anarchy, autonomy, antagonism, and abolition each brought an added layer of radicalism to the tradition that was unapologetic in its choice of tactics that brazenly challenged Fascism, particularly the Fascism-corporativism that Jackson decried. Black Anarchism's commitment to challenging state domination converges powerfully with the contemporary Abolitionist movement's attack on the prison-industrial complex. In our next chapter, we will examine how Abolitionism itself is steeped in the Black Antifascist Tradition and has helped push the tradition into the mainstream of the Black freedom struggle.

— CHAPTER 7 —

ABOLITIONIST ANTIFASCISM

Put simply, this is the era of the prison industrial complex.
The prison has become a black hole into which the detritus of
contemporary capitalism is deposited.
>   —**Angela Davis**, *Are Prisons Obsolete?*[1]

We assert that the documented and lived experiences of young
people of color in Chicago constitute torture and CIDT at the hands
of law enforcement. We echo the claim made by the Civil Rights
Congress in their 1951 "We Charge Genocide" petition:
*We maintain, therefore, that the oppressed Negro citizens of the United
States, segregated, discriminated against and long the target of violence,
suffer from genocide as the result of the consistent, conscious, unified
policies of every branch of government.*
>   —**We Charge Genocide report to the United Nations Committee
Against Torture**, Geneva, Switzerland, September 2014[2]

The long historical praxis of abolition is grounded in a Black radical
genealogy of revolt and transformative insurgency against racial
chattel enslavement and the transatlantic trafficking of captive
Africans. Understood as part of the historical present tense,
abolitionist critique, organizing, and collective movement (across
scales of geography and collectivity) honor and extend this tradition.
>   —**Dylan Rodriguez**, "Abolition as Praxis
of Being Human: A Foreword"[3]

WHEN DID ABOLITIONISM BEGIN? The question animates the living present of the Black Antifascist Tradition. If Black Antifascism may be defined as the project to topple what abolitionist Ruth Wilson Gilmore calls "the constructed character of U.S. hierarchies,"[4] Abolitionist Antifascism is the end point of a tradition as old as racial capitalism itself. For prison abolitionist and Critical Resistance cofounder Dylan Rodriguez, the "praxis" of abolition covers a *longue durée* intersecting Black lived history and the master narrative of the West. As Rodriguez puts it, Abolitionism names

> the duress that some call dehumanization, others name colonialism, and still others identify as slavery and incarceration. Abolition, then, is constituted by so many acts long overlapping, dispersed across geographies and historical moments, that reveal the underside of the New World and its descendant forms—the police, jail, prison, criminal court, detention center, reservation, plantation, and "border."[5]

Rodriguez's vital definition of Abolitionism returns us to its place in a Black Antifascist Tradition, without which it is not fully legible. Specifically, it returns us to an inception point of Abolitionist Antifascism: abolitionist organizer Angela Davis's 1971 articulation of Fascism as state-sponsored resistance to "latent-revolutionary trends among nationally oppressed people."[6] Adopting Davis's words to the historical present it anticipates, Abolitionist Antifascism may be said to name the twenty-first-century wave of freedom struggle against racial capitalism and anti-Black racism in all its forms. As the Abolitionist Critical Resistance National Anti-Policing Group has defined it:

> Fascism is an aggressive political ideology and system, and a form of far-right populism. Fascism is a reactionary politic rooted in authoritarian nationalism, hetero-patriarchy, hyper-militarism, dominance, exclusion, elitism, and supremacy . . . Fascism opposes liberalism, Marxism, socialism, communism, Third World

4A BLACK ANTIFASCISM

and Indigenous self- determination, anarchism, anti-authoritarian politics, feminism, and queerness.[7]

This chapter will explore and delineate Abolitionism as a keyword and master trope in the Black Antifascist Tradition, past and present. It will show that the contemporary social movement known variously as Abolitionism or Prison Abolitionism is a vital tributary in the Black Antifascist Tradition, one that has resurrected many of its most salient features and figures, while conscripting them to a new language and new political tactics. This feature of Abolitionist Antifascism is sharply and poetically captured in the epigraph to this chapter from the Chicago-based Prison Abolitionist organization We Charge Genocide. Fashioning its name and organizing strategies after those of the 1951 Civil Rights Congress (CRC) campaign, We Charge Genocide embraced the Black Antifascist Tradition as what Rodriguez calls "historical present tense," crafting a taxonomy of police killings and appealing to the United Nations Committee Against Torture for genocidal relief. We Charge Genocide mindfully bridged more than sixty years of Black Antifascist organizing, infusing it with a contemporary Abolitionist spirit embodied in its generational resurrection of a key moment in the Black Radical Tradition.

We Charge Genocide is but one index to a wide range of contemporary social movement theory and praxis beholden to the Black Antifascist Tradition. This range of theory and practice might be seen as stepping-stones in an as yet unfinished road in the Black Antifascist Tradition. Its major articulating agents include figures such as Mariame Kaba, Angela Davis, Ruth Wilson Gilmore, Frank Wilderson, Mumia Abu Jamal, and Achille Mbembe, on one hand, and a wide terrain of contemporary Abolitionist Antifascist organizing on the other. In addition to We Charge Genocide, named above, these include groups and movements such as the Malcolm X Grassroots Movement, Why Accountability?, TGI Justice Initiative, BYP100, Critical Resistance, the Black Anarchist tradition, and the Movement for Black Lives. Each of these movement actors helps us understand and define Abolitionist

Antifascism as a continuous present of imaginative organizing and intervention within the tradition of Black Antifascism.

In her 2003 book *Are Prisons Obsolete?*, Angela Davis recalls once considering that the mass incarceration of more than two million Americans—a statistical fact at the time of her writing—could never take place "unless this country plunges into fascism."[8] Davis's book was written nearly midpoint between Abolitionist Antifascism's founding epoch in the late 1960s and our historical present. It might be considered the manifesto of the contemporary Abolitionist movement and an updated sequel to her 1971 book *If They Come in the Morning*. There, Davis had first defined Fascism as a "protracted social process," based largely in the use of the law, courts, and prisons to quell opposition to racial capitalism.[9] In *Are Prisons Obsolete?*, Davis named that "social process" the "prison industrial complex" (PIC), a term first coined both by prisoners and the radical social theorist Mike Davis.[10] With its clear echoes of what George Jackson and the Black Panthers called "fascist corporativism," Davis described the PIC as a conjuncture of mass incarceration, predatory legislation, the globalization of capitalist discipline, and widespread privatization. Whereas in 1971 Davis had named the battle against Fascism as the key battle of her generation, in *Are Prisons Obsolete?* she named it Abolitionism:

> Radical opposition to the global prison industrial complex sees the antiprison movement as a vital means of expanding the terrain on which the quest for Democracy will unfold. This movement is thus antiracist, anticapitalist, antisexist, and antihomophobic. It calls for the abolition of the prison as the dominant mode of punishment but at the same time recognizes the need or genuine solidarity with the millions of men, women, and children who are behind bars.[11]

For Davis and others seeking to build it, the Abolitionist movement has become a necessary second act to history. The staggering fact of two million US prisoners has demanded a tactical shift from the prisons to the streets. Indeed, what might be called First Wave Antifascist Abolitionism was the movement by prisoners *themselves* to abolish the conditions of their lives. As Davis's *If They Come in the Morning* documented, in 1970 and 1971, prisoner uprisings and strikes had occurred at Folsom Prison, San Quentin Prison, the Marin County Court House, Long Island City Prison, the Queens Men's House of Detention, the Brooklyn Men's House of Detention, Soledad Prison, and the Men's Colony at San Luis Obispo. In each of these instances, prisoners were murdered, wounded, beaten, or otherwise physically abused by prison guards. At Folsom, during a work stoppage, prison authorities unleashed a reign of terror named "night riding" by the prisoners, in reference to the Ku Klux Klan's terrors in the American South. Because US prisons by this time had active chapters of the Black Panther Party (BPP) and Chicano prisoners' organizations, their responses to these brutalities carried the same political interpretation of events. "The Folsom Prisoners' Manifesto of Demands and Anti-Oppression Platform" emulated the BPP's 10-point platform, expanded to twenty-nine demands for reform, ranging from adequate medical care and visiting conditions to an end to segregation in prisons (a demand also put forward by the CRC against the California prison system some twenty years earlier). As in the work of Angela Davis and the committee to free her, the Folsom prisoners' analysis was also a class analysis: demanding that industries be allowed to enter institutions and employ inmates to work eight hours, that inmates be allowed to form or join unions, and that inmates have the right to support their own families. The manifesto also left no doubt that prisoners viewed their occupying space as Fascist: "It is a matter of documented record and human recognition," they wrote, "that the administrators of the California prison system have restructured the institutions which were designed to socially correct men into the FASCIST CONCENTRATION CAMPS OF MODERN AMERICA."[12]

A second grounding conception of First Wave Abolitionist Antifascism lay in the idea of prisoners (and citizens) as their own legislators. A good example is the manifesto produced by the Panther 21, BPP members arrested in 1969 in New York City, charged with conspiracy to commit murder and possession of explosives (all were eventually acquitted). In the 1971 book *Look for Me in the Whirlwind*, their own Black Antifascist manifesto, they compared their arrests to abolitionist-era laws like the 1851 Fugitive Slave Act and 1847 Dred Scott decision. Panther 21 member Curtis Powell referred to US judicial history as "legalized grand larceny and fascism"[13] and endeavored to countercharge the US state with genocide. Like the Folsom manifesto authors, the Panther 21 imagined their Abolitionist Antifascism as litigation from below of a system whereby prisoners would become the authors of new laws and new justice. As Kuwasi Balagoon put the matter, "We blacks who felt we were marked men, on whom designs had been made to take care of 208-style, looked at the injustices on the post, had a secret meeting, and formed an organization based on fucking up racists. We called ourselves De Legislators, because we were going to make and enforce new laws that were fair. We were De Judge, De Prosecutor, De Executioner, Hannibal, and De Prophet."[14]

Abolitionist Antifascism, from its inception, imagined the Black poor and working classes as legislators of the world. Seizing the means of *legal* production was seen as fundamental to enabling the revolutionary transformation of racial capitalism. This through line conjoined the Black Panther Party to the Free Angela Davis Committee to the Soledad Brothers to Davis herself. The event that arguably kick-started modern Abolitionist Antifascism as a mass movement was the 1971 Attica Prison rebellion. The summer uprising of prisoners against the upstate New York prison took direct and literal inspiration from the Folsom and other prison uprisings. After prisoners seized conditions within the prison, five men in the Attica Liberation Faction delivered a "July Manifesto," which tweaked—while otherwise copying verbatim—points of demand from the Folsom manifesto. Formally titled "The Attica Liberation Faction Manifesto of Demands and Anti-Depression Platform," the document opened with a reiteration of the Folsom manifesto declaration, "IT IS A MATTER OF DOCUMENTED RECORD AND HUMAN RECOGNITION THAT THE ADMINISTRATION

OF THE NEW YORK PRISON SYSTEM HAVE RESTRUC-
TURED THE INSTITUTIONS WHICH WERE DESIGNED
TO SOCIALLY CORRECT MEN INTO THE FASCIST CON-
CENTRATION CAMPS OF MODERN AMERICA," with "New
York Prison System" swapped for "California." The demands were ad-
dressed up and down the chain of legal command that the Free Angela
Davis Committee had deemed, contra charges against Davis, a "con-
spiracy": "The Governor of New York State The N.Y.S. Department
of Corrections The N.Y.S. Legislature The N.Y.S. Courts The United
States Courts The N.Y.S. Parole Board."[15]

The rebellion inside Attica lasted from September 9 to 13 after
the prison administration's refusal to comply with these demands and
proved to be a tipping point in the history of Abolitionist Antifascism.[16]
The twenty-nine inmates massacred inside Attica after Governor Nelson Rockefeller ordered a fifteen-minute attack on the rebellion by state
police drew more widespread attention to prison conditions in the US
than any previous moment. The New York State Special Commission
on Attica (also known as the McKay Commission), appointed to investigate the uprising, suggested, "With the exception of Indian mas-
sacres in the late 19th century, the State Police assault which ended the
four-day prison uprising was the bloodiest one-day encounter between
Americans since the Civil War."[17] In Washington, DC, the Pepper
Commission recommended serious prison reform bills. In New York,
eight prison reform bills were passed in the 1972 legislative session. The
Department of Correctional Services requested $2.7 million for the
"inauguration of Department-wide inmate food service and clothing
programs."[18]

At the same time, prompted by the Attica uprising, the American
Correctional Association (ACA) conducted a major prison study that
concluded that there was a "New Type of Prisoner" in the United States,
who was a threat to "a majority of prisons and jails in the nation."[19]
According to the ACA, this new prisoner type had acquired "a knowledge—superficially and otherwise—of history, race problems, street
fighting and the vocabulary of radicalism." This was a "new breed of

politically radical young prisoners," who sought to build a "'Holy War' against racist oppressors."[20] The ACA report helped ignite efforts by New York's commissioner of correctional service, Russell Oswald, to move prisoners to "Maxi-maxi" facilities, to isolate political militants, and to begin stricter measures toward isolation, segregation, and overall discipline.[21] As Michelle Alexander has documented, the Attica rebellion also inspired Rockefeller to pass the most draconian drug laws in the US to date, soon emulated by states across the country as well as by the federal government. The "war on drugs" was on. In short, Attica and the ACA report triggered what scholar Heather Ann Thompson calls "an anti-civil-rights and anti-rehabilitative ethos" in the US, which, in the Abolitionist movement would come to be known as the "prison-industrial complex."[22]

What the American Correctional Association was recognizing as a "New Type of Prisoner" was in fact an Abolitionist. Because of the force of state resistance to prison rebellions, Attica had helped to produce a new wave in the urgent conception of Abolitionism as a political approach to incarceration. In 1974, Norwegian scholar and activist Thomas Mathiesen published the influential book *The Politics of Abolition*, a treatise describing the efforts, beginning around 1968, by Norwegian prisoners, activists, and social scientists, working in collaboration under the acronym KROM (The Norwegian Association of Penal Reform), to seek a nonviolent and policy-driven approach to the reform of Norwegian prisons. Its organizers intended to produce a "moral community" to challenge features of incarceration, from drug criminalization to the use of pre-trial hearings.[23] A second, more influential development in the United States, was the long-term work of Quaker radical Fay Honey Knopp. Knopp had begun visiting prisoners in 1955 and in 1962 was named a Quaker "minister of record" to increase her access.[24] In 1968, she founded Prison Visitation and Support to extend her work to conscientious objectors to the Vietnam War. From there, Knopp developed the Prison Research Education Action Program (PREAP) and the organization Instead of Prisons. After the Attica uprising, a group of women led by Virginia Mackey, in Rochester, New York, came together to form a faith-based group seeking solutions and alternatives to prison. Knopp joined with them, and PREAP became the Safe Society Committee. In 1976, PREAP published the first Abolitionist prison manifesto in the US: *Instead of Prisons*. The book's nine-point perspective for abolition was rooted in a moral and empathic critique of prisons; a call for "reconciliation, not punishment"; for the empowerment of prisoners; and for the creation of a "caring community," in which "corporate and individual redemption can take place."[25] "Caring community" was defined further as one in which "power and equality" are distributed to all members and where the "spirit of reconciliation" prevails. An Abolitionist, by PREAP's definition, was one invested in building the caring community.[26]

Between the two groups, Mathiesen and PREAP (Safe Society Committee) laid out what would become essential planks of long-term Prison Abolitionist politics, broadly conceived: calls for the decriminalization of minor and nonviolent offenses; decarceration and excarceration as alternatives to imprisonment; the defunding of prisons and refunding of social welfare and provisioning; and recognition of the racist, violent, and xenophobic nature of incarceration. At the same time, they endorsed a broader and more gradual conception of the "united front" supported by the BPP. It would include elected officials, judges, social workers, clergy, and lay people committed to a general vision of a caring community. For Mathiesen and PREAP, Abolitionism might best be understood as radical reformism. Accordingly, the terms "genocide," "Fascism" and "revolution" were not part of their Abolitionist lexicons.

In total, the first wave of Abolitionist Antifascism of the 1960s and 1970s left distinctive legacies for both the US state and its incipient new layer of dissidents. As Dan Berger has summarized the matter:

> The prison rebellions of the 1960s and 1970s left officials believing that prisoners had too much freedom. As prisons modernized their technology, they limited their capacities for collective action, seeking ever more ways to separate prisoners from each other and the outside world. The prison construction binge that began in the 1980s included new experiments in isolation—including whole units and facilities devoted to

190 THE BLACK ANTIFASCIST TRADTION

isolation. By the 1990s, whole prisons were structured around solidarity confinement, which has been used to punish the thoughts and actions of dissident prisoners, to break people's spirits, and to reinscribe racial distinctions as political divisions among the prison population.[27]

It was this combination of a racialized bonanza of prison construction and new techniques of political repression of inmate populations that produced the starting point for the most important incubator of second wave Abolitionist Antifascism, namely Critical Resistance (CR). Founded in 1997 in Oakland, CR and its analytical and organizational framework are only fully legible via reference to its roots in first wave Abolitionist Antifascism. Critical Resistance officially launched in 1998 as a conference in Berkeley, where more than 3,500 activists came together united under the banner "Critical Resistance: Beyond the Prison Industrial Complex."[28] Its origins lay in both grassroots prisoner family and rights organizing, especially in the state of California, and intellectual theorizing about the massive rise of prisons in the US and ways of fighting against them. Its architects included prisoner families, like those in the group MOTHERS ROC, described by participant activist Ruth Wilson Gilmore, and the work of prisoners themselves, community organizers, organic intellectuals, cultural workers, and academic organizers like Angela Davis and Dylan Rodriguez.

What has characterized the work of Critical Resistance since its 1998 inception is a fine-tuned attention to the relationship between the PIC, authoritarian politics, and the specter of Fascism. For example, in his book *Forced Passages: Imprisoned Radical Intellectuals and the U.S. Prison Regime*, Rodriguez borrows from George Jackson's critique of "reformism" as Fascism to ask, "How might our political understanding of the United States be altered or dismantled if we were to conceptualize fascism as the *restoration* of a liberal hegemony, a *way out* of crisis, rather than as the *symptom* of crisis or the *breakdown* of "democracy" and "civil society"?[29] This question, what Rodriguez calls the "fascism problematic," informs much of Abolitionist Antifascism. The neoliberal efforts to establish a political economy of mass incarceration has drawn special

4A BLACK ANTIFASCISM 191

attention to neoliberalism as a constituent element of the "fascism problematic." In 1998, the same year as the founding CR conference, Angela Davis, a CR cofounder along with Ruth Wilson Gilmore and Rose Braz, published the essay "Masked Racism: Reflections on the Prison Industrial Complex."[30] Davis's metaphor of a "mask" to describe the prison comported with George Jackson's earlier description of corporative reformism as a "disguise" for Fascism. Central to Davis's argument was that mass incarceration and the exploitation of prison labor by public and private prisons produce a new regime or "hierarchy" of race and class: "By segregating people labeled as criminals, prison simultaneously fortifies and conceals the structural racism of the U.S. economy."[31] The Critical Resistance Anti-Policing Workgroup, meanwhile, has focused on neoliberalism dating to the Reagan administration, World Bank Structural Adjustments, and the Clinton-era NAFTA agreement as helping to maintain the "status quo of racial capitalism by entrenching poverty and marginalization of communities of color within the US." It has also cited the neoliberal "war on gangs" and "war on drugs" as constituent elements of neoliberalism's role in midwiving the new forms of Fascism as cited at the head of this chapter.[32]

Davis's 2003 book *Are Prisons Obsolete?* likewise situated the PIC within the wider frame of neoliberalism and neoliberal politics:

> Since the 1980s, the prison system has become increasingly ensconced in the economic, political, and ideological life of the United States and the transnational trafficking in U.S. commodities, culture, and ideas. Thus, the prison industrial complex is much more than the sum of all the jails and prisons in this country. It is a set of symbiotic relationships among correctional communities, transnational corporations, media conglomerates, guards' unions, and legislative and court agendas.[33]

Like Rodriguez and George Jackson, Davis here targets the PIC as part of a liberal (and neoliberal) "restoration" of hegemony and a tributary of "corporative" reformism. Yet, Davis slightly shifts the analytic of abolition. Whereas she described the rise and presence of US prisons as a harbinger of Fascism and Fascist process in 1971, in *Are Prisons Obsolete?*, Davis describes prisons as part of a "history of antiblack racism. . . . the prison reveals congealed forms of antiblack racism that operate in clandestine ways."[34] A likely source of Davis's claims for "antiblack racism" is revealed elsewhere in the text. A page earlier in her book, Davis cites the then recent 2001 World Conference against Racism, Racial Discrimination, Xenophobia, and Racial Intolerances in Durban, South Africa. Held to commemorate the downfall of South African apartheid in 1993, the conference, Davis argues, exhibited a "global consensus that racism should not define the future of the planet."[35] The Durban conference also helped to globalize the idea of "Anti-Black" racism as a descriptor of the particular discrimination faced by Black people—what one Durban report called the "negation" of the essence of people of African descent under the transatlantic slave trade.[36] "Anti-Black" racism could also refer to the special discriminations faced by Black Africans (or Bantu, as described under apartheid) from White, Coloured (Mixed Race), and Indian citizens.[37] Though she didn't attend the Durban conference, Davis had visited South Africa, in 1991, where because of the intense racist conditions faced by the Black population, she argued for a continuation of sanctions against the de Klerk regime.

Davis's reference to Durban surfaces a subplot and political turn in second wave Abolitionist Antifascism. For many years, apartheid South Africa had been the most sustainable example for Black Antifascists of the prospects for Black people under Fascism. This is because South Africa had historically been one of the countries with the highest per capita prison population in the world, and because its white-supremacist settler-colonial state bore the imprint of Europe's twentieth-century genocidal campaigns, backed by heavy US support. W. E. B. Du Bois in the 1930s and 1940s, the "We Charge Genocide" campaign in the 1950s, the prisoner abolitionist movement of the 1960s, the anti-apartheid divestment movement of the 1970s and 1980s all used the South African example as a warning of what a Fascist state could look like for Black people. Indeed, while incarcerated in Marin County in 1971, the Free Angela Davis Committee received a letter of support from the

Women's Secretariat of the African National Congress, claiming that the fight against white supremacy in South Africa had "everything in common with you and the just struggle of your people against racism and all the unjust deeds that go with it." Davis herself had warned from jail that the US was headed toward a "South African-style fascism."[38] The 1970s in the US ended with a statement from Assata Shakur, on November 5, 1979, which had been deemed "Black Solidarity Day: We Charge Genocide." Reviving again the ghosts of the Civil Rights Congress, the political prisoner Shakur stated, "The prisons of Amerika are rapidly becoming replicas of Nazi of South Afrikan Koncentration Kamps; and with the reinstitution of the death penalty, prisons will shortly become extermination kamps."[39] In 1986, responding to South Africa's state-sponsored attacks on rebels in bordering Mozambique, Amiri Baraka described the South African regime as "a fascist state. . . . almost every other week new more extreme fascist racial-oriented laws are put in place as desperate measures to stop the black liberation juggernaut that will smash apartheid and its bearers."[40] Davis ended *Are Prisons Obsolete?* with an example from South Africa of how it had attempted to move past its apartheid past.

To be sure, Davis adds to "Anti-Black racism" in *Are Prisons Obsolete?* the oppressions faced by other non-white groups (and immigrants), gays and lesbians, and workers. Yet, the shift in terminology from Fascism to "Anti-Black racism" as a core of mass incarceration helped launch what might be called *Intersectional Abolitionist Antifascism*. Intersectional Abolitionist Antifascism added to the Comintern analysis of Fascism as monopoly capitalism, or the overt BPP analysis of "corporative" Fascism, a radical intersectional analysis of racial capitalism. The term *abolition*, in turn, became an inclusive descriptor for wide-scale social transformation and maximal political horizons. This phraseological shift was intentionally inclusive and expansive: different from first wave Abolitionist Antifascism, Intersectional Abolitionist Antifascism has considered more prominently in its theory of liberation the gender and sexual oppressions faced by women, gays, lesbians, trans, and working-class people. As Davis puts it in her concluding chapter to *Are Prisons Obsolete*, "Alternatives that fail to address racism, male dominance, homophobia, class bias, and other structures of domination will not, in the final analysis, lead to decarceration and will not advance the goal of abolition."[41] The book thus pays special attention to "battered women's syndrome" and intimate partner violence as part of the critique of systems of "domination" and "networks of social domination,"[42] language derived from intersectional analysis. To take the most famous example, Patricia Hill Collins's 1990 book, *Black Feminist Thought*, had famously coined the phrase "matrix of domination" to describe four interrelated and intersecting "domains of power": structural, disciplinary, hegemonic, and interpersonal. In her 1993 essay "Mapping the Margins," intersectional theorist Kimberlé Crenshaw referred to battering and rape as "broad-scale structures of domination" affecting Black women.[43]

Following Davis, Collins, and Crenshaw, the political and rhetorical shift toward Intersectional Abolitionist Antifascism within the Black Antifascist Tradition is a reminder, as Vaughn Rasberry has noted, that Black diasporic writing on Fascism conjures a "different epistemological view of the political history of the twentieth century"—as well as the twenty-first.[44] This epistemological difference can also help illuminate how other discursive and political trends in our time carry forward the Black Antifascist Tradition. To take one example, Davis's invocation of "Anti-Black racism" at the heart of mass incarceration can be considered a revisionist neologism for the combination of white supremacy and Black genocide charged by the Civil Rights Congress. Following directly from the UN definition, "We Charge Genocide" referenced genocide as "mass slayings on the basis of race."[45] In more concentrated philosophical form, "Anti-Black racism" has become, under Intersectional Abolitionist Antifascism, "anti-Blackness." Significant to this chapter, the term, perhaps first popularized by scholar and activist Frank Wilderson, germinates from the same source as Davis's. As has been widely documented, Wilderson went to South Africa in 1989 and joined the African National Congress (ANC). He also worked clandestinely for Umkhonto weSizwe (MK), the armed wing of the ANC. Arms were used in direct battle with the South African Defence Force and the government-supported Inkatha Freedom Party (IFP).[46] In a 2020 interview, Wilderson explains that "anti-blackness is the essential grammar of South African suffering." Where non-Black South Africans under capitalism experience exploitation, Black South Africans suffer particular forms of "structural violence" rooted in the differentiation between the human and the Black. For Wilderson, anti-Blackness explains Black ontology as what scholar Orlando Patterson calls "social death." It is a form of ideology produced by racial capitalism that provides a standpoint version of what Marx termed *alienation*. As Wilderson puts it, "Anti-Blackness cuts through and organizes the unconscious of everyone; it just doesn't benefit Black people when we are deployed as its implements and turn it on ourselves."[47]

Missing, however, from many explanatory frameworks of Wilderson's theory of anti-Blackness is its grounding in Black Antifascist thought. Elsewhere in the same interview, for example, Wilderson elaborates on anti-Blackness with reference to teaching Kwame Nkrumah's novel *The Beautiful Are Not Yet Born*, which he describes as rendering the "social death of the people of Ghana." This is a novel, writes Wilderson,

> that tells you what happens if you don't push all the way for communism; this is a novel that tells you what happens if you don't line the apartheid generals against the wall—or at least give them life without parole. Fidel Castro tried to tell this to Salvador Allende, who wouldn't listen—and we know what happened there.
>
> In a way, this is a novel that tells you what happens when you go through the TRC [Truth and Reconciliation Commission], an unethical exercise in which revolutionaries must atone as well as fascist security officers; then you give black people the vote without the return of their own land or control of the means of production. It tells you that you will find yourself in a dystopic universe in which Black people are poorer than they were during colonialism.[48]

Wilderson's explanatory framework for anti-blackness sits comfortably between first wave Abolitonist Antifascism's theory of Fascism as "preventive counterrevolution," while more explicitly naming its "structural violence" as Anti-Black Fascism. South Africa's place in the Black Antifascist matrix (as well as that of Pinochet's 1973 Fascist coup) is thus again unveiled as a cornerstone of Intersectional Abolitionist Antifascism.

This analysis helps explain the concomitant rise in second wave Abolitionist Antifascism with a political rhetoric of anti-Blackness in the service of Intersectional Abolitionist Antifascism. A powerful example is the work of Mariame Kaba. A cofounder of the Chicago Freedom School and numerous other political projects, Kaba is also director of the New York City–based NIA (meaning "with purpose" in Swahili).[49] A primary entry point for Kaba into Abolitionist organizing was her reading of the Civil Rights Congress's "We Charge Genocide" document and her cofounding and participation in the Chicago group of that name. Kaba's theory of change is rooted in the Intersectional Abolitionist Antifascism of the movement's second wave. She has described structures of oppression as "white supremacy, misogyny, ableism, classism, homophobia, and transphobia,"[50] while rooting her analysis in a lineage of Black Antifascist thought that resonates with Wilderson's:

> Prisons are the iteration of structural racism in the United States, which allows some people to be treated as less than human and therefore reasonably subject to all manner of exploitation, torture, and abuse. This is the legacy of anti-Blackness in the United States. Even when the system ensnares a non-Black person, the prison-industrial complex remains a structurally anti-Black apparatus, firmly rooted in the United States' ongoing reliance on the financial exploitation and social control of Black people.[51]

Kaba's argument for the prison as the violent instrumentalization of Black ontology as the "less than human" also resonates with Achille Mbembe's sense of Black "necropolitics." For Mbembe, the category of "race" and the conditions of the prison and colony provide the sovereign power to grant life and death. More than Kaba, Mbembe explicitly situates his theory of necropolitics in a tradition of analytical writing on Fascism, from Hannah Arendt's notion that race is "not the natural birth of man, but his unnatural death" to Foucault's conception of the Third Reich as a combination of the "racist state, the murderous state, and the suicidal state."[52] For Mbembe, the colony, and slavery, are the racial incubators for an ontological Fascism. "Slave life," he writes, "in many ways, is a form of death-in-life."[53] Mbembe, like Davis and Wilderson, also draws on South African apartheid as well as Palestine as examples of what becomes the site of modernity's profound anti-Blackness. Indeed, both Mbembe and Angela Davis have included Israel in what might be called an Intersectional Abolitionist Antifascist triangulation of South Africa, US Jim Crow South, and Israel. In a 2013 speech at the School of African and Oriental Studies in London, on the role of the global Israeli security company G4S, Davis ended her speech thus: "Just as we say 'never again' with respect to the fascism that produced the Holocaust, we should also say 'never again' with respect to apartheid in South Africa, and in the Southern U.S."[54]

Ruth Wilson Gilmore's own long leadership in the politics of abolition also discloses roots in thinking through the contours of anti-Black Fascism. In March 1992, Gilmore delivered a paper at a day-long conference at UC Berkeley. The paper described a rising conjuncture of American racial nationalism and state-sponsored violence as "tending toward fascism through the brutal romance of identity, forged in the always already of the American national project."[55] In an early 1993 essay, titled "Public Enemies and Private Intellectuals: Apartheid USA," Gilmore described the dissolution of a fifty-year "reich" of California's economic miracle—deindustrialization, layoffs, unemployment, and the "browning" of the state's population—as laying the groundwork for a "more secure fascism, through American apartheid's geographical enclavism and separate-but-unequal institutions, most notably education and the legal system."[56] Notably, Gilmore's book delineating the historical arc of these conditions assumed a starkly authoritarian nomenclature: *Golden Gulag*. In the same essay, Gilmore cites Stuart Hall's *Policing the Crisis* as an apt analytic for defining the lineaments of a more "secure" US Fascism: "An appeal to an originary nativism (not aboriginal, but rather founding—as in the Founding Fathers) has the warfare state armed and active against 'all enemies foreign and domestic' (as the US loyalty oath reads). Such are the master's tools."[57]

As an Abolitionist, meanwhile, racism for Gilmore may be defined as one arm of this warfare state: she names racism as "the state-sanctioned and/or legal production and exploitation of group-differentiated vulnerabilities to premature death."[58] The prison is, in turn, a primary agent for racism's processes. "The rationality underlying prison growth," she writes, "uses both rhetoric and practices of violence to make mass incarceration seem other than it is—a machine for producing and exploiting group-differentiated vulnerability to premature death."[59] Gilmore, here, too, asks us to look back on the Black Antifascist Tradition. As we noted in our introduction to this book, "premature death" was the Civil Rights Congress's clarion keyword for Anti-Black Fascism in "We Charge Genocide." Finally, Gilmore's Intersectional Abolitionist Antifascism looks to abolition as a horizon for revolution: at the 2022 Socialism conference, in Chicago, Gilmore referred to the current US state as demonstrating an uneven but momentous "tendency" towards Fascism, and Abolitionism as its greatest counterforce.[60] Gilmore's remarkable, long career as an activist, organizer, and writer, beginning with MOTHERS ROC (Mothers Reclaiming Our Children), cofounding CR, continuing to her contemporary organizing for abolition is a testament to her commitment to the fight against Anti-Black Fascism.

Wilderson, Mmembe, Kaba, Davis, and Gilmore constitute a radical vanguard of a new Black Antifascist Tradition that sits at the crossroads of contemporary Abolitionist theory and practice. Given the extraordinary proliferation of their organizing work and ideas, it should not surprise us that Black Antifascist thought has helped to produce something like one hundred flowers of Intersectional Abolitionist Antifascism. The vital conjuncture of Black Antifascist theory and practice in our time would include, for example, the Malcolm X Grassroots Project, a direct descendant of the New Afrika Movement. Rooted in principles of self-defense and self-determination, the Malcolm X Grassroots Project has called for demonstrations against so-called Three-Percent Fascists in Wisconsin, analyzed the January 6, 2021, Capitol riot as an example of American Fascism, and forwarded "We Charge Genocide" as an organizing slogan for their political calls for reparations, an end to violence against women, and release of political prisoners.[61] In 2021, it celebrated and commemorated George Jackson, the Soledad Brothers, and "Black August" with a tribute to "Black/New Afrikan prisoners held within . . . concentration camps."[62] Its platform for Black liberation is also decidedly intersectional. "We understand," they write, "that the collective institutions of white supremacy, patriarchy and capitalism have been at the roots of our people's oppression."[63] The Malcolm X Grassroot Project work is a symmetrical offshoot of the ongoing prison writing and organizing of former BPP member Mumia Abu Jamal, still imprisoned on America's death row for the alleged shooting of a Philadelphia police officer in 1981 and, in late 2022, denied a new trial. Abu Jamal, who was radicalized in part by being beaten for taking part in a demonstration against racist political candidate George Wallace in 1968, has kept alive and embodied first wave Abolitionist Antifascist analysis of the prison as the most visible site of the US Fascist process. In a series of prison radio broadcasts since his incarceration, Abu Jamal has combined an analysis of Fascism as "the merger of state and corporate power," evidence of state repression of political dissidents by operations like COINTELPRO, and repressive legislation like the Patriot Act to lay allegations of Fascism at the door of American government. In January 2021, from prison, Abu Jamal published "The American Way of Fascism," in response to the January 6, 2021, Capitol riots.[64] Abu Jamal has also developed an intersectional analysis of the Black Freedom Struggle, foregrounding the role of Black women in the BPP and the contributions of organizer Ella Baker to the Student Nonviolent Coordinating Committee.[65] His ongoing incarceration as a political prisoner is a living totem of the Black Antifascist Tradition's grounding in incarcerated Black Lives.

Another important Intersectional Abolitionist Antifascist group is BYP100. BYP, or Black Youth Project, was created in response to the acquittal of George Zimmerman in the murder of Trayvon Martin and draws on the organizing work of Dr. Cathy Cohen with a Black Youth Project advisory council in Chicago. In 2012, Cohen was working with the National Black Justice Coalition to help represent the voices of queer, trans, and labor organizers. In July 2013, she held the "Beyond November Movement Convening" outside of Chicago. Also in 2013, after an event to commemorate the fiftieth anniversary of the March on Washington, a group of thirty BYP members wrote the founding document for a national collective. BYP centers its work through a "Black, queer, feminist lens,"[66] and focuses on ending "systems of anti-Blackness" and building an inclusive network of radicals between the ages of eighteen and thirty-five. In August 2017, in the wake of the Charlottesville "Unite the Right" Rally, BYP published its own Antifascist organizing manifesto, "What to Do if White Supremacists Hold a Rally in Your Hood."[67] The manifesto included step-by-step instructions for building a "counteraction" against white supremacists and included the fight against Fascism as a cornerstone of the BYP's long-term project for liberation. "As we rise up, like the people of Charlottesville, to fight for our freedom, we must prepare ourselves to confront the rising threat of neo-Nazis and neo-Confederates. We must remember: the goal of any counteraction is *still* to build Black power long term."[68]

Perhaps the second wave Abolitionist Antifascism group most beholden to the deep history of the Black Antifascist Tradition is Chicago's We Charge Genocide. As noted earlier, NIA founder Mariame Kaba first approached Chicago activists about forming the group after reading the original 1951 CRC petition in the wake of the murder of Trayvon Martin. We Charge Genocide applied CRC's techniques to the public chronicling of Chicago Police Department killings, torture, tasings, and arrests, as well as complaints of police brutality, to demonstrate a two-tiered system of racial violence in Chicago. Borrowing from the CRC's playbook, it classified these crimes as violations of the UN Conventions against Torture, ratified in 1994, and presented its findings to the UN in Geneva in November 2014.[69] The UN responded by officially condemning the actions of the CPD. In an interview with Christina Heatherton and Jordan Camp, Page May, a We Charge Genocide delegate to Geneva, also located the CPD as a modality of Anti-Black Fascism, stating: "There are a lot of silences we're speaking to. Primarily, we're naming anti-Blackness. We're saying that this is not just about police violence, it's not just that the police are racist; we're saying that they are an anti-Black institution."[70] We Charge Genocide has also featured women and queer organizers in leadership positions.

Intersectional Abolitionist Antifascism has also yielded Black women–led organizing in groups such as the New York City-based Why Accountability? The collective organized a march against white nationalism on Donald Trump's inauguration day and has subsequently marched in New York City against the far-right Proud Boys. Although focused on police brutality, Why Accountability's Gem Isaac has described contemporary Black Antifascism as an ancestral heir to previous Abolitionist and self-defense movements in US history: "When you talk about Nat Turner or Sojourner Truth to take up arms against your oppressor and push back against them, that is antifascist work. When you talk about Nanny of the Maroons in the Caribbean or the Haitian Revolution, that is antifascist work. History has shown us, time and again, African people participating in antifascist work."[71]

Intersectional Abolitionist Antifascism has also generated a vital new current of Black Antifascism rooted in trans lives and their self-defense. A key moment in this upsurge was the arrest and imprisonment of Black trans radical Cece McDonald. On June 5, 2011, McDonald and some friends were walking on the streets of Minneapolis, when McDonald was attacked by a white supremacist neo-Nazi shouting transphobic and racist epithets. The attacker gashed McDonald's face before McDonald killed him in self-defense. McDonald was sentenced to four years in prison, a sentence eventually commuted after nineteen months. She was freed on January 13, 2014. McDonald's attack and her self-defense helped birth national attention to far-right, neo-Nazi attacks and murders of trans people in the US, particularly Black trans women. Mainstream civil rights organizations like the Southern Poverty Law Center began tracking the voluminous attacks on trans people by the far right.[72] Meanwhile, a flurry of Abolitionist trans organizing and writing in response has been mobilized by groups like the TGI Justice Project, dedicated to organizing transgender, gender variant, and intersex people inside and outside of prisons to help incarcerated and formerly incarcerated Black and Brown people.[73] TGI's work has developed a strong theoretical cast, consonant with Intersectional Abolitionist Antifascism. For example, in their important 2015 book *Captive Genders: Trans Embodiment and the Prison Industrial Complex*, Morgan Bassichis, Alexander Lee, and Dean Spade ground a history of trans and queer organizing in the lineages of the BPP and CR. They invoke histories of internal colonization and state-sponsored repression such as COINTELPRO to describe the parallel histories of repression of trans and queer people as "counter-revolution—the attempt to squash the collective health and political will of oppressed people."[74] Key examples of trans Intersectional Abolitionist Antifascist organizing include the Sylvia Rivera Law Project, which seeks to provide legal and mutual aid to self-determining gender expression, free from violence.[75] As noted in our previous chapter, Rivera's STAR organization, cofounded with Marsha P. Johnson, was itself rooted in the Antifascist politics of the 1960s and 1970s. In total, Intersectional Abolitionist Antifascism builds upon the important Antifascist organizing of queer ancestors in US- and European-based movements, such as ACT UP, which deployed the pink triangle used by the Nazis to stigmatize homosexuals in their queering of Antifascist history. Intersectional Abolitionist Antifascism contains its own powerful racialized queering of that history.

The Black Anarchist Antifascist tradition introduced in our previous chapter has also continued into what Rodriguez calls the "historical present" of Abolitionist history. In their 2018 book *As Black as Resistance*, Zoé Samudzi and William C. Anderson describe US "societal fascism" as the exclusion of racial subjects from the social contract, a result of

US history's rootedness in slavery and settler colonialism.[76] For Black Anarchists, under societal Fascism, African Americans are "pre-contractually excluded because they have never been a part of a given social contract and never will be, or they are ejected from a contract they were previously a part of and are only able to enjoy conditional exclusion at best."[77] In her foreword to the book, Mariame Kaba argues, "As an abolitionist, the Black anarchism espoused by Anderson and Samduzi resonates with me. Abolishing the prison industrial complex (PIC) is not just about ending prisons but also about creating an alternative system of governance that is not based on domination, hierarchy, and control. In that respect, abolitionism and anarchism are positive rather than negative projects."[78]

Black Anarchist Antifascism's conjuncture with Intersectional Abolitionist Antifascism may be seen as an important political mirror held up to our present. In 2019 and 2020, both president Donald Trump and attorney general William Barr set out to conflate Black Lives Matter protests broadly with the movement known as Antifa. Trump tweeted that Black Lives Matter as a movement was a form of "treason," while Barr described anti-police protests as "fascistic."[79] Trump and Barr articulated the state-centric perspective that has infused the far right in its own street war with Black Lives Matter. Though the Movement for Black Lives has itself avoided using the explicit language of "Fascism" and "genocide" against the US state, describing the current neoliberal crisis of racial capitalism as a manifold "war on Black people," its platform preamble to the call to end that war echoes without naming the tenets of Intersectional Abolitionist Antifascism: "We are intentional about amplifying the particular experiences of racial, economic, and gender-based state and interpersonal violence that Black women, queer, trans, gender nonconforming, intersex, and disabled people face. Cisheteropatriarchy and ableism are central and instrumental to anti-Blackness and racial capitalism and have been internalized within our communities and movements."[80] Yet, the current Anti-Black Fascist movement has had no trouble decoding the Movement for Black Lives as an attack on Anti-Black Fascism. As

Adam Turl and others have noted, Black Lives Matter protests have been a repeated and special target for Fascist and far-right demonstrators since the movement's inception, cresting at the 2017 Charlottesville killing of BLM activist Heather Heyer and resounding with Kyle Rittenhouse's murder of two BLM activists in Kenosha, Wisconsin, in August 2020.[81] Far-right street attacks have repeatedly targeted Black Lives Matter organizing.[82] These attacks on Intersectional Abolitionist Antifascist activists are the interracial collateral violence to the police murders of Black people, which have spawned the largest protest movement in US history, involving some 26 million people.[83]

This state of perpetual war between Intersectional Abolitionist Antifascism, Anti-Black Fascists, and the US state shows no signs of ending or letting up. It has brought the Black Antifascist Tradition dead center to American politics, making visible the crossroads between Black protest and a distinctively Anti-Black Fascist tradition. In 2017, a year after the election of Donald Trump and in the wake of his notorious "Muslim Ban," the CR project dedicated an entire issue of its journal to the topic, "Organizing against Fascism." In light of what the issue called "extreme right-wing forces" emboldened by Trump, and "in the face of intensified racism, sexism, transphobia, and imperialist war-mongering," the issue offered a variety of tools for building Intersectional Abolitionist Antifascism. These included articles by political prisoner Herman Bell against state repression; David Stein's assessment of Trump's contribution to mass incarceration and state repression; an interview with Tarso Luis Ramos, comparing Trump's authoritarian rule to the Bolsonaro regime in Brazil; and an interview with Arab-American organizer Lara Kiswami on the public fight against Trump's Muslim ban. The issue also reprinted an interview with Ruth Wilson Gilmore and Mariame Kaba of the New York–based group Survived and Punished, which works to assist women who are victims of domestic violence. In the interview, Gilmore reflected on her work with the grassroots organization Making the Road:

> If abolition is a form of consciousness, historically it has also become this incredible road that we've all met on. Like, we

4A BLACK ANTIFASCISM

205

didn't know each other before, but we met on this road, and we met on this road that we make by walking it, by walking it, and it's the most exciting and thrilling thing imaginable almost twenty years, eighteen years after that first Critical Resistance conference. To think about abolition as something that is tied exactly to the ending of unfreedom in the form of slavery, but that ending of unfreedom, tied as it is to the necessity for structural inequality that is the precondition of capitalism valorizing itself, means that abolition has an ambition, has an ambition that says, if the prison industrial complex can't be fixed by reworking it within its own logic, then by definition, the world has to be different.[84]

More recently, in the winter of 2021, in the wake of the January 6, 2021, Capitol riot, CR member Woods Ervin, in an article entitled "Finding Our Way Forward: Past Neoliberalism, Fascism, Austerity and the Prison Industrial Complex," considers the future of Antifascism and Abolitionism as one:

In order to understand the connection between neoliberalism and fascism, we must consider the violent character of neoliberalism and its support of authoritarianism, both in the US and abroad. As neoliberalism emerged, so did a growing resentment across the political spectrum. In the absence of a more liberatory program, it further ripened conditions for authoritarianism to fester. In other words, neoliberalism creates conditions where a cycle of state and extra-legal violence can thrive. The slashing of the social welfare net, as well as the rise in unemployment of the working class and the shrinking of the middle class, creates the conditions of powerlessness and inequality. This then produces desperation, division, and increased violence—by the state and within our communities. The state's disavowal to take responsibility for the needs of the people feeds into the people's disillusionment with government, creating a perfect storm for a populist, Fascist leader, party, or forces to make things "great

206   **THE BLACK ANTIFASCIST TRADTION**

again," to restore glory, and so on. Neoliberalism has created conditions of despair and disillusion. Through "organized abandonment," as coined by Ruthie Gilmore, in this way, neoliberalism facilitated Trumpism and its fascistic tendencies to rise with political efficacy in the 21st century. . . .

. . . we must continue the diligent work of rooting out neoliberalism, white supremacy, militarism, and the PIC from our communities, and we must seriously contest their legitimacy and remove them from positions of power. We need to find places of weakness within our enemies and win over those who can be won, de-platform those who must be de-platformed, and eradicate the structures of policing, imprisonment, and militarism that threaten our future. The work of building true safety, peace, and liberation through abolition remains an ever-present need for us to take on with rigor and seriousness.[85]

Even more recently, Black British feminist Abolitionists Aviah Sarah Day and Shanice Octavia McBean have drawn directly on the fight against Fascism and for Socialism to advocate for an Intersectional Abolitionist Antifascism merging "transformative justice" and social justice into what they call "revolutionary justice:"

A serious project to end police violence and the siege of marginalized communities cannot be anything but revolutionary: a total transformation of the international world order, the unequivocal abolition of the conditions that give rise to policing and a rebuilding in the interests of ordinary folk—as equals, as collaborators, as comrades. Abolition. Revolution. Now.[86]

Gilmore, Day, McBean, and Ervin point to the aspirational futurism of what we have been calling in this book the Black Antifascist Tradition and its imagination of political horizons beyond the present. Because there can be no last word in the Black Antifascist Tradition until there is no Anti-Black Fascism, we leave a lingering call to its future to Black Antifascist organizers JoNina Abron-Ervin and Lorenzo Kom'boa Ervin. Ervin is a former member of the BPP and a founder of the civil rights group Concerned Citizens for Justice in Chattanooga, Tennessee. In 2012, they helped organize the Memphis Black Autonomy Federation to address Black unemployment and mistreatment of Black prisoners. They have called for a renewed commitment of Black community organizing around Black Antifascist principles as a means to "bring together the movement against police terrorism with the movement against mass incarceration." For them, the lessons of the Black Antifascist Tradition must be the source and wellspring for its next chapter and for the vision of a new world:

> We need to create alternatives. We need to create people's assemblies that are independent and autonomous . . . And by doing this we can reach people and educate, organize, and put them in opposition to the government, the State. We should be fighting for dual power. We need to build a mass movement to free political prisoners, end mass imprisonment, especially among communities of color. We need to combat state violence from police and vigilantes, fight austerity and poverty imposed by the government. We need to defeat fascists in the streets *and* in the government and corporate suites. Start survival campaigns that begin to build a new economy to soften the blow of the collapse of this system, which is coming. We also need to build a black partisan/workers' militia. . . . we need to be doing these things if we are gonna go from oppression to liberation. I guess the main thing we can say is that we have to build an antifascist movement that is a movement fighting for revolution—for social revolution.[87]

— EPILOGUE —

THE MODERN GLOBAL FASCIST ECHO CHAMBER AND BLM-ANTIFA

N 1995, Toni Morrison delivered a riveting speech, "Racism and Fascism," at Howard University's Charter Day celebration. In the tradition of the many Black Antifascists written about in this book, Morrison cautioned the audience about the twin systems—Fascism and racism—during an era marked by a "war on drugs" and the rise of mass incarceration. She asserted that Fascism can "only reproduce the environment that supports its own health: fear, denial, and an atmosphere in which its victims have lost the will to fight"—an environment whereby multinational companies can become Fascist political structures, public services are transformed into private entrepreneurship (Fascist-corporativism), parenting manifests as "panicking" and voting against our children, "their health care, their education, their safety from weapons." Furthermore, she reminded us that the allure of Fascism was not limited to a particular political party, surmising that "fascism talks ideology, but it is really just marketing—marketing for power." Morrison's nearly thirty-year-old assessment of Fascism, which she specifically chose to give at a Black institution, still holds much truth, as many of her prophecies have unfortunately become a dark reality for so many.

For both of us, *The Black Antifascist Tradition* has been a long time in the making, as much of our research, organizing, and activist work has long pointed to the salience and prominence of Anti-Black Fascism across space and time. With the rise of the Tea Party movement in 2009 and the election of Donald Trump in 2016, it became glaringly apparent that the US—and much of the Western world—was not only moving further toward the political right but also embracing a more authoritarian style of governance, accompanied by a commitment to elevating what can best be summed up as overtly white supremacist rhetoric, policy, and values, all while decrying facts and reality as "misinformation."

The grip of Anti-Black Fascism in the US has insidiously shaped the Black experience, but now, when overtly "fascist solutions to national problems" are being normalized and legalized for so many, some people, but not enough of them, are finally ready to mount a resistance to Fascism.[1] The contemporary global Fascist era has been ushered in by Donald J. Trump, Jair Bolsonaro, Rodrigo Duterte, Narendra Modi, Viktor Orbán, and Giorgia Meloni, all forging their own stake in the whittling away of democracy. Voting rights and elections integrity, public education, and the restriction of personal freedoms have been clear targets of this movement. Trump's denial of the 2020 election results, which culminated with the failed January 6, 2021, insurrection, has not only sparked a wave of legislation to restrict voting rights (which has grossly disenfranchised Black people across the American South) but also served as a direct inspiration for the similarly failed January 8, 2023, insurrection in Brazil following Bolsonaro's ouster.[2] As polarizing far-right demagogues, both Trump and Bolsonaro have galvanized their bases by touting deeply anti–working class, nationalist, racist, and anti-Indigenous talking points, harking back to the "good old days." Authoritarian force and state-sanctioned violence have been heralded as *necessary* to "reclaim" the nations from immigrants, shifting racial demographics, LGBTQIA+ people and movements, and those on the left—and, moreover, as a means to further cement white supremacist cisheteropatriarchy. *When one's supporters call for the declaration of martial law, as has happened under both Trump's and Bolsonaro's presidencies, that must be understood as the weaponization of Fascism being both normalized and seen as the methods by which the far right intends to use and govern. The gloves have come off.*

At the same time, since 2020, public schools across the US have increasingly been under attack by conservatives and the far right. Critical Race Theory (CRT), a legal framework for interrogating systemic racism that was introduced by legal scholars like Derrick Bell and Kimberlé Crenshaw, has morphed into a political punching bag, reduced and anti-intellectualized to mean anything and everything in public education that aims to further diversity, equity, inclusion, and justice, and foster the creation of more culturally responsive curriculum and instructional materials.[3] State legislatures and school boards, hijacked by conservative parent groups, political action committees (PACs), and members of far-right organizations, have launched a full-on assault on public education, starting with the banning of a litany of Black- and LGBTQIA+ authored books; the exclusion, censoring, and rewriting of ethnic studies and social studies through a conservative lens; and the elimination of policies meant to protect nonbinary and transgender students. In states like Texas and Florida, where the largest K–12 school districts are considered "minority majority," it is often Black and Brown students and parents who are most harmed by these developments. These attacks have also ushered in a mass exodus of K–12 teachers, who were already grossly underpaid and undervalued, curtailing any work to repopulate the already dwindling teacher pipeline. Instead of being incentivized to become educators, under "anti-CRT" and "anti-woke" laws, teachers are now threatened with termination and incarceration.[4] The erosion of public education and academic freedom in an effort to prop up "school choice," which boils down to the privatization and charterization of education, is no more than an attempt to apply corporativism to one of the longstanding bedrocks of Western democracy. *When books are being banned, curricular materials censored, critical and analytical scholarship substituted with political propaganda and anti-intellectualism, and far-right militia members and groups overrunning and presiding over school board meetings, we understand that to be the systematic Fascist restructuring of education.*

As many mourned the reversal of the landmark *Roe v. Wade* decision in 2022, and with it the right to safe and accessible abortion services, birthing people across all racial lines were once again reminded that their personal and bodily freedoms could be legislated. Indeed, white women's reproductive rights had been eroded as a means of supporting the pro-natalist politics of the modern Fascist movement that seeks to increase the white population. Conversely, Fascist and pro-natalist ideology has also shaped the violent imaginations of an increasing number of white male mass shooters who have explicitly targeted Black, Brown, Asian American, and Jewish people.[5] While murmurs of a burgeoning "race war" have long animated far-right rhetoric and racial resentment, pro-natalist legislation and violence have resulted in real material consequences for those on the margins of race and gender lines, including poor maternal health outcomes, limited reproductive healthcare access, and increasing infant mortality and poverty rates.[6] Following the decision to reverse *Roe*, Justice Clarence Thomas signaled in his opinion that the court should also take up similar cases that would limit personal freedoms as related to same-sex marriage (*Obergefell v. Hodges*), opening onto a slippery slope to the possible overturning of interracial marriage (*Loving v. Virginia*). *When birthing people are used as political pawns and are seen as no more than vessels in which to shape racial demographics and produce bodies for a supposed race war, and the literal composition of intimate relationships is in part dictated by an increasingly hostile and authoritarian state and court system, that, too, must be understood as Fascism seeping further into one of the most intimate aspects of our lives—the right to choose whom we love, marry, and build a family with.*

This modern Fascist movement has only cemented the inextricability of anti-Blackness and Fascism. The 2020 #blacklivesmatter rebellion in response to a relentless cycle of violent killings of Black people by law enforcement, and the January 6, 2021, Capitol insurrection, will stand as two pivotal events of modern US history. Both were shaped and deeply informed by Black Antifascist and Anti-Black Fascist politics and organizing. From the very outset, Trump and leaders across the far-right cast the 2020 protests as an "anti-police" movement led by "professional anarchists, violent mobs, arsonists, looters, criminals, rioters, Antifa," and the truncated "BLM-ANTIFA."[7] In response, Black leadership and political pundits of the establishment class sought to distance #blacklivesmatter from Antifa, who were largely being scapegoated as the main provocateurs of "non-peaceful protesting." There was an insistence that Black people were *not* Antifa or, by extension, Antifascists. But this was so far from the truth.

As cities across the US were upended by protests and calls for racial justice, police reform, the defunding of law enforcement agencies, and, ultimately, the abolition of police, the Trump administration responded with brute force, deploying federal agents in unmarked vehicles to "liberal cities" like Portland and Denver, endorsing further brutality.[8] This type of authoritarianism was cheered on by those on the far right. Neofascist groups like the Proud Boys and the Boogaloo Bois mounted a campaign to infiltrate Antifa and leftist networks, stoking divisions and stirring up violence as bait to entice additional Trumpian response and, overall, to undermine the #blacklivesmatter protests.[9] In just three days (May 28–30, 2020) at least nine Proud Boys and Boogaloo Bois members had committed arson, lobbed Molotov cocktails at buildings, damaged public property, fired random shots, and shot law enforcement officers, with each act committed under the cover of the protests. This concerted movement destabilization, disconcertingly similar to COINTELPRO provocateur tactics, continued in the following weeks. What became abundantly clear after the summer of 2020 was that (1) Black people were indeed organizing under the banner of Antifascism; (2) to be aligned with Antifa or Antifascist politics was understood to be a form of domestic terrorism in this warped modern Fascist and Trumpian reality; (3) any response by Black people to police brutality, no matter how righteous the response, was perceived as a domestic threat deserving of brute force and the trampling of civil liberties; and (4) various levels of the US government had effectively emboldened, sided with, and provided cover for far-right militias and the effective rise of modern-day Fascism.

In contrast, in the weeks leading up to the January 6, 2021, insurrection, thousands of far-right militia members (including the Proud Boys, Boogaloo Bois, Patriot Prayer, and others), Trump supporters, and neofascists like Nick Fuentes gathered in Washington, DC, on December 12, 2020, to voice discontent over Trump's election loss and the Supreme Court's refusal to take up additional cases surrounding bogus claims of election fraud and the "Big Steal."[10] They called on the Trump administration to overrule the democratic process by declaring martial law in a last-ditch effort to retain power. Trump, notably, responded to the seditious rally with support and admiration, tweeting, "Wow! Thousands of people forming in Washington (D.C.) for Stop the Steal. Didn't know about this, but I'll be seeing them! #MAGA," a far cry from the state-sanctioned violence inflicted on #blacklivesmatter protesters months earlier.[11] Later that day, Trump would go even further, riding by the event in a presidential motorcade eerily reminiscent of the motorcades Hitler had deployed through the streets of Germany to galvanize supporters. The rally evolved into a march to the two-block area north of the White House that had been christened "Black Lives Matter Plaza" by DC mayor Muriel Bowser during the previous summer. Along the way, armed militia members donning explicitly Nazi and Fascist paraphernalia, including a shirt that read "PINOCHET DID NOTHING WRONG," beat, terrorized, and accosted random Black civilians. When the militia arrived at the plaza, they clashed with a small contingent of #blacklivesmatter counterprotesters. The group also vandalized the African Methodist Episcopal Church, which had once hosted the funerals of Frederick Douglass and Rosa Parks, because the church had raised its own #blacklivesmatter sign. While the intent of the rally was to galvanize support for Trump's campaign to overturn the 2020 election results, much of its vitriol and violence was directed at Black people and #blacklivesmatter. The far right's calls for full-on Fascist governance and acts of anti-Black violence happened in tandem. Just as we've pointed to in this book, Fascism and anti-Blackness are inseparable, as so much of white supremacy and Fascism is predicated on the control and subjugation of Black people. Trump's loss was perceived as a blow to the supposed freedom of his supporters. They refused to return to a pre-Trumpian status quo, where more overtly Fascist rhetoric, governance and policy would presumably not be tolerated.

During the December 12, 2020, rally, several members of the Proud Boys were photographed in sweatshirts with "Uhuru," the Swahili word for freedom, emblazoned on the back, along with other noticeable Proud

Boys iconography. In the 1950s and 1960s, "Uhuru" was often chanted and evoked as Kenyans fought for their independence from the British. Since then, the word has carried deep anticolonial and Pan-African meaning across generations of Black people. The Proud Boys' depraved use of "Uhuru" wasn't just one of the many contradictions or poor attempts by the far right to co-opt Black liberation movement cultural production, it also served as an unintentional (or not) call back to Fascism's colonial roots.[12] They were aligning neofascism with resistance efforts to the most enduring Fascist project of them all—the colonization of Africa. But the Proud Boys are not of the Mau Mau or Black liberation tradition, as Aimé Césaire and W.E.B. Du Bois would remind us; they are the fruits of and testament to European colonialism.

Just a few short weeks later, many of the attendees of the December rally made their way back to Washington, DC, on January 6, 2021, this time swarming and breaking into the US Capitol, threatening elected officials and staffers with death, beating law enforcement, and, overall, desecrating the nation's effigy of democracy. For hours, law enforcement failed to control the riotous acts that resulted in the deaths of four people. With Nazi, Confederate, QAnon, Trump, and "Blue Lives Matter" paraphernalia on full display, the images from January 6, 2021, showcased a collage of Fascist and far-right imagery. Despite an overwhelming preponderance of evidence pointing to far-right groups being the main, if not only, provocateurs of violence on that day, in the hours, days, and weeks to follow, somehow Antifa was blamed repeatedly, as if that level of violence were inconceivable from groups that had long aligned themselves with anti-government, pro-secessionist, and pro-gun beliefs. False equivalencies, comparing the insurrection to #blacklivesmatter protests, were, and still are, also in abundance. *January 6, 2021, was a tipping point within US history, one that will certainly be written about for generations to come, but we must also hold the fact that the failed insurrection represents a major stride on the long road toward Fascism in the US, a type of Fascism that is distinctly informed and undergirded by anti-Blackness and anti-Black violence.*

In the final pages of Octavia Butler's cautionary tale *The Parable of the Sower*, Lauren Olamina and her Earthseed community are burying their dead and looking for a place to settle. Lauren reminds them (and Butler reminds the reader) that, despite the perils that surround them—whether that be slavery, police violence, drugs, disease, Fascist leaders, or other—there is a constant need to grow and build anew. Butler's concept of Earthseed signifies that commitment to radically rebuilding a new society through the lens of Antifascism—Black Antifascism—led by the likes of Black youth. As we stare down a resounding global Fascist echo chamber, it is imperative that we not only plant new seeds of Antifascism but also uplift and refashion the tactics, strategies, writings, and struggles of past Black Antifascists.

THE BLACK ANTIFASCIST TRADITION SYLLABUS

Course Description

This course takes at its starting point Aimé Césaire's thesis in *Discourse on Colonialism* that twentieth-century Fascism is rooted in white supremacy, colonialism, and settler colonialism, including in the United States. Throughout the semester, students will trace a new genealogy of Fascism—one that contends with Césaire's thesis and identifies anti-Blackness as an intrinsic feature of Fascism. Students will analyze a range of writings (cultural texts, autobiographies, political newspapers and newsletters, and more) and social movements from the late nineteenth century through the early twenty-first century (from the anti-lynching movement to the contemporary Abolitionist movement) that critically grapple with Anti-Black Fascism: slavery; targeted state and mass vigilante violence; colonial-style occupation; disproportionate police surveillance; egregious movement restriction; political suppression. The course will foreground Black self-organizing and self-activity in the face of Anti-Black Fascism: the Black Antifascist Tradition. Students will engage new strategies, tactics, and histories that will tie the history of Anti-Black Fascism and Antifascist organizing in the United States to current social movements and discourse on the rise of neofascism and the enduring legacy of Black Antifascist organizing. Overall, this course will provide students with a "Black Antifascist toolkit" that can be used beyond the classroom, serving as a guide for real-world Antifascist application.

COURSE OUTLINE AND READINGS

(please see reading list for full citations)

Week 1: Introducing the Black Antifascist Tradition

Ida B. Wells-Barnett, *Southern Horrors and Other Writings: The Anti-Lynching Campaign of Ida B. Wells, 1892–1900* (excerpt)

Aimé Césaire, *Discourse on Colonialism* (excerpt)

Civil Rights Congress, "We Charge Genocide" (excerpt)

Walter Rodney, *How Capitalism Underdeveloped Africa* (excerpt)

James Whitman, *Hitler's American Model: The United States and the Making of Nazi Race Law* (excerpt)

Week 2: Anti-Lynching and Premature Black Antifascism

Amii Larkin Barnard, "The Application of Critical Race Feminism to the Anti-Lynching Movement: Black Women's Fight against Race and Gender Ideology, 1892–1920," *UCLA Women's Law Journal* 3, no. 1 (1993)

Beverly Guy-Sheftall, *Daughters of Sorrow: Attitudes Toward Black Women, 1880–1920* (excerpt)

Equal Justice Initiative, *Lynching in America: Confronting the Legacy of Racial Terror*

Ida B. Wells-Barnett, *Crusade for Justice: The Autobiography of Ida B. Wells* (excerpt)

Ida B. Wells-Barnett, *Southern Horrors and Other Writings: The Anti-lynching Campaign of Ida B. Wells, 1892–1900* (excerpts from *Red Record*)

Week 3: Pan-African and Anticolonial Antifascism

Albert Memmi, *The Colonizer and the Colonized* (excerpt)

THE BLACK ANTIFASCIST TRADITION SYLLABUS   219

W. E. B. Du Bois, "The African Roots of War," *Atlantic Monthly*, May 1915

Paul Robeson, "Robeson Visions an Africa Free of Rule by Europeans," *New York Herald-Tribune*, January 12, 1936, in *Paul Robeson Speaks: Writings, Speeches, Interviews*, ed. Philip S. Foner

Abraham Lincoln Brigade Archive, "Salaria Kea: A Negro Nurse in Republican Spain"

Week 4: Black Marxist Antifascism

Langston Hughes, "Love Letter from Spain"

James Yates, *Mississippi to Madrid: Memoirs of a Black American in the Spanish Civil War 1936-1938* (excerpt)

George Padmore, "Hitler, Mussolini and Africa," *Crisis*, September 1937

Robin D. G. Kelley, "This Ain't Ethiopia but It'll Do: African Americans and the Spanish Civil War," in *Race Rebels: Culture, Politics, and the Black Working Class*

Harry Haywood, *Black Bolshevik* (excerpt)

Week 5: Double Victory Antifascism

W. E. B. Du Bois, *Dusk of Dawn: An Essay Toward an Autobiography of a Race Concept* (excerpt)

"Blitz over Georgia," *Chicago Defender*, September 28, 1940

Euell A. Nielsen, "The Double V Campaign 1942–1945," Black Past (website), July 1, 2020, accessed September 21, 2023, https://www.blackpast.org/african-american-history/events-african-american-history/the-double-v-campaign-1942-1945/

Langston Hughes, "Beaumont to Detroit: 1943"

Jackie Ormes, political cartoons, *Chicago Defender*

Gwendolyn Brooks, "Gay Chaps at the Bar," "the progress"

Week 6: Legal Antifascism: We Charge Genocide

Civil Rights Congress, "We Charge Genocide: The Crime of Government Against the Negro People"

Charisse Burden-Stelly. "Claudia Jones, the Longue Durée of McCarthyism, and the Threat of U.S. Fascism," *Journal of Intersectionality* 3, no. 1 (July 2019): 46–66

Lloyd Brown, *Stand Up for Freedom: The Negro People vs. the Smith Act* (excerpt)

Week 7: Black Power Antifascism

Kathleen Cleaver, "Racism, Fascism, and Political Murder (1968)," in *The U.S. Anti-Fascism Reader*, ed. Bill Mullen and Christopher Vials

Georgi Dimitrov, *United Front: The Struggle Against Fascism and War* (excerpts)

Huey Newton and Vladmir Lenin, *Revolutionary Intercommunalism and the Right of Nations to Self-Determination*

Robert F. Williams, *Negroes with Guns* (excerpts)

Robert and Mabel Williams, select issues of *The Crusader*

Week 8: Queer and Anarchist Antifascism

Angela Davis, ed., *If They Come in the Morning* (excerpts)

Assata Shakur, *Assata: An Autobiography* (excerpts)

Lorenzo Kom'boa Ervin, *Anarchism and the Black Revolution* (excerpts)

"George Jackson: Dragon Philosopher and Revolutionary Abolitionist," *Black Perspectives* (blog), accessed December 21, 2018, https://www.aaihs.org/george-jackson-dragon-philosopher-and-revolutionary-abolitionist/

Street Transvestite Action Revolutionaries, *Street Transvestite Action Revolutionaries: Survival, Revolt, and Queer Antagonist Struggle* (excerpts)

Week 9: Abolitionist Antifascism

Angela Davis, *Are Prisons Obsolete?* (excerpt)

We Charge Genocide, *Police Violence Against Chicago's Youth of Color*, http://report.wechargegenocide.org

Ruth Wilson Gilmore, "Terror Austerity Race Gender Excess Theater." *Abolition Geography: Essays Towards Liberation*

Malcolm X Grassroots Movement, "New Curriculum, We Charge Genocide Again, Notes the Importance of *Operation Ghetto Storm* Findings for Younger Generations"

Black Youth Project, "What to Do if White Supremacists Hold a Rally in Your Hood"

Critical Resistance National Anti-Policing Working Group and *The Abolitionist* Editorial Collective, "What is Fascism? What is Neoliberalism? Definitions"

Week X: Black Antifascism Now!

Octavia Butler, *Parable of the Sower*

THE BLACK ANTIFASCIST TRADITION
A Reading List

Abraham Lincoln Brigade Archive. Tamiment Library, New York University. https://guides.nyu.edu/tamimentlibrary/alba.

Abu Jamal, Mumia. "The American Way of Fascism," Change-Links, January 30, 2021, https://change-links.org/mumia-abu-jamal-the-american-way-of-fascism/.

Alexander, Michelle. *The New Jim Crow: Mass Incarceration in the Age of Colorblindness*. New York: New Press, 2020.

Anderson, Carol. *Eyes Off the Prize: The United Nations and the African American Struggle for Human Rights, 1944–1955*. Cambridge: Cambridge University Press, 2003.

Andrews, Gregg. *Thyra B. Edwards: Black Activist in the Global Freedom Struggle*. Columbia: University of Missouri Press, 2011.

Arendt, Hannah. *The Origins of Totalitarianism*. New York: Harcourt, Brace and Jovanovich, 1973.

"The Attica Liberation Faction Manifesto of Demands and Anti-Depression Platform," Freedom Archives. https://freedomarchives.org/Documents/Finder/DOC510_scans/Attica/510.Prisons.AtticaManifesto.pdf.

Bailey, Moya. *Misogynoir Transformed: Black Women's Digital Resistance*. New York: New York University Press, 2022.

Bay, Mia. *To Tell the Truth Freely: The Life of Ida B. Wells*. New York: Hill and Wang, 2009.

Berger, Dan. *Captive Nation: Black Prison Organizing in the Civil Rights Era*. Durham: University of North Carolina Press, 2016.

Blain, Kesha and Tiffany Gill, eds. *To Turn the Whole World Over: Black Women and Internationalism*. Urbana: University of Illinois, 2019.

Bohn, John. "Crisis, Struggle, Counter-Revolution: A Brief Guide to Racial Capitalism in the U.S." Columbia Journal. July 21, 2020. https://www.columbiajournal.org/articles/2020-crisis-struggle-counter-revolution-a-brief-guide-to-racial-capitalism-in-the-us.

Brown, Lloyd. *Stand Up for Freedom: The Negro People vs. the Smith Act*. New York: New Century Publishers, 1952.

Burden-Stelly, Charisse. "Claudia Jones, the Longue Durée of McCarthyism, and the Threat of US Fascism." *Journal of Intersectionality* 3; no. 1 (July 2019): 46–66.

———.*Black Scare/Red Scare*. University of Chicago Press, 2023.

Burton-Rose, Daniel. *Guerrilla USA: The George Jackson Brigade and the Anticapitalist Underground of the 1970s*. Berkeley: University of California Press, 2010.

———.*Creating a Movement with Teeth: A Documentary History of the George Jackson Brigade*. Oakland: PM Press, 2010.

Camp, Jordan and Christina Heatherton. "An Interview with Breanna Champion, Page May, and Asha Rosa Ransby-Spore." *Policing the Planet: Why the Policing Crisis Led to Black Lives Matter*. New York: Verso, 2016.

Carmichael, Stokely and Charles Hamilton. *Black Power: The Politics of Liberation in America*. New York: Random House, 1967.

Césaire, Aimé. *Discourse on Colonialism*. New York: Monthly Review Press, 2001.

THE BLACK ANTIFASCIST TRADITION: A READING LIST 225

Chigumadzi, Panashe. "Who Is Afraid of Race?" *Boston Review.* March 11, 2021. https://www.bostonreview.net/articles/who-is-afraid-of-race/.

Cooper-Owens, Deirdre. *Medical Bondage: Race, Gender, and the Origins of American Gynecology.* Athens: University of Georgia Press, 2018.

Critical Resistance. "Critical Resistance: Beyond the Prison Industrial Complex." https://criticalresistance.org/updates/critical-resistance-beyond-the-prison-industrial-complex-1998-conference/

Davies, Carol Boyce. *Left of Karl Marx: The Political Life of Black Communist Claudia Jones.* Durham: Duke University Press, 2008.

Davis, Angela. *Are Prisons Obsolete?* New York: Seven Stories Press, 2003.

———.*Freedom Is a Constant Struggle: Ferguson, Palestine, and the Foundations of a Movement.* Chicago: Haymarket Books, 2016.

Davis, Angela, ed. *If They Come for Us in the Morning: Voices of Resistance.* New York: Verso, 2016.

Davis, Mike. "Hell Factories in the Field." *Nation.* February 20, 1995.

Day, Aviah Sarah and Shanice Octavia McBean. *Abolition Revolution.* London: Pluto Press, 2022.

Du Bois, W. E. B. "The African Roots of War." *Atlantic Monthly.* May 1915. https://www.theatlantic.com/magazine/archive/1915/05/the-african-roots-of-war/528897/

———.*Black Reconstruction in America, 1860–1880.* New York: Free Press, 1998.

———."Writings on National Socialism." *Pittsburgh Courier,* December 12, 1936. In *The U.S. Antifascism Reader.* Edited by Bill V. Mullen and Christopher Vials. New York: Verso, 2020.

Fanon, Frantz. *The Wretched of the Earth.* New York: Grove Press, 2005 (reprint).

———.*A Dying Colonialism*. New York: Grove Press, 1994 (reprint).

———.*Black Skin White Masks*. New York: Grove Press, 2008 (reprint).

Featherstone, David. *Solidarity: Hidden Histories and Geographies*. London: Zed Books, 2012.

"The Folsom Prisoners Manifesto Of Demands and Anti-Oppression Platform," Freedom Archives. http://www.freedomarchives.org/Documents/Finder/DOC510_scans/Folsom_Manifesto/510.folsom.manifesto.11.3.1970.pdf

Fraenkel, Ernst. *The Dual State: A Contribution to the Theory of Dictatorship*. Oxford: Oxford University Press, 2017.

Frederickson, George. *White Supremacy: A Comparative Study of American and South African History*. New York: Oxford University Press, 1982.

Giddings, Paula. *Ida: A Sword Among Lions; Ida B. Wells and the Campaign Against Lynching*. New York: Amistad, 2009.

Gilmore, Ruth Wilson. *Golden Gulag: Prisons, Surplus, Crisis, and Opposition in Globalizing California*. Berkeley: University of California Press, 2006.

———."Terror Austerity Race Gender Excess Theater." *Abolition Geography: Essays Towards Liberation*. New York: Verso, 2022.

Glenn, Susan A. "'We Charge Genocide': The 1951 Black Lives Matter Campaign." Mapping American Social Movements Project. Civil Rights and Labor History Consortium. University of Washington. https://depts.washington.edu/moves/CRC_genocide.shtml.

Goldstein, Nancy. *Jackie Ormes: The First African American Woman Cartoonist*. Ann Arbor: The University of Michigan Press, 2008.

Hall, Stuart. *Policing the Crisis: Mugging, the State, and Law and Order*. London: The Macmillan Press, 1978.

Haney-Lopez, Ian. *White by Law: The Legal Construction of Race*. New York: New York University Press, 2006.

Hayes Edwards, Brent. "Langston Hughes and the Futures of Diaspora." *American Literary History* 19, no. 3 (Autumn 2007): 689–711.

Haywood, Harry. *Black Bolshevik: Autobiography of an Afro-American Communist*. Minneapolis: University of Minnesota Press, 1978.

Hoffman, Frederick. "The Race Traits and Tendencies of the American Negro." *American Economic Association* 11, nos. 1–3 (1896).

Hope, Jeanelle K. "Black Antifa AF: The Enduring Legacies of Black Antifascism." *Essence*. June 20, 2020. https://www.essence.com/feature/fascism-black-antifa-rallies/.

———."Roe's Reversal and the Specter of American Fascism," *Forum*, July 1, 2022. https://forummag.com/2022/07/01/roes-reversal-and-the-specter-of-american-fascism/.

Horne, Gerald. *Communist Front? The Civil Rights Congress, 1946–1956*. Madison, NJ: Fairleigh Dickinson University Press, 1988.

———.*Black Revolutionary: William Patterson and the Globalization of the African American Freedom Struggle*. Champaign: University of Illinois Press, 2013.

———.*The Counter-Revolution of 1776: Slave Resistance and the Origins of the United States of America*. New York: New York University Press, 2016.

———.*The Dawning of the Apocalypse: The Roots of Slavery, White Supremacy, Settler Colonialism, and Capitalism in the Long Sixteenth Century*. New York: Monthly Review Press, 2020.

Hughes, Langston. *The Collected Poems of Langston Hughes*. New York: Vintage, 1995.

———.*Langston Hughes and the Chicago Defender: Essays on Race, Politics and Culture, 1942–1962*. Edited by Christopher DeSantis. Champaign: University of Illinois Press, 1995.

James, C. L. R. "Revolution and the Negro." *Selected Writings of C. L. R. James 1939–1949*. Edited by Scott McLemee and Paul LeBlanc. Chicago: Haymarket Books, 2018.

Kaba, Mariame. *We Do This 'Til We Free Us: Abolitionist Organizing and Transforming Justice*. Chicago: Haymarket Books, 2021.

Kakel, Carroll. *The American West and the Nazi East: A Comparative Perspective*. New York: Palgrave Macmillan, 2011.

Kelley, Robin D. G. "Births of a Nation, Redux: Surveying Trumpland with Cedric Robinson." *Boston Review*, November 5, 2020. https://www.bostonreview.net/articles/robin-d-g-kelley-births-nation/.

———."The Future of L. A. Is Here: Robin D. G. Kelley's Radical Imagination Shows Us the Way." *Los Angeles Times*. March 17, 2021. https://www.latimes.com/lifestyle/image/story/2021-03-17/robin-dg-kelley-black-marxism-protests-la-politics.

———."This Ain't Ethiopia but It'll Do: African Americans and the Spanish Civil War." In *Race Rebels: Culture, Politics, and the Black Working Class*. New York: The Free Press, 1994.

Keyes, Allison. "The East St. Louis Race Riot Left Dozens Dead, Devastating a Community on the Rise." *Smithsonian Magazine*, June 30, 2017.

New York 21. *Look For Me in the Whirlwind: The Collective Autobiography of the New York 21*. New York: Random House, 1971.

Malcolm X Grassroots Movement. http://www.mxgm.org/

Makalani, Minkah. *In the Cause of Freedom: Radical Black Internationalism from Harlem to London, 1917–1939*. Durham: University of North Carolina Press, 2014.

McDuffie, Erik. *Sojourning for Freedom: Black Women, American Communism, and the Making of Black Left Feminism.* Durham: Duke University Press, 2011.

Memmi, Albert. *The Colonizer and the Colonized.* London: Earthscan Publications Ltd., 1974.

Moore, Hilary, and James Tracy. *No Fascist USA: The John Brown Anti-Klan Committee and Lessons for Today's Movements.* San Francisco: City Lights Books, 2020.

Mullen, Bill V. *Popular Fronts: Chicago and African-American Cultural Politics, 1935–1946.* Champaign: University of Illinois Press, 1999.

Mullen, Bill V. and Christopher Vials, eds. *The U.S. Antifascism Reader.* New York: Verso, 2020.

Murch, Donna Jean. *Living for the City: Migration, Education, and the Rise of the Black Panther Party in Oakland, California.* Chapel Hill: University of North Carolina Press, 2010.

Nelson, Alondra. *Body and Soul: The Black Panther Party and the Fight against Medical Discrimination.* Minneapolis: University of Minnesota Press, 2013.

Newton, Huey, and Vladmir Lenin. *Revolutionary Intercommunalism and the Right of Nations to Self-Determination.* Edited by Amy Gdala. Wales, UK: Superscript, 2004.

Padmore, George. "Hitler, Mussolini and Africa." *Crisis*, September 1937. In *The U.S. Antifascism Reader.* Edited by Bill V. Mullen and Christopher Vials. New York: Verso, 2020.

Patterson, William L. *The Man Who Cried Genocide: An Autobiography.* New York: International Publishers, 2017.

Patterson, William L., ed. *We Charge Genocide: The Crime of Government Against the Negro People.* New York: International Publishers, 2017.

Paxton, Robert. *The Anatomy of Fascism.* New York: Vintage, 2005.

Perez, Jasson. "Snatching Victory: Weak American Democracy Lends Strength to Trump's Insurgent Right." *Spectre*. January 25, 2021. https://spectrejournal.com/snatching-victory/.

Rasberry, Vaughn. *Race and the Totalitarian Century: Geopolitics in the Black Literary Imagination*. Cambridge: Harvard University Press, 2016.

Retish, Aaron. "Robin D. G. Kelley on Antifascism Then and Now." *The Volunteer*. October 23, 2020.

Richards, Johnetta. "Fundamentally Determined: James E. Jackson and Esther Cooper Jackson and the Southern Negro Youth Congress, 1937–1946," *American Communist History* 7, no. 2 (2008): 191–202.

Roberto, Michael Joseph. *The Coming of the American Behemoth: The Origins of Fascism in the United States, 1920–1940*. New York: Monthly Review Press, 2018.

Roberts, Dorothy. *Killing the Black Body: Race, Reproduction, and the Meaning of Liberty*. New York: Vintage Books, 1997.

Robeson, Paul. *Paul Robeson Speaks: Writings, Speeches, Interviews*. Edited by Philip S. Foner. New York: Brunner/Mazel Publishers, 1978.

Robinson, Cedric. *Black Marxism: The Making of the Black Radical Tradition*. Chapel Hill: University of North Carolina Press, 2021.

———.*Cedric J. Robinson: On Racial Capitalism, Black Internationalism, and Cultures of Resistance*. Edited by H. L. T. Quan. London: Pluto Press, 2019.

Rodriguez, Dylan. "Abolition as the Praxis of Being Human: A Foreword." *Harvard Law Review* 132*(6): 1575–1612*.

———.*Forced Passages: Imprisoned Radical Intellectuals and the U. S. Prison Regime*. Minneapolis: University of Minnesota Press, 2005.

THE BLACK ANTIFASCIST TRADITION: A READING LIST   231

————.*White Reconstruction: Domestic Warfare and the Logics of Genocide*. New York: Fordham University Press, 2020.

Samudzi, Zoé, and William C. Anderson. *As Black as Resistance: Finding the Conditions for Liberation*. Chico, CA: AK Press, 2018.

Stanley, Eric A., Nat Smith, and CeCe McDonald, eds. *Captive Genders: Trans Embodiment and the Prison Industrial Complex*. Oakland: AK Press, 2013.

Thompson, Heather Ann. *Blood in the Water: The Attica Prison Uprising of 1971 and Its Legacy*. New York: Pantheon, 2016.

Thyra Edwards Collection. Chicago Historical Museum.

Trotsky, Leon. *Fascism: What It Is and How to Fight It*. Atlanta: Pathfinder Press, 1996 (reprint).

Vials, Christopher. *Haunted by Hitler: Liberals, the Left, and the Fight against Fascism in the United States*. Amherst: University of Massachusetts Press, 2014.

We Charge Genocide. "Police Violence Against Chicago's Youth of Color." September 2014. http://report.wechargegenocide.org.

Wells-Barnett, Ida. B. *Southern Horrors and Other Writings: The Anti-Lynching Campaign of Ida B. Wells, 1892–1900*, 2nd ed. Edited by Jacqueline Jones Royster Boston, MA: Bedford/St. Martin's, n.d.

Whitman, James. *Hitler's American Model: The United States and the Making of Nazi Race Law*. New Haven: Yale University Press, 2018.

Wilderson, Frank. *Incognegro: A Memoir of Exile and Apartheid*. Boston: South End Press, 2008.

Williams, Dana. "Black Panther Radical Factionalization and the Development of Black Anarchism." *Journal of Black Studies* 46, no. 7 (October 2015): 678–703.

Wright, Richard. *Native Son*. New York: Harper Collins, 1993.

———. *The Man Who Lived Underground: A Novel*. New York: New American Library, 2021.

Yates. James. *Mississippi to Madrid: Memoirs of a Black American in the Spanish Civil War 1936–1938*. New York: Shamal Books, 1986.

NOTES

Introduction

1 Walter Rodney, *How Capitalism Underdeveloped Africa* (London: Bogle-L'Ouverture Publications, 1972), 316.

2. Angela Davis, "Political Prisoners, Prisons, and Black Liberation," in *If They Come in the Morning: Voices of Resistance*, ed. Angela Y. Davis (New York: Verso, 2016), 42.

3. Vinson Cunningham, "The Future of L.A. Is Here. Robin D. G. Kelley's Radical Imagination Shows Us the Way," *Los Angeles Times*, March 17, 2021, accessed December 13, 2022, https://www.latimes.com/lifestyle/image/story/2021-03-17/robin-dg-kelley-black-marxism-protests-la-politics.

4. Davis, "Political Prisoners."

5. Aimé Césaire, *Discourse on Colonialism* (New York: Monthly Review Press, 2001), 62. See also Panashe Chigumadzi, "Who Is Afraid of Race?," *Boston Review* (2021), accessed December 13, 2022, https://www.bostonreview.net/articles/panashe-chigumadzi-caste-review-2/.

6. Angela Y. Davis and Bettina Aptheker, Preface, in Davis, *If They Come in the Morning*, xiv.

7. Cunningham, "The Future of L.A. Is Here."

8. See, for example, Enzo Traverso, *The New Faces of Fascism: Populism and the Far Right* (New York: Verso, 2019); Jason Stanley, *How Fascism Works: The Politics of Us and Them* (New York: Random House, 2018); Sarah Churchwell, *Behold America: A History of America First and the American Dream* (London: Bloomsbury, 2019); Shane Burley, *Fascism Today: What It Is and How to End It* (Oakland: AK Press, 2017). See also an earlier, important study by Roger Griffin, *Fascism* (London: Oxford, 1995).

9. See Stuart Hall, et al., *Policing the Crisis: Mugging, the State, and Law and Order* (New York: Palgrave, 1978); Ugo Palheta, "Fascism, Fascisation, Antifascism," *Monthly Review Online*, January 9, 2021, https://mronline.org/2021/01/09/fascism-fascisation-antifascism/;

David Renton, *The New Authoritarians: Convergence on the Right* (London: Pluto Press, 2019); Prabhat Patnaik, "Neoliberalism and Fascism," *Agrarian South: Journal of Political Economy* 9, no. 1 (April 2020): 33–49; Jasson Perez, "Snatching Victory," *Spectre*, January 25, 2021, https://spectrejournal.com/snatching-victory/; Charisse Burden-Stelly, "Claudia Jones, the Longue Durée of McCarthyism, and the Threat of US Fascism," *Journal of Intersectionality* 3; no. 1 (July 2019): 46–66. See also Burden-Stelly's forthcoming *Black Scare/Red Scare* (Chicago: University of Chicago Press, 2023); Alyosha Goldstein and Simon Ventura Trujillo, *For Antifascist Futures* (Brooklyn: Common Notions, 2022).

10. Cedric J. Robinson, "Fascism and the Response of Black Radical Theorists," in *On Racial Capitalism, Black Internationalism, and Cultures of Resistance* (London: Pluto Press, 2019), 152–153.

11. William Anderson and Zoé Samudzi, *As Black as Resistance: Finding the Conditions for Liberation* (Chico, CA: AK Press, 2018), 6.

12. Anderson and Samudzi, *As Black as Resistance.*

13. James Whitman, *Hitler's American Model: The United States and the Making of Nazi Race Law* (Princeton: Princeton University Press, 2018), 15.

14. The Negro Act, 1740. Acts of the South Carolina Assembly, #670.

15. Perez, "Snatching Victory."

16. Jennifer Devroye, "The Rise and Fall of the American Institute of Criminal Law and Criminology," *Journal of Criminal Law and Criminology* 100, no. 1 (Winter 2010): 11.

17. Frederick Hoffman, "The Race Traits and Tendencies of the American Negro," *American Economic Association* 11, nos. 1–3 (1896): i–x; 1–329.

18. Alondra Nelson, *Body and Soul: The Black Panther Party and the Fight against Medical Discrimination* (Minneapolis: University of Minnesota Press, 2013), 44.

19. Hoffman, "The Race Traits," 236.

20. Hoffman, "The Race Traits," 217–236.

21. Equal Justice Initiative, *Lynching in America: Confronting the Legacy of Racial Terror* (Montgomery, AL: Equal Justice Initiative, 2017).

22. See Alex Ross, "How American Racism Influenced Hitler," *New Yorker*, April 30, 2018, accessed December 13, 2022, https://www.newyorker.com/magazine/2018/04/30/how-american-racism-influenced-hitler;

NOTES

235

Edwin Black, *War Against the Weak: Eugenics and America's Campaign to Create a Master Race* (Washington, DC: Dialog Press, 2012).

23. Martin Kitchen, "The Antisemite's Vade Mecum: Theodor Fritsch's *Handbuch der Judenfrage*," *Antisemitism Studies* 2, no. 2 (February 2018): 199–200.

24. Whitman, *Hitler's American Model*.

25. For more on reproductive rights and justice, see Deirdre Cooper-Owens, *Medical Bondage: Race, Gender, and the Origins of American Gynecology* (Athens: University of Georgia Press, 2018); Dorothy Roberts, *Killing the Black Body: Race, Reproduction, and the Meaning of Liberty* (New York: Vintage Books, 1997); Loretta Ross and Rickie Solinger, *Reproductive Justice: An Introduction* (Oakland: University of California Press, 2017); Harriet Washington, *Medical Apartheid: The Dark History of Medical Experimentation on Black Americans from Colonial Times to the Present* (New York: Harlem Moon, 2008).

26. Bill Mullen, "J. D. Vance & Replacement Theory," *Tempest*, May 23, 2022, accessed December 14, 2022, https://www.tempestmag.org/2022/05/j-d-vance-replacement-theory-and-the-2022-u-s-elections/?utm_source=rss&utm_medium=rss&utm_campaign=j-d-vance-replacement-theory-and-the-2022-u-s-elections.

27. Mullen, "J. D. Vance."

28. Michael Omi and Howard Winant, *Racial Formation in the United States*, 3rd ed. (New York: Routledge, 2014), 62.

29. For more on forced sterilization and reproductive justice movements in Latin America see *La Operación*, directed by Ana Maria Garcia, Latin American Film Project, 1982; *No Más Bebés*, directed by Renee Tajima-Peña, ITVS International, 2016.

30. Whitman, *Hitler's American Model*, 77.

31. Whitman, *Hitler's American Model*, 77.

32. Whitman, *Hitler's American Model*, 77.

33. Michael Livingston, *The Fascists and Jews of Italy: Mussolini's Race Laws, 1938–1943* (New York: Cambridge University Press, 2014), 15–23; Aaron Gillette, "The Origins of the 'Manifesto of Racial Scientists'," *Journal of Modern Italian Studies* 6, no. 3 (2001).

34. Livingston, *The Fascists and Jews of Italy*, 15–23.

35. Richard Pankhurst, "Racism in the Service of Fascism, Empire-Building and War: The History of the Italian Fascist Magazine 'La

Difesa della Razza,'" Marxists Internet Archive, accessed December 14, 2022, https://www.marxists.org/archive/pankhurst-richard/2007/03/x01.htm.

36. Pankhurst, "Racism in the Service of Fascism, Empire-Building and War."

37. Whitman, *Hitler's American Model*, 84.

38. Whitman, *Hitler's American Model*, 84.

39. Whitman, *Hitler's American Model*, 86.

40. Ian Haney Lopez, *White by Law: The Legal Construction of Race* (New York: New York University Press, 2006), 7–8.

41. Steve Martinot, "The Question of Fascism in the United States," *Socialism and Democracy* 22, no. 2 (July 2008): 29.

42. It should be noted that many European immigrants, including Italians, Jews, Irish, Polish, and others, experienced a great deal of marginalization and discrimination during the nineteenth century and first half of the twentieth century in the US. Many European immigrants were stigmatized, often associated with various types of crime.

43. W. E. B. Du Bois, *The World and Africa: An Inquiry Into the Part Which Africa Has Played in World History* (New York: International Publishers, 2015), 43.

44. *Autobiography of W. E. B. Dubois: A Soliloquy on Viewing My Life from the Last Decade of Its First Century*, ed. Herbert Aptheker (New York: International Publishers, 1968), 305–306.

45. W. E. B. Du Bois, "The African Roots of War," *Atlantic Monthly* (May 1915), https://www.theatlantic.com/magazine/archive/1915/05/the-african-roots-of-war/528897/; W. E. B. Du Bois, *Dusk of Dawn: An Essay Toward an Autobiography of a Race Concept* (New York, NY: Oxford University Press, 2014).

46. Bill Mullen and Christopher Vials, eds., *The U.S. Anti-Fascism Reader* (Brooklyn: Verso Books, 2020), 197.

47. Mullen and Vials, *The U.S. Anti-Fascism Reader*, 11.

48. Mullen and Vials, *The U.S. Anti-Fascism Reader*, 197.

49. William L. Patterson, ed., *We Charge Genocide: The Crime of Government Against the Negro People* (New York: International Publishers, 2017), 3.

NOTES   237

Chapter 1

1. See Mia Bay, *To Tell the Truth Freely: The Life of Ida B. Wells* (New York: Hill and Wang, 2009); Daina Ramey Berry and Nicole Kali Gross, eds., *A Black Women's History of the United States* (Boston: Beacon Press, 2021); Brittney Cooper, *Beyond Respectability: The Intellectual Thought of Race Women* (Urbana: University of Illinois Press, 2017); Paula Giddings, *Ida: A Sword Among Lions: Ida B. Wells and the Campaign Against Lynching* (New York: Amistad, 2009); Beverly Guy-Sheftall, ed., *Words of Fire: An Anthology of African-American Feminist Thought* (New York: The New Press, 1995).

2. Lynch law: the substitution of the court of law with white mob rule and/or the sanctioning of extrajudicial lynchings by the law.

3. Vinson Cunningham, "The Future of L.A. Is Here. Robin D. G. Kelley's Radical Imagination Shows Us the Way," *Los Angeles Times*, March 17, 2021, accessed December 14, 2022, https://www.latimes.com/lifestyle/image/story/2021-03-17/ robin-dg-kelley-black-marxism-protests-la-politics.

4. Robin D. G. Kelley, "Births of a Nation, Redux: Surveying Trumpland with Cedric Robinson," *Boston Review*, November 5, 2020, accessed December 14, 2022, https://www.bostonreview.net/articles/ robin-d-g-kelley-births-nation/.

5. Ida B. Wells-Barnett, *Southern Horrors and Other Writings: The Anti-Lynching Campaign of Ida B. Wells, 1892–1900*, 2nd ed., ed. Jacqueline Jones Royster (Boston: Bedford/St.Martin's, n.d.), 148.

6. Equal Justice Initiative, *Lynching in America: Confronting the Legacy of Racial Terror* (Montgomery, AL: Equal Justice Initiative, 2017).

7. *The Memphis Appeal-Avalanche*, "A Darky Damsel Obtains a Verdict for Damages Against the Chesapeake & Ohio Railroad," December 25, 1884, Ida B. Wells Papers, 1884–1976, University of Chicago Library, Special Collections Research Center, Chicago, IL.

8. Maureen Moss Browning, foster daughter of Ida B. Wells, photograph, Ida B. Wells Papers, 1884–1976, University of Chicago Library, Special Collections Research Center, Chicago, IL.

9. Ida B. Wells-Barnett, "Lynch Law in All Its Phases," speech, Tremont Temple, Boston, MA, February 13, 1893.

10. Amii Larkin Barnard, "The Application of Critical Race Feminism to the Anti-Lynching Movement: Black Women's Fight against Race and Gender Ideology, 1892–1920," *UCLA Women's Law Journal* 3, no. 1 (1993): 9.

11. Barnard, "The Application of Critical Race Feminism to the Anti-Lynching Movement," 3.

12. Wells-Barnett, *Southern Horrors*, 51.

13. Wells-Barnett, *Southern Horrors*, 52.

14. Jeanelle K. Hope, "Roe's Reversal and the Specter of American Fascism," *The Forum*, July 1, 2022, accessed December 14, 2022, https://forummag.com/2022/07/01/roes-reversal-and-the-specter-of-american-fascism/.

15. Ruwe Dalitso, "Eugenic Caricatures of Black Male Death from the Nineteenth- to Twenty-first Centuries," *Theory & Event* 25, no. 3 (July 2022): 668.

16. Oscar Riddle, "Biographical Memoir of Charles Benedict Davenport," *National Academy of Sciences of the United States*, 1947, 84.

17. Stefan Kuhl, *The Nazi Connection: Eugenics, American Racism, and German National Socialism* (New York: Oxford University Press, 2002).

18. See: Beverly Guy-Sheftall, *Daughters of Sorrow: Attitudes Toward Black Women, 1880–1920* (Brooklyn: Carlson Publishing, 1990).

19. Wells-Barnett, *Southern Horrors*, 55.

20. For more on misogynoir see Moya Bailey, *Misogynoir Transformed: Black Women's Digital Resistance* (New York: New York University Press, 2022).

21. Wells-Barnett, *Southern Horrors*, 63.

22. *Cleveland Gazette*, April 9, 1898, reprinted in Herbert Aptheker, ed., *A Documentary History of the Negro People in the United States,* vol. 2, (New York: Citadel Press, 1970), 798.

23. Keisha Blain and Tiffany Gill, eds., *To Turn the Whole World Over: Black Women and Internationalism* (Urbana: University of Illinois, 2019), 194, 199, 206.

24. For more on Black women Communists, see Erik McDuffie, *Sojourning for Freedom: Black Women, American Communism, and the Making of Black Left Feminism* (Durham: Duke University Press, 2011); Charisse Burden-Stelly, *Black Scare/Red Scare* (Chicago: University of Chicago Press, forthcoming, 2023).

NOTES 239

25. Evelyn Brooks Higginbotham, *Righteous Discontent: The Women's Movement in the Black Baptist Church, 1880–1920* (Cambridge: Harvard University Press, 1994).
26. Blain and Gill, *To Turn the Whole World Over*, 198.
27. Blain and Gill, *To Turn the Whole World Over*, 263.
28. Ida B. Wells, *Crusade for Justice: The Autobiography of Ida B. Wells*, 2nd ed. (Chicago: University of Chicago Press, 2020).
29. Neighborhood Union, "Anti-lynching Statement 'to the President, the Cabinet, the Congress of the United States, the Governors and Legislators of the Several States of the United States of America,'" letter, March 1, 1918, Neighborhood Union Collection, Atlanta University Center Robert W. Woodruff Library, Atlanta, GA.
30. Letter by Neighborhood Union, "Anti-lynching Statement."
31. Allison Keyes, "The East St. Louis Race Riot Left Dozens Dead, Devastating a Community on the Rise," *Smithsonian Magazine*, June 30, 2017.
32. Chad Williams, "World War I in the Historical Imagination of W. E. B. Du Bois," *Modern American History* 1, no. 1 (March 2018).
33. Harry Haywood, *Black Bolshevik: Autobiography of an Afro-American Communist* (Morrisville, NC: Lulu Press, 2020).
34. Letter by Neighborhood Union, "Anti-lynching Statement."
35. The Emmett Till Antilynching Act was passed by the 117th United States Congress in 2022.
36. Mike German, "The FBI Warned for Years That Police Are Cozy with the Far Right. Is No One Listening?," *Guardian*, August 28, 2020, accessed December 14, 2022, https://www.theguardian.com/commentisfree/2020/aug/28/fbi-far-right-white-supremacists-police.
37. Malcolm X Grassroots Movement and Every 36 Hours Campaign, *Operation Ghetto Storm: 2012 Annual Report on Extrajudicial Killings of 313 Black People by Police, Security Guards, and Vigilantes* (MXGM, 2013), 20.

Chapter 2

1 David Featherstone, *Solidarity: Hidden Histories and Geographies* (London: Zed Books, 2012), 127.

2. Albert Memmi, *The Colonizer and the Colonized* (London: Earthscan Publications Ltd., 1974), 12.

3. C. L. R. James, "Revolution and the Negro," in *Selected Writings of C. L. R. James 1939–1949*, ed. Scott McLemee and Paul LeBlanc (Chicago: Haymarket Books, 2018), 78.

4. Langston Hughes, "Love Letter From Spain," *The People's Daily World Magazine*, January 22, 1938, p. 8. https://www.marxists.org/history/usa/pubs/peoples-world/n529-v1n19-sec2-mag-jan-22-1938-MPDW.pdf.

5. W. E. B. Du Bois, "The African Roots of War," *Atlantic Monthly*, May 1915. https://www.theatlantic.com/magazine/archive/1915/05/the-african-roots-of-war/528897/.

6. Du Bois, "The African Roots of War."

7. W. E. B. Du Bois, "As the Crow Flies," in *Newspaper Columns by W. E. B. Du Bois*, vol. 1, 1883–1944, ed. Herbert Aptheker (White Plains: Kraus-Thomson Organization, Ltd.), 376.

8. George Steinmetz, "The First Genocide of the Twentieth Century and Its Postcolonial Afterlives: Germany and the Namibian Overherero," *Journal of the International Institute* 12, no. 2 (Winter 2005): 3.

9. Vaughn Raspberry, *Race and the Totalitarian Century: Geopolitics in the Black Literary Imagination* (Cambridge: Harvard University Press, 2016), 34.

10. Harry Haywood, *Black Bolshevik: Autobiography of an Afro-American Communist* (Minneapolis: University of Minnesota Press, 1978), 49.

11. Haywood, *Black Bolshevik*, 72.

12. Featherstone, *Solidarity*, 92.

13. Mikah Makalani, *In the Cause of Freedom: Radical Black Internationalism From Harlem to London, 1917–1939* (Durham: University of North Carolina Press, 2014), 192.

14. Makalani, *In the Cause of Freedom*, 194.

15. Makalani, *In the Cause of Freedom*, 203.

16. Makalani, *In the Cause of Freedom*, 204.

NOTES 241

17. Robin D. G. Kelley, "This Ain't Ethiopia but It'll Do: African Americans and the Spanish Civil War," in *Race Rebels: Culture, Politics, and the Black Working Class* (New York: The Free Press, 1994), 131.
18. Makalani, *In the Cause of Freedom*, 204.
19. Featherstone, *Solidarity*, 102.
20. Featherstone, *Solidarity*, 105.
21. Featherstone, *Solidarity*, 107.
22. Makalani, *In the Cause of Freedom*, 200.
23. George Padmore, "Hitler, Mussolini and Africa," *Crisis*, September 1937, reprinted in *The U.S. Antifascism Reader*, ed. Bill V. Mullen and Christopher Vials (New York: Verso, 2020), 89.
24. James Yates, *Mississippi to Madrid: Memoirs of a Black American in the Spanish Civil War 1936–1938* (New York: Shamal Books, 1986), 73.
25. Yates, *Mississippi to Madrid*, 73.
26. Yates, *Mississippi to Madrid*, 15.
27. Yates, *Mississippi to Madrid*, 79.
28. David Walker, *David Walker's Appeal: To the Coloured Citizens of the World, but In Particular, and Very Expressly, to Those of the United States of America* (New York: Hill and Wang, 1995).
29. Kelley, "Ethiopia," 128.
30. Haywood, *Black Bolshevik*, 217.
31. Haywood, *Black Bolshevik*, 221.
32. Featherstone, *Solidarity*, 106.
33. Unemployed Councils, Branch 1, "Resolution from Unemployed Councils, Branch 1 in Rockford, Illinois, to Governor Miller in Alabama," Scottsboro Boys Trials, accessed July 17, 2023, https://scottsboroboysletters.as.ua.edu/items/show/584.
34. Benjamin Balthaser, *Anti-Imperialist Modernism: Race and Transnational Radical Culture From the Great Depression to the Cold War* (Ann Arbor: University of Michigan Press, 2011), 28.
35. Barry B. Witham, *The Federal Theatre Project: A Case Study* (New York: Cambridge University Press, 2003), 3.
36. Paul Robeson, "Robeson Visions an Africa Free of Rule by Europeans," *New York Herald-Tribune*, January 12, 1936, reprinted in *Paul Robeson Speaks: Writings, Speeches, Interviews*, ed. Philip S. Foner (New York: Brunner/Mazel Publishers, 1978), 104.

37. Zinn Education Project, "Dec. 11, 1917: Black Soldiers Executed for Houston Riot," https://www.zinnedproject.org/news/tdih/black-soldiers-executed/.

38. Thyra Edwards Collection. Chicago Historical Museum, Box 1, Folder 1, p. 5.

39. Thyra Edwards Collection. Chicago Historical Museum, Box 1, Folder 1, p. 5.

40. Gregg Andrews, *Thyra B. Edwards: Black Activist in the Global Freedom Struggle* (Columbia: University of Missouri Press, 2011), 96.

41. Andrews, *Thyra B. Edwards*, 98.

42. Andrews, *Thyra B. Edwards*, 102.

43. Andrews, *Thyra B. Edwards*, 103.

44. Erik McDuffie, *Sojourning for Freedom: Black Women, American Communism, and the Making of Black Left Feminism* (Durham: Duke University Press, 2011), 109.

45. McDuffie, *Sojourning for Freedom*, 107.

46. Andrews, *Thyra B. Edwards*, 104.

47. Featherstone, *Solidarity*, 119.

48. Yates, *Mississippi to Madrid*, 91.

49. Yates, *Mississippi to Madrid*, 141.

50. Kelley, "This Ain't Ethiopia," 139.

51. Yates, *Mississippi to Madrid*, 136.

52. Abraham Lincoln Brigade Archives, "Garland, Walter Benjamin, Biography," https://alba-valb.org/volunteers/walter-benjamin-garland/ ; Kelley, "This Ain't Ethiopia," 145.

53. "Brother of Angelo, Freed From Georgia Chain Gang, Is One of Nine Americans Slain," *New York Times*, October 20, 1937, p. 18.

54. Abraham Lincoln Brigade Archives, "Law, Oliver, Biography," https://alba-valb.org/volunteers/oliver-law/.

55. "Salaria Kea: A Negro Nurse in Republican Spain," Abraham Lincoln Brigade Archive, https://alba-valb.org/resource/salaria-kea-a-negro-nurse-in-republican-spain/.

56. Emily Robins Sharpe, "Salaria Kea's Spanish Memoirs," *The Volunteer*, December 4, 2011, https://albavolunteer.org/2011/12/salaria-keas-spanish-memoirs/.

57. Kelley, "This Ain't Ethiopia," 130.

58. "Salaria Kea: A Negro Nurse."

NOTES 243

59. "Salaria Kea: Nurse and Freedom Fighter." New York State Nurses Association. https://www.nysna.org/salaria-kea-nurse-and-freedom-fighter#.YjzMm5rMKbt.
60. Brent Hayes Edwards, "Langston Hughes and the Futures of Diaspora," *American Literary History* 19, no. 3 (Autumn 2007): 693.
61. Edwards, "Langston Hughes and the Futures of Diaspora," 694.
62. Edwards, "Langston Hughes and the Futures of Diaspora," 695.
63. Edwards, "Langston Hughes and the Futures of Diaspora," 696.
64. Thyra Edwards Collection, Box 1, Folder 3.
65. Kelley, "This Ain't Ethiopia," 146.
66. Kelley, "This Ain't Ethiopia," 152.
67. Andrews, *Thyra B. Edwards*, 111.
68. Andrews, *Thyra B. Edwards*, 148.
69. Thyra Edwards Collection, Box 1, Folder 4.
70. Thyra Edwards Collection, Box 1, Folder 5.
71. Sharpe, "Salaria Kea's Spanish Memoirs."
72. Kelley, "This Ain't Ethiopia," 150.
73. Abraham Lincoln Brigade Archives, "Garland, Walter Benjamin, Biography."
74. Kelley, "This Ain't Ethiopia," 152.
75. Kelley, "This Ain't Ethiopia," 150.
76. Kelley, "This Ain't Ethiopia," 156.

Chapter 3

1. W. E. B. Du Bois, *Dusk of Dawn: An Essay Toward an Autobiography of a Race Concept* (New York: Routledge, 1983), 169.
2. Grace Tompkins, *Negro Story* 1, no. 2 (July–August 1944), 50.
3. Margaret Burroughs, *Chicago Defender*, August 31, 1940, p. 24.
4. *Langston Hughes and the* Chicago Defender: *Essays on Race, Politics and Culture, 1942–1962*, ed. Christopher DeSantis (Champaign: University of Illinois Press, 1995), 158.
5. Hughes, *Langston Hughes and the* Chicago Defender, 123.
6. See W. E. B. Du Bois, *Black Reconstruction in America, 1860–1880* (New York: Free Press, 1998) and C. L. R. James, *The Black Jacobins: Toussaint L'Ouverture and the San Domingo Revolution* (New York: Vintage, 1989).

7. W. E. B. Du Bois, "Writings on National Socialism," *Pittsburgh Courier*, December 12, 1936, in *The U.S. Antifascism Reader*, eds. Bill V. Mullen and Christopher Vials (New York: Verso, 2020), 86.
8. Du Bois, "Writings on National Socialism," 86.
9. W. E. B. Du Bois, "Forum of Fact and Opinion," in *Newspaper Columns by W. E. B. Du Bois, vol. 1, 1883–1944*, ed. Herbert Aptheker, (White Plains: Kraus-Thomson Organization Limited, 1986), 148.
10. Frantz Fanon, "Concerning Violence," in *The Wretched of the Earth* (New York: Grove Weidenfeld, 1968), 40.
11. John Dower, *War without Mercy: Race and Power in the Pacific* (New York, NY: Pantheon Books, 1987).
12. "Blitz over Georgia," *Chicago Defender*, September 28, 1940, 1.
13. "Blitz over Georgia."
14. Brooks E. Hefner, "How it Happened Here: Race and American Antifascist Literature," *Los Angeles Review of Books*, November 26, 2016, https://lareviewofbooks.org/article/happens-race-american-antifascist-literature/.
15. Hughes, *Langston Hughes and the* Chicago Defender, 147.
16. Bobby Harrison, "The Bilbo Statue, Still Missing, Was First Removed by Gov. William Winter in the 1980s," *Mississippi Today*, February 4, 2022, https://mississippitoday.org/2022/02/04/theodore-bilbo-statue-made-by-gov-winter-on-football-saturday/.
17. Albert Norman, "Mississippi's Most Racist Member of Congress," *Greenville Recorder*, December 3, 2018, https://www.recorder.com/my-turn-norman-21818864.
18. *Chicago Defender*, September 28, 1940, 1.
19. Harry Haywood, *Black Communist in the Freedom Struggle: The Life of Harry Haywood* (Minneapolis: University of Minnesota Press, 2012), 245.
20. Haywood, *Black Communist in the Freedom Struggle*, 249.
21. Vaughn Rasberry, *Race and the Totalitarian Century: Geopolitics in the Black Literary Imagination* (Cambridge: Harvard University Press, 2016), 29.
22. Jacey Forten and Alexa Mills, "Felix Hall, a Soldier Lynched at Fort Benning, Is Remembered After 80 Years," *New York Times*, August 20, 2021, https://www.nytimes.com/2021/08/20/us/felix-hall-soldier-lynching-wwii.html.

NOTES   245

23. History News Network, "White Workers Riot After Black Workers Promoted in Mobile, Alabama," Columbia College of Arts & Sciences, George Washington University, https://historynewsnetwork.org/article/175677.

24. Langston Hughes, *The Collected Poems of Langston Hughes* (New York: Vintage, 1995), 281.

25. Hughes, *Langston Hughes and the* Chicago Defender, 28.

26. Hughes, *Langston Hughes and the* Chicago Defender, 28.

27. Erika Doss, "Commemorating the Port Chicago Naval Magazine Disaster of 1944: Remembering the Racial Injustices of the 'Good War' in Contemporary America," *American Studies Journal*, no. 59 (2015), http://www.asjournal.org/59-2015/commemorating-port-chicago-naval-magazine-disaster-1944/.

28. Bill V. Mullen, *Popular Fronts: Chicago and African-American Cultural Politics, 1935–1946* (Champaign: University of Illinois Press, 1999), 4.

29. Paul Robeson, *Paul Robeson Speaks: Writings, Speeches, Interviews*, ed. Philip S. Foner. (New York: Brunner/Mazel Publishers, 1978), 131.

30. Robeson, *Paul Robeson Speaks*, 96.

31. Robeson, *Paul Robeson Speaks*, 119.

32. Frantz Fanon, *The Wretched of the Earth* (New York: Grove Press, 2005), 168.

33. *Chicago Defender*, September 12, 1942, 1.

34. Mullen, *Popular Fronts*, 1.

35. Mullen, *Popular Fronts*, 115.

36. Mullen, *Popular Fronts*, 112.

37. Mullen, *Popular Fronts*, 112.

38. Grace Tompkins, "The Birth Pangs of a New Order," *Negro Story* 2, no. 1 (August–September 1945), 50.

39. Gwendolyn Brooks, *Selected Poems* (New York: Harper and Row, 1963), 28.

40. Rasberry, *Race and the Totalitarian Century*, 46.

41. Hughes, *Collected Poems*, 244.

42. Quoted in Bill V. Mullen, "Object Lessons: Fetishization and Class Consciousness in Ann Petry's *The Street*," in *Revising the Blueprint: Ann Petry and the Literary Left*, ed. Alex Lubin (Jackson: University Press of Mississippi, 2007), 35–48.

43. Hughes, *Collected Poems*, 102.

44. Ann Petry, *The Street: A Novel* (Boston: Mariner Books, 1998), 275.
45. Richard Wright, *Native Son* (New York: Harper Collins, 1993), 521.
46. Richard Wright, *The Man Who Lived Underground: A Novel* (New York: New American Library, 2021).
47. Thyra Edwards Collection. Box 1, Folder 4.
48. *The FBI: A Comprehensive Reference Guide* (Westport, CT: Greenwood Annotated Edition, 1998), 366.
49. Nancy Goldstein, *Jackie Ormes: The First African American Woman Cartoonist* (Ann Arbor: The University of Michigan Press, 2008), 87.
50. Brian Dolinar, "Battling Fascism for Years with the Might of His Pen," in *The Black Cultural Front: Black Writer and Artists of the Depression Generation* (Jackson: University of Mississippi Press, 2004), 171–224.
51. Goldstein, *Jackie Ormes*, 56.
52. *Langston Hughes and the* Chicago Defender, 121.
53. *Langston Hughes and the* Chicago Defender, 123–124.
54. *Langston Hughes and the* Chicago Defender, 124.
55. W. E. B. Du Bois, *W. E .B. Du Bois Speaks: Speeches and Addresses 1920–1963* (New York: Pathfinder Press, 1971), 163.
56. Du Bois, *W. E .B. Du Bois Speaks*, 159.
57. Du Bois, *W. E .B. Du Bois Speaks*, 151.

Chapter 4

1. William L. Patterson, ed., *We Charge Genocide: The Crime of Government Against the Negro People* (New York: International Publishers, 2017), 4.
2. Charisse Burden-Stelly, *Black Scare/Red Scare* (Chicago: University of Chicago Press, forthcoming, 2023).
3. William L. Patterson, *The Man Who Cried Genocide* (New York: International Publishers, 2017); Gerald Horne, *Communist Front? The Civil Rights Congress, 1946–1956* (New York: International Publishers, 2021), 45.
4. *Labor Defender*, April 4, 1933, p. 1. https://www.marxists.org/history/usa/pubs/labordefender/1933/v09n04-apr-1933-lab-def.pdf .
5. *Labor Defender*, April 4, 1933, p. 1.
6. *Labor Defender*, April 4, 1933, p. 1.
7. Steven Skinner, ed., *Fascism and Criminal Law: History, Theory, Continuity* (Oxford: Hart Publishing, 2017), 6.

NOTES 247

8. "Racism in the Service of Fascism, Empire-Building and War: The History of the Italian Fascist Magazine *La Defessa Della Razza*," https://www.marxists.org/archive/pankhurst-richard/2007/03/x01.htm.

9. Claude McKay, "To The White Fiends," https://poets.org/poem/white-fiends-0.

10. Charisse Burden-Stelly, "Claudia Jones, the Longue Durée of McCarthyism, and the Threat of U.S. Fascism," *Journal of Intersectionality* 3, no. 1 (July 2019): 46–66.

11. National Federation for Constitutional Liberties Pamphlet (Washington DC, 1940).

12. US Congress. Alien Registration Act, 1940, https://loveman.sdsu.edu/docs/1940AlienRegistrationAct.pdf.

13. *New York Times*, "1,250 Ask Abolition of Dies Committee," February 5, 1943, p. 13, https://timesmachine.nytimes.com/timesmachine/1943/02/05/85082949.html?pageNumber=13.

14. NFCL, *Investigate Martin Dies!* (Washington, DC: National Federation for Constitutional Liberties, 1942), 8.

15. NFCL, *They Still Carry On! Native Fascists: How to Spot Them and Stop Them* (New York: National Federation for Constitutional Liberties, 1945).

16. United Nations, "Preparatory Years: UN Charter History," https://www.un.org/en/about-us/history-of-the-un/preparatory-years.

17. Charter of the United Nations, Chapter XII, International Trusteeship System, Article 76, https://legal.un.org/repertory/art76.shtml.

18. Carol Anderson, *Eyes Off the Prize: The United Nations and the African American Struggle for Human Rights, 1944–1955* (Cambridge: Cambridge University Press, 2003), 3.

19. Anderson, *Eyes Off the Prize*, 4.

20. W. E. B. Du Bois, "The Winds of Time," July 19, 1947, reprinted in *Newspaper Columns, vol. 2, 1944–1961*, ed. Herbert Aptheker (White Plains: Kraus-Thompson Organization Limited, 1986), 727.

21. Du Bois, "The Winds of Time," 727.

22. National Association for the Advancement of Colored People, "An Appeal to the World," (New York: National Association for the Advancement of Colored People, 1947), https://www.crmvet.org/info/470000_naacp_appeal_un-r.pdf.

23. Anderson, *Eyes Off the Prize*, 88.

24. National Negro Congress, "A Petition on Behalf of 13,000,000 Oppressed Negro Citizens of the United States of America," Florida Atlantic University Digital Library, https://fau.digital.flvc.org/islandora/object/fau%3A5359.

25. Civil Rights Congress Papers, Schomburg Center for Research in Black Culture, New York City, Part 1, Reel 1.

26. Civil Rights Congress Papers.

27. Horne, *Communist Front?*, 13.

28. Death Penalty Information Center, "'Martinsville 7' Granted Posthumous Pardons 70 Years After Their Execution," September 3, 2021, https://deathpenaltyinfo.org/news/martinsville-7-granted-posthumous-pardons-70-years-after-their-executions.

29. Horne, *Communist Front?*, 129.

30. Marine Guillame, "Napalm in US Bombing Doctrine and Practice, 1942–1975," *Asia-Pacific Journal* 14, no. 5 (December 1, 2016), https://apjjf.org/2016/23/Guillaume.html.

31. Patterson, *We Charge Genocide*, 32.

32. *We Charge Genocide*, 4.

33. *We Charge Genocide*, 5.

34. *We Charge Genocide*, 7.

35. *We Charge Genocide*, 22.

36. *We Charge Genocide*, 24.

37. Hugh Collins, *Marxism and Law* (Oxford: Oxford University Press, 1982), 19.

38. *We Charge Genocide*, 25.

39. *We Charge Genocide*, 31.

40. *We Charge Genocide*, 49.

41. *We Charge Genocide*, 57.

42. Civil Rights Congress Papers, Part 3, Reel 1.

43. Civil Rights Congress Papers, Part 3, Reel 1.

44. Civil Rights Congress Papers, Part 3, Reel 2.

45. Civil Rights Congress Papers, Part 3, Reel 2.

46. Lloyd Brown, *Stand Up for Freedom: The Negro People Vs. the Smith Act* (New York: New Century Publishers, 1952), 8.

47. Brown, *Stand Up for Freedom*, 7, 11.

48. Civil Rights Congress Papers, Part 1, Reel 2; Horne, 447.

49. Anderson, *Eyes Off the Prize*, 203.

NOTES   249

50. Graham Glusman, "The Long Afterlife of the Bricker Amendment," Columbia Journal of Transnational Law Bulletin (blog), December 2, 2021, https://www.jtl.columbia.edu/bulletin-blog/the-long-afterlife-of-the-bricker-amendment-jim-crow-human-rights-and-the-genocide-convention.
51. Anderson, *Eyes Off the Prize*, 254.
52. Burden-Stelly, "Claudia Jones, the Longue Durée of McCarthyism, and the Threat of U.S. Fascism," 46.
53. Stokely Carmichael, "Let Another World Be Born," speech at the Spring Mobilization to End the War in Vietnam, United Nations Headquarters, New York City, April 15, 1967.

Chapter 5

1. Raymond "Masai" Hewitt, speech, *Black Panther*, July 5, 1969, 14.
2. The Black Panther Party, "What is the United Front Against Fascism? Interview with Bobby Seale by Liberation News Service," *Black Panther*, July 12, 1969, 8. Courtesy of the African American Museum and Library at Oakland.
3. Charles Jones, ed., *Black Panther Party [Reconsidered]* (Baltimore, MD: Black Classic Press, 2005), 44.
4. For more on the TWLF, see Harvey Dong and Janie Chen, eds., *Power of the People Won't Stop: Legacy of the TWLF at UC Berkeley* (Berkeley: Eastward Books of Berkeley, 2020).
5. For more on the YPO and the CPD, see Hy Thurman, *Revolutionary Hillbilly: Notes from the Struggle on the Edge of the Rainbow* (Berkeley: Regent Press, 2020); Laurence Ralph, *The Torture Letters: Reckoning with Police Violence* (Chicago: The University of Chicago Press, 2020).
6. For more on the Young Lords, see Johanna Fernandez, *Young Lords: A Radical History* (Chapel Hill: University of North Carolina Press, 2022).
7. See Joe Burns, *Class Struggle Unionism* (Chicago: Haymarket Books, 2022).
8. The Black Panther Party, "Black Panther Party Book List 1968," It's About Time Black Panther Legacy and Alumni.
9. Timothy Tyson, "'Black Power' and the Roots of the African American Freedom Struggle," *Journal of African American History* 85, no. 2 (September 1998): 549.

10. Robert F. Williams, *Negroes with Guns* (Eastford, CT: Martino Fine Books, 2013), 26.
11. Founded in 1964, the Deacons for Defense and Justice were a civil rights organization composed of African American WWII veterans whose aim was to protect activists and community members during marches and protests. They were a major proponent of armed self-defense. At their height, Deacons for Defense and Justice maintained more than twenty chapters across Louisiana, Mississippi, and Alabama.
12. Martin Luther King Jr., "The Social Organization of Nonviolence," October 1, 1959, King Papers, Stanford University, The Martin Luther King, Jr. Research and Education Institute, Palo Alto, CA.
13. King, "The Social Organization of Nonviolence."
14. King, "The Social Organization of Nonviolence."
15. *Negroes with Guns* chronicled Williams's experience confronting racism in Monroe, North Carolina, during the civil rights era. Williams specifically advocates for the use of armed self-defense. He also begins to frame the conditions of "American fascism."
16. Robin D. G. Kelley and Betsy Esch, "Black Like Mao: Red China and Black Revolution," in *Afro Asia: Revolutionary Political & Cultural Connections Between African Americans & Asian Americans*, ed. Fred Ho and Bill Mullen (Durham, NC: Duke University Press, 2008), 99.
17. Judy Tzu-Chun Wu, *Radicals on the Road: Internationalism, Orientalism, and Feminism During the Vietnam Era* (Ithaca, NY: Cornell University Press, 2013), 4.
18. Mao Tse-Tung, "On the International United Front Against Fascism," in *Quotations from Chairman Mao* (Shanghai: People's Press, 1964).
19. J. T. Murphy, *Fascism! The Socialist Answer* (London.: The Socialist League, 1935), accessed December 15, 2022, https://www.marxists.org/archive/murphy-jt/1935/x01/fascism.htm.
20. Robert F. Williams, "Why I Propose to Return to Racist America," *The Crusader* 9, no. 3 (December 1967): 2, courtesy of the Freedom Archives (Mabel and Robert F. Williams Collection).
21. Williams, "Why I Propose to Return to Racist America," 10.
22. Robert F. Williams, "Reaction without Positive Change," *The Crusader* 9, no. 3 (March 1968): 7, courtesy of the Freedom Archives (Mabel and Robert F. Williams Collection).

NOTES

23. Robert F. Williams, "The Potential of a Minority Revolution Part III," *The Crusader* 9, no. 2 (September/October 1967): 12, courtesy of the Freedom Archives (Mabel and Robert F. Williams Collection).

24. Susan Glisson, ed., *The Human Tradition in the Civil Rights Movement* (Lanham, MD: Rowman & Littlefield Publishers, 2006), 242.

25. For more on the Black Panther Party and migration, see Donna Murch, *Living for the City: Migration, Education, and the Rise of the Black Panther Party in Oakland, California* (Chapel Hill: University of North Carolina Press, 2010).

26. For more on Asian American migration, see Ronald Takaki, *Strangers from a Different Shore: A History of Asian Americans* (Boston: Little, Brown and Company, 1998).

27. Murch, *Living for the City*, 3.

28. For more on the history of Blacks in the West/California, see Albert Broussard, *Black San Francisco: The Struggle for Racial Equality in the West, 1900–1954* (Lawrence: University of Kansas Press, 1993); Allison Rose Jefferson, *Living the California Dream: African American Leisure Sites During the Jim Crow Era* (Lincoln: University of Nebraska Press, 2022); Lynn Hudson, *West of Jim Crow: The Fight against California's Color Line* (Urbana: University of Illinois Press, 2020); Robert Self, *American Babylon: Race and the Struggle for Postwar Oakland* (Princeton: Princeton University Press, 2005); Herbert Ruffin, *Uninvited Neighbors: African Americans in Silicon Valley, 1769–1990* (Norman: University of Oklahoma Press, 2014).

29. The Black Panther image and iconography was first adopted by the Lowndes County Freedom Organization.

30. For more on the Black Panther Party, see Joshua Bloom and Waldo Martin Jr., *Black Against Empire: The History and Politics of the Black Panther Party* (Berkeley: University of California Press, 2013).

31. See Sean Malloy, *Out of Oakland: Black Panther Party Internationalism during the Cold War* (Ithaca, NY: Cornell University Press, 2013).

32. Elaine Brown, *A Taste of Power: A Black Woman's Story* (New York: Anchor Books, 1993), 137.

33. Tzu-Chun Wu, *Radicals on the Road*.

34. The Bandung Conference of 1955 was the first major convening of newly independent African and Asian countries. The major aims of the conference were to increase Afro-Asian collaboration and to collectively

strategize on how to oppose colonization. The conference is often touted as being an exemplar of Afro-Asian solidarity. However, the conference resulted in very few, if any, major advancements toward meaningful solidarity and has been critiqued as largely symbolic.

35. David Hilliard, interview by Jeanelle Hope, 2013.

36. The Black Panther Party, "Chairman Bobby Speaks to Scandinavia," *Black Panther*, October 25, 1969, courtesy of the African American Museum and Library at Oakland.

37. Huey Newton and Vladmir Lenin, *Revolutionary Intercommunalism and the Right of Nations to Self-Determination* (Wales: Superscript, 2004), 29–30.

38. Huey P. Newton, "Intercommunalism," speech, Boston College, Boston, MA, November 18, 1970.

39. Newton and Lenin, *Revolutionary Intercommunalism*, 31.

40. Newton and Lenin, *Revolutionary Intercommunalism*, 33.

41. Kathleen Cleaver, "Racism, Fascism, and Political Murder (1968)," in *The U.S. Anti-Fascism Reader*, ed. Bill Mullen and Christopher Vials (Brooklyn: Verso, 2020), 265–266.

42. Georgi Dimitrov, *United Front: The Struggle Against Fascism and War* (Paden, OK: Bolsheviki Press, 2019), 7.

43. Dimitrov, *United Front*, 19–20.

44. The Black Panther Party, "Black Panther Party, 'Call for a United Front against Fascism,' Old Mole, July 1969," in Mullen and Vials, *The U.S. Anti-Fascism Reader*, 268.

45. Old Mole, "UFAF Conference, Old Mole, August 1969," in Mullen and Vials, *The U.S. Anti-Fascism Reader*, 274–275.

46. Eldridge Cleaver, "Message to Sister Ericka Huggins of the Black Panther Party," *Black Panther*, July 5, 1969, courtesy of the African American Museum and Library at Oakland.

47. Ashley Farmer, et al., "Women in the Black Panther Party: A Roundtable," *International Socialist Review*, no. 111 (Winter 2018).

48. "Ericka Huggins' Statement Read by Elaine Brown (Episode 8 of 12); United Front against Fascism Conference," Pacifica Radio Archives, American Archive of Public Broadcasting (GBH and the Library of Congress), Boston, MA and Washington, DC, accessed December 15, 2022, http://americanarchive.org/catalog/cpb-aacip-28-6h4cn6z74m.

NOTES

253

49. The Black Panther Party, "U.F.A.F. Women's Panel: Roberta Alexander at Conference," *Black Panther*, August 2, 1969, p. 7, courtesy of the African American Museum and Library of Oakland.

50. Penny Nakatsu, "Penny Nakatsu, speech at the United Front Against Fascism Conference, 1969," in Mullen and Vials, *The U.S. Anti-Fascism Reader*, 270.

51. "Nakatsu, speech," in Mullen and Vials, *The U.S. Anti-Fascism Reader*, 271.

52. Mary Phillips, "The Feminist Leadership of Ericka Huggins in the Black Panther Party," *Black Diaspora Review* 4, no. 1 (Winter 2014): 198.

53. Robyn Spencer, "The Black Panther Party and Black Anti-Fascism in the United States," *Duke Press* (blog), entry posted January 26, 2017, accessed December 15, 2022, https://dukeupress.wordpress.com/2017/01/26/the-black-panther-party-and-black-anti-fascism-in-the-united-states/.

54. JoNina Abron, "Serving the People: The Survival Programs of the Black Panther Party," in *The Black Panther Party [Reconsidered]*, ed. Charles Jones (Baltimore: Black Classic Press, 1998).

55. Alondra Nelson, *Body and Soul: The Black Panther Party and the Fight Against Medical Discrimination* (Minneapolis: University of Minnesota Press, 2011), 121.

56. Tolbert Small, interview by Emily Schiller, Michigan, 2011.

57. The Black Panther Party, "The Intercommunal Committee to Combat Fascism," It's About Time Black Panther Legacy and Alumni, accessed December 15, 2022, http://www.itsabouttimebpp.com/Our_Stories/Chapter1/The_iccf.html.

58. Ericka Huggins, "The Oakland Community School: A BPP Community Survival Program," (unpublished manuscript, 2016), accessed December 15, 2022, https://www.erickahuggins.com/_files/ugd/1610f9_d498c6e495674b88a03407432e5c3880.pdf. In his seminal work, *Pedagogy of the Oppressed*, Paulo Freire argues that education and teaching should be in the service of developing critically conscious students who are equipped with knowledge, skills, and tools to help liberate them from various forms of oppression. Furthermore, Freire argued that the old ways of teaching, which he characterized as "the

banking method," needed to be disrupted to allow students to have a greater role in their own education.

59. Sarah Alkhafaji, "Activist Mariame Kaba Calls Mutual Aid Key to Ending Prison Industrial Complex at BARS Event," *Daily Pennsylvanian*, February 2, 2021, accessed December 15, 2022, https://www.thedp.com/article/2021/02/penn-bars-conference-mariame-kaba.

60. The Black Panther Party, "The Intercommunal Committee."

61. Red Army Faction, *Urban Guerrilla Concept* (Montreal: Kersplebedeb Publishing, 2005), 105.

Chapter 6

1. As quoted in Huey Newton, *Revolutionary Suicide* (New York: Penguin Books, 2009), 200.

2. See Jeanelle Hope, "The Black Antifascist Roots of Black August," *The Forum*, August 26, 2022, accessed December 16, 2022,https://forummag.com/2022/08/26/the-black-antifascist-roots-of-black-august/; Joy James, "George Jackson: Dragon Philosopher and Revolutionary Abolitionist," *Black Perspectives* (blog), accessed December 21, 2018, https://www.aaihs.org/george-jackson-dragon-philosopher-and-revolutionary-abolitionist/.

3. Newton, *Revolutionary Suicide*, 331.

4. Angela Davis, ed., *If They Come in the Morning* (New York: The Third Press, 1971), 27.

5. Davis, *If They Come in the Morning*, 35–36.

6. Coordinating Committee of Black Liberation Army, Message to the Black Movement: A Political Statement from the Black Underground (n.p., 1976), 22–33.

7. Davis, *If They Come in the Morning*, 17–18.

8. The proceeds from the sale of George Jackson's books were directed to the Black Panther Party.

9. Hilary Moore and James Tracy, *No Fascist USA!: The John Brown Anti-Klan Committee and Lessons for Today's Movements* (San Francisco: City Lights Books, 2020), 75.

10. George Jackson, *Soledad Brother: The Prison Letters of George Jackson* (Chicago: Lawrence Hill Books, 1994), 18.

11. Roderick Ferguson, *We Demand: The University and Student Protests* (Oakland: University of California Press, 2017), 37.

NOTES

12. Ferguson, *We Demand*, 40.
13. Davis, *If They Come in the Morning*, 173.
14. Benito Mussolini and Giovanni Gentile, "The Doctrine of Fascism," 1932.
15. George Jackson, *Blood in My Eye* (Baltimore: Black Classic Press, 1990), 136.
16. In recent years, Davis has weighed in on contemporary economic and political issues, particularly during the Trump era, highlighting how those on the right have been increasingly drawn to a "fascist appeal." See Angela Davis and Amy Goodman, "Angela Davis on Not Endorsing Any Presidential Candidate: 'I Think We Need a New Party,'" *Democracy Now*, March 28, 2016, accessed December 16, 2022, https://www.democracynow.org/2016/3/28/angela_davis_on_the_fascist_appeal.
17. Davis, *If They Come in the Morning*, 183.
18. Jackson, *Blood in My Eye*, 127.
19. Jackson, *Blood in My Eye*, 137.
20. See Dylan Rodriguez, *Forced Passages: Imprisoned Radical Intellectuals and the U.S. Prison Regime* (Minneapolis: University of Minnesota Press, 2006).
21. See Keeanga Yamahtta-Taylor, *From #BlackLivesMatter to Black Liberation* (Chicago: Haymarket Books, 2016).
22. Dylan Rodriguez, *White Reconstruction: Domestic Warfare and the Logics of Genocide* (New York: Fordham University Press, 2021).
23. Lou Cannon, "From Skyscrapers to Seaport, Bradley Brought Growth to L.A.," *Washington Post*, July 1, 1993.
24. Yamahtta-Taylor, *From #BlackLivesMatter to Black Liberation*.
25. Assata Shakur, *Assata: An Autobiography* (Chicago: Lawrence Hill Books, 2001), 10–11.
26. Jeanelle K. Hope, "The Black Antifascist Tradition: A Primer," in *No Pasarán! Antifascist Dispatches from a World in Crisis*, ed. Shane Burley (Chico, CA: AK Press, 2022), 81–85.
27. The Black Liberation Army, *Documents of the Black Liberation Army* (n.p.: Pattern Books, 2021), 8.
28. *Documents of the Black Liberation Army*, 15.
29. Coordinating Committee of Black Liberation Army, *Message to the Black Movement*, 17.

THE BLACK ANTIFASCIST TRADTION

30. *Message to the Black Movement*, 17.
31. *Message to the Black Movement*, 2–4.
32. *Documents of the Black Liberation Army*, 61.
33. Lorenzo Kom'boa Ervin, *Anarchism and the Black Revolution* (London.: Pluto Press, 2021), 3.
34. *Frame-Up!*, directed by Steven Fischler, Howard Blatt, and Joel Sucher, 1974.
35. Ervin, *Anarchism and the Black Revolution*, 7, 45.
36. Ervin, *Anarchism and the Black Revolution*, 7, 45.
37. Ervin, *Anarchism and the Black Revolution*, 11.
38. Black Autonomy Federation, "Autonomy as a Revolutionary Tendency," *Black Autonomy Federation* (blog), accessed December 16, 2022, https://blackautonomyfederation.blogspot.com/2014/09/autonomy-as-revolutionary-tendency.html.
39. William C. Anderson and Lorenzo Kom'Boa Ervin, "Ungovernable: An Interview with Lorenzo Kom'boa Ervin," *Black Rose Anarchist Federation* (blog), accessed December 16, 2022, https://blackrosefed.org/ungovernable-interview-lorenzo-komboa-ervin-anderson/; Lorenzo Ervin and his wife, JoNina Ervin, created a podcast with a similar moniker—The Black Autonomy Podcast—where they continue to discuss Black social movements and Black anarchisms.
40. Seattle's 2020 autonomous zone was also known as Capitol Hill Autonomous Zone (CHAZ) and the Capitol Hill Occupied Protest (CHOP).
41. See Hizkias Assefa, *The MOVE Crisis in Philadelphia: Extremist Groups and Conflict Resolution* (Pittsburgh: University of Pittsburgh Press, 1990); Kathleen Neal Cleaver, "Philadelphia Fire," *Transition* 51 (January 1991): 150–157.
42. Tajah Ebram. "'Can't Jail the Revolution': Policing, Protest, and the MOVE Organization in Philadelphia's Carceral Landscape," *Pennsylvania Magazine of History and Biography* 143 (3): 333–62.
43. Say Burgin and Jeanne Theoharis, "Targeting Bail Funds and Stop Cop City Activists Is an Old Tactic," *Washington Post*, June 9, 2023, https://www.washingtonpost.com/made-by-history/2023/06/09/cop-city-bail-funds/.

NOTES

44. Akinyele Umoja, "Maroon: Kuwasi Balagoon and the Evolution of Revolutionary New African Anarchism," *Science & Society* 79, no. 2 (April 2015): 196–197.

45. Kuwasi Balagoon, "Anarchy Can't Fight Alone," The Anarchist Library, accessed August 3, 2023, https://theanarchistlibrary.org/library/kuwasi-balagoon-anarchy-can-t-fight-alone.

46. William Anderson, *The Nation on No Map: Black Anarchism and Abolition* (Chico, CA: AK Press, 2021), 92; Umoja, "Maroon: Kuwasi Balagoon."

47. See Edward Onaci, *Free the Land: The Republic of New Afrika and the Pursuit of a Black Nation-State* (Chapel Hill: University of North Carolina Press, 2020).

48. Balagoon, "Anarchy Can't Fight Alone."

49. Sam Bick and David Zinman, *Treyf Podcast*, season 1, episode 47, "Ashanti Alston," July 28, 2020, podcast video, accessed August 3, 2023, https://www.treyfpodcast.com/2020/07/28/47-ashanti-alston/.

50. Bick and Zinman, *Treyf Podcast*.

51. Cathy Cohen, "Punks, Bulldaggers, and Welfare Queens: The Radical Potential of Queer Politics?," *GLQ: A Journal of Lesbian & Gay Studies* 3 (1997): 439.

52. Hope, *No Pasarán*, 84.

53. See Donn Teal, *Gay Militants* (New York: Stein & Day, 1971).

54. Street Transvestite Action Revolutionaries, *Street Transvestite Action Revolutionaries: Survival, Revolt, and Queer Antagonist Struggle* (Untorelli Press, 2013).

55. New York Public Library, "Street Transvestites Action Revolutionaries," *1969: The Year of Gay Liberation*, http://web-static.nypl.org/exhibitions/1969/revolutionaries.html.

56. Puar's conception of homonationalism rightly critiques the nationalist ideology within the LGBT movement and spaces that tends to focus on rights and neoliberal progress as opposed to addressing the systemic forms of oppression that directly harm LGBTQIA people, particularly those of color.

57. Arthur Bell, "STAR Trek," *Village Voice*, July 1971, 46.

58. Marsha P. Johnson, "Rapping with a Street Transvestite Revolutionary: An Interview with Marsha P. Johnson," in *Street Transvestite Action Revolutionaries: Survival, Revolt, and Queer Antagonist Struggle*, 22.

258   **THE BLACK ANTIFASCIST TRADTION**

59. Bell, "STAR Trek."
60. Frank Leon Roberts, "There's No Place Like Home: A History of House Ball Culture," *Wire Tap Magazine*, June 6, 2007, accessed August 7, 2023, https://transgriot.blogspot.com/2008/02/theres-no-place-like-home-history-of.html.
61. Roberts, "There's No Place Like Home."
62. Avery Gordon, "Some Thoughts on Haunting and Futurity," *Borderlands* 10, no. 2 (October 2011): 8.
63. William C. Anderson, *The Nation on No Map: Black Anarchism and Abolition* (Chico, CA: AK Press, 2021).
64. Anarkata, "Anarkata: A Statement," *Anarkata* (blog), October 19, 2019, accessed December 16, 2022, https://anarkataastatement.wordpress.com.

Chapter 7

1. Angela Davis, *Are Prisons Obsolete?* (New York: Seven Stories Press, 2003), 11.
2. We Charge Genocide, "Police Violence Against Chicago's Youth of Color," September 2014, p. 12, ,http://report.wechargegenocide.org.
3. Dylan Rodriguez, "Abolition as the Praxis of Being Human: A Foreword," *Harvard Law Review* 132*(6): 1575–1612.*
4. Ruth Wilson Gilmore, "Terror Austerity Race Gender Excess Theater," *Abolition Geography: Essays Towards Liberation* (New York: Verso, 2022), 159.
5. Rodriguez, "Abolition as the Praxis of Being Human: A Foreword."
6. Angela Davis, "Political Prisoners, Prison, and Black Liberation," in *If They Come in the Morning: Voices of Resistance*, ed. Angela Davis (New York: Verso, 2016), 17.
7. Critical Resistance, *The Abolitionist* 34, no. 4 (March 2021).
8. Davis, *Are Prisons Obsolete?*, 12.
9. Angela Davis and Bettina Aptheker, preface, *If They Come in the Morning*, xiv.
10. Mike Davis, "Hell Factories in the Field," *Nation*, February 20, 1995, 229–234.
11. Davis, *Are Prisons Obsolete?*, 113.
12. "The Folsom Prisoners Manifesto Of Demands and Anti-Oppression Platform," 1, Freedom Archives, http://www.freedomarchives.org/

NOTES 259

Documents/Finder/DOC510_scans/Folsom_Manifesto/510.folsom.manifesto.11.3.1970.pdf.

13. New York 21, *Look for Me in the Whirlwind: The Collective Autobiography of the New York 21* (New York: Random House, 1971), 283.

14. New York 21, *Look for Me in the Whirlwind*, 202.

15. "The Attica Liberation Faction Manifesto of Demands and Anti-Depression Platform." Freedom Archives, https://freedomarchives.org/Documents/Finder/DOC510_scans/Attica/510.Prisons.AtticaManifesto.pdf.

16. "The Attica Liberation Faction Manifesto," 1.

17. Attica Prison Uprising," Zinn Education Project, https://www.zinnedproject.org/materials/attica-prison-uprising/.

18. Heather Ann Thompson, *Blood in the Water: The Attica Prison Uprising of 1971 and Its Legacy* (New York: Pantheon, 2016), 559, 560.

19. Thompson, *Blood in the Water*, 561.

20. Thompson, *Blood in the Water*, 562.

21. Thompson, *Blood in the Water*, 562.

22. Thompson, *Blood in the Water*, 562.

23. Thomas Mathiesen, *The Politics of Abolition* (New York: Wiley, 1974), 3.

24. Fay Honey Knopp, *Instead of Prisons: A Handbook for Abolitionists* (New York: Prison Research Education Project, 1976), iii.

25. Knopp, *Instead of Prisons*, 11.

26. Knopp, *Instead of Prisons*, 10.

27. Dan Berger, *Captive Nation: Black Prison Organizing in the Civil Rights Era* (Durham: University of North Carolina Press, 2016), 270.

28. Critical Resistance, "Critical Resistance: Beyond the Prison Industrial Complex," https://criticalresistance.org/updates/critical-resistance-beyond-the-prison-industrial-complex-1998-conference/.

29. Dylan Rodriguez, *Forced Passages: Imprisoned Radical Intellectuals and the U.S. Prison Regime* (Minneapolis: University of Minnesota Press, 2005), 137.

30. Angela Davis, "Masked Racism: Reflections on the Prison Industrial Complex," *Colorlines*, September 10, 1998, https://www.colorlines.com/articles/masked-racism-reflections-prison-industrial-complex.

31. Davis, "Masked Racism."

32. Critical Resistance National Anti-Policing Working Group and *The Abolitionist* Editorial Collective, "What Is Fascism? What Is Neoliberalism? Definitions," *The Abolitionist* 34 (March 2021).
33. Davis, *Are Prisons Obsolete?*, 107.
34. Davis, *Are Prisons Obsolete?*, 25.
35. Davis, *Are Prisons Obsolete?*, 24.
36. United Nations, "World Conference against Racism, Racial Discrimination, Xenophobia and Related Intolerance," https://www.un.org/WCAR/durban.pdf.
37. United Nations, "World Conference"; see also Zulaikah Patel, "Abolish Anti-Blackness: Hair and Racism in South Africa," Aljazeera.com, December 6, 2020, https://www.aljazeera.com/opinions/2020/12/6/abolish-anti-blackness-hair-and-racism-in-south-africa.
38. Davis, *If They Come in the Morning*, 183, 284.
39. NewAfrican77, "Black Solidarity Day November 5 1979 We Charge Genocide Assata Shakur's Statement," November 2017, https://newafrikan77.wordpress.com/2017/11/05/black-solidarity-day-november-5-1979-we-charge-genocide-assata-shakurs-statement/.
40. Amiri Baraka, "Death to Apartheid! Smash South African Fascism," *Unity Newspaper*, June 9, 1986, https://unityarchiveproject.org/article/death-to-apartheid-smash-south-african-fascism/.
41. Davis, *Are Prisons Obsolete?*, 108.
42. Davis, *Are Prisons Obsolete?*, 111.
43. Kimberlé Crenshaw, "Mapping the Margins: Intersectionality, Identity Politics, and Violence Against Women of Color," *Stanford Law Review* 43, no. 6 (July 1991): 1241–1299.
44. Vaughn Rasberry, *Race and the Totalitarian Century: Geopolitics in the Black Literary Imagination* (Cambridge: Harvard University Press, 2016), 22.
45. Civil Rights Congress, *We Charge Genocide: The Crime of Government Against the Negro People* (New York: International Publishers, 1970), xxv.
46. Frank Wilderson, *Incognegro: A Memoir of Exile and Apartheid* (Boston: South End Press, 2008).
47. Zamansele Nsele, "Part I: Afro-Pessimism and the Rituals of Anti-Black Violence," *Mail & Guardian*, June 24, 2020, https://mg.co.

NOTES 261

za/article/2020-06-24-frank-b-wilderson-afropessimism-memoir-structural-violence/.

48. Nsele, "Part I: Afro-Pessimism and the Rituals of Anti-Black Violence."

49. Project NIA, "About Us," https://project-nia.org/mission-history.

50. Mariame Kaba, *We Do This 'Til We Free Us: Abolitionist Organizing and Transforming Justice* (Chicago: Haymarket Books, 2021), 4.

51. Kaba, *We Do This 'Til We Free Us*, 60.

52. See Hannah Arendt, *The Origins of Totalitarianism* (New York: Harcourt, Brace, Jovanovich, 1973), 17; see also Achille Mbembe, "Necropolitics," *Public Culture* 15, no. 1 (Winter 2003): 11–40.

53. Mbembe, "Necropolitics," 21.

54. Angela Davis, "On Palestine, G4S, and the Prison-Industrial Complex," *Freedom Is a Constant Struggle: Ferguson, Palestine, and the Foundations of a Movement* (Chicago: Haymarket Books, 2016), 51–61.

55. Gilmore, "Terror," 166.

56. Ruth Wilson Gilmore, "Public Enemies and Private Intellectuals," *Abolition Geography: Essays Towards Liberation* (New York: Verso, 2022), 86.

57. Gilmore, "Public Enemies and Private Intellectuals," 87.

58. Ruth Wilson Gilmore, *Golden Gulag: Prisons, Surplus, Crisis and Opposition in Globalizing California* (Berkeley: University of California Press, 2006), 28.

59. Ruth Wilson Gilmore, "Race, Prisons, and War: Scenes from the History of U.S. Violence," *Socialist Register* 45 (2009): 82–83.

60. Ruth Wilson Gilmore, speech, "The Dig LIVE: What Now? Perspectives on the Conjuncture," Socialism 2022 Conference, Chicago, Illinois, September 4, 2022, https://www.youtube.com/watch?v=W7skTDBWH3E.

61. Malcolm X Grassroots Movement, http://www.mxgm.org/; Malcolm X Grassroots Movement, "For Immediate Release: New Curriculum, We Charge Genocide Again, Notes the Importance of *Operation Ghetto Storm* Findings for Younger Generations," May 13, 2013, https://www.facebook.com/MXGMnational/posts/for-immediate-release-new-curriculum-we-charge-genocide-again-notes-the-importan/10151427060297960/; see also Malcolm X Grassroots

262   **THE BLACK ANTIFASCIST TRADITION**

Project, "Operation Ghetto Storm," https://www.prisonpolicy.org/scans/Operation-Ghetto-Storm.pdf.

62. See Malcolm X Grassroots Movement. http://www.mxgm.org/.

63. See Malcolm X Grassroots Movement. http://www.mxgm.org/.

64. Mumia Abu Jamal, "The American Way of Fascism," Change-Links, January 30, 2021, https://change-links.org/mumia-abu-jamal-the-american-way-of-fascism/.

65. Mumia Abu Jamal, "Women & The Movement," YouTube, January 8, 2013, https://www.youtube.com/watch?v=DsAIOg5l5Eo.

66. BYP100, "About BYP 100," https://www.byp100.org/about.

67. Black Youth Project, "What to Do if White Supremacists Hold a Rally in Your Hood," August 16, 2017, https://blackyouthproject.com/white-supremacists-hold-rally-hood/.

68. Black Youth Project, "What to Do if White Supremacists Hold a Rally in Your Hood."

69. Jason Mast, "We Charge Genocide Issues Damning Report on Abuse and Brutality in Chicago," Juvenile Justice Information Exchange, October 24, 2014, https://jjie.org/2014/10/24/we-charge-genocide-issues-damning-report-on-abuse-and-brutality-in-chicago/.

70. Jordan Camp and Christina Heatherton, "An Interview with Breanna Champion, Page May and Asha Rosa Ransby-Spore," in *Policing the Planet: Why the Policing Crisis Led to Black Lives Matter* (New York: Verso, 2016), 201, http://aworldwithoutpolice.org/wp-content/uploads/2016/08/jordan-t-camp-policing-the-planet-why-the-policing-crisis-led-to-black-lives-matter.pdf.

71. Ashoka Jegroo, "Fighting Cops and the Klan: The History and Future of Black Antifascism," Truthout, February 21, 2017, https://truthout.org/articles/fighting-cops-and-the-klan-the-history-and-future-of-black-antifascism/.

72. Southern Poverty Law Center, "White Nationalist Threats Against Transgender People are Escalating," June 26, 2019, https://www.splcenter.org/hatewatch/2019/06/26/white-nationalist-threats-against-transgender-people-are-escalating.

73. TGI Justice Project, http://www.tgijp.org.

74. Eric A. Stanley, Nat Smith, and CeCe McDonald, eds., *Captive Genders: Trans Embodiment and the Prison Industrial Complex* (Oakland: AK Press, 2013), 27.

NOTES **263**

75. Sylvia Rivera Law Project, https://srlp.org.
76. Zoé Samudzi and William C. Anderson, *As Black As Resistance: Finding the Conditions for Liberation* (Oakland: AK Press, 2018), 6.
77. Samudzi and Anderson, *As Black As Resistance*, 6.
78. Mariame Kaba, foreword, *As Black As Resistance*, xvii.
79. Jaclyn Peisler, "'Their Tactics are Fascistic': Barr Slams Black Lives Matter, Accuses the Left of 'Tearing Down the System,'" *Washington Post*, August 10, 2020, https://www.washingtonpost.com/nation/2020/08/10/barr-fox-antifa-blm/.
80. Movement for Black Lives, "End the War on Black People," https://m4bl.org/end-the-war-on-black-people/.
81. Chris Vials and Bill V. Mullen, "Black Antifascism and Fighting Today's Far Right," Verso Blog, November 18, 2020, https://www.versobooks.com/blogs/4918-black-antifascism-and-fighting-today-s-far-right.
82. Mihir Chaudhary and Joseph Richardson Jr., "Violence Against Black Lives Matter Protesters: A Review," *Current Trauma Reports* 8 (2022): 96–104, https://link.springer.com/article/10.1007/s40719-022-00228-2.
83. A good example of the innovative Black Antifascism produced by the Black Lives Matter movement broadly is the documentary film *We Charge Genocide*, produced by the In the Spirit of Mandela International Tribunal, https://www.maysles.org/calendar/2021/10/21/in-the-spirit-of-mandela-international-tribunal-2021-we-charge-genocide-virtual-short-film-program-and-live-tribunal-viewing-party.
84. Critical Resistance, *The Abolitionist*, no. 28 (Winter 2018): 8.
85. Woods Ervin, "Finding Our Way Forward: Past Neoliberalism, Fascism, Austerity and the Prison Industrial Complex," *The Abolitionist*, no. 34 (Winter, 2021): 1.
86. Aviah Sarah Day and Shanice Octavia McBean, *Abolition Revolution* (London: Pluto Press, 2022), 204.
87. JoNina Abron-Ervin and Lorenzo Kom'boa Ervin, "Black Antifascism: A Conversation," *Propter Nos* 3 (Winter 2019): 138.

Epilogue

1. Toni Morrison, "Racism and Fascism," *Journal of Negro Education* 64, no. 3 (Summer 1995).

2. For voting rights post–2020 election, see Brennan Center for Justice, Voting Laws Roundup: May 2022 (Washington, DC: Brennan Center for Justice, 2022), accessed February 19, 2023, https://www.brennancenter.org/our-work/research-reports/voting-laws-roundup-may-2022.

3. Sam Adler-Bell, "Behind the CRT Crackdown: Racial Blamelessness and the Politics of Forgetting," *Forum* magazine, January 13, 2022, accessed February 19, 2023, https://www.aapf.org/theforum-critical-race-theory-crackdown.

4. Scott Neuman, "The Culture Wars Are Pushing Some Teachers to Leave the Classroom," NPR, November 13, 2022, accessed February 19, 2023, https://www.npr.org/2022/11/13/1131872280/teacher-shortage-culture-wars-critical-race-theory.

5. Henry Giroux, "Mass Shootings and the Culture of Violence in the U.S.," *Yes* magazine, June 2022, accessed February 19, 2023, https://www.yesmagazine.org/opinion/2022/06/13/end-mass-shootings-violent-culture.

6. Eugene Declercq, et al., "The U.S. Maternal Health Divide: The Limited Maternal Health Services and Worse Outcomes of States Proposing New Abortion Restrictions," The Commonwealth Fund, December 14, 2022, accessed February 19, 2023, https://www.commonwealthfund.org/publications/issue-briefs/2022/dec/us-maternal-health-divide-limited-services-worse-outcomes.

7. Donald Trump, "Statement by the President," in the White House Archives, last modified June 1, 2020, accessed February 19, 2023, https://trumpwhitehouse.archives.gov/briefings-statements/statement-by-the-president-39/.

8. Luke Mogelson, "In the Streets with Antifa," *New Yorker*, October 2020, accessed February 19, 2023, https://www.newyorker.com/magazine/2020/11/02/trump-antifa-movement-portland.

9. Mike Fitts, "Second Arrest of a 'Boogaloo Boy' Suspect Made after Violent Columbia Demonstrations," *Post and Courier* (Charleston), June 2020, accessed February 19, 2023, https://www.postandcourier.com/news/second-arrest-of-a-boogaloo-boy-suspect-made-after-violent-columbia-demonstrations/article_9e4fdf5c-a76f-11ea-8217-ef9830925b24.html.

NOTES

10. Jason Slotkin, Suzanne Nuyen, and James Dubek, "4 Stabbed, 33 Arrested after Trump Supporters, Counterprotesters Clash in D.C.," NPR, December 12, 2020, accessed February 19, 2023, https://www.npr.org/2020/12/12/945825924/trump-supporters-arrive-in-washington-once-again-for-a-million-maga-march.
11. "4 Stabbed, 33 Arrested After Trump Supporters, Counterprotesters Clash in D.C."
12. It should also be noted that the Proud Boys have invoked "Uhuru" as a mocking response to Gazi Kodzo, a former member of the African People's Socialist Party, who frequently used the word as a greeting and chant throughout his YouTube videos, particularly one entitled "White People Are Paying Reparations."

INDEX

Page numbers in *italic* refer to illustrations. "Passim" (literally "scattered") indicates intermittent discussion of a topic over a cluster of pages.

AAPA. *See* Asian American Political Alliance (AAPA)

abolition and abolitionism, 5, 28, 151, 165–68 passim, 176–207 passim. *See also* police abolition

Abraham Lincoln Brigade, 20, 60–66, 70, 71, 80, 120

Abron-Ervin, JoNina, 206–7

Abu Jamal, Mumia, 154, 183, 199–200

Abyssinia. *See* Ethiopia

Abzug, Bella, 111

Acoli, Sundiata, 163

Africa: Du Bois on, 19–20; Germany in, 19, 49, 50, 54, 95; World War I, 95–96. *See also* Ethiopia; Libya; South Africa

Africa, John, 169

Afrofuturism, 1–2, 167, 177–79, 26

Afrofuturist Abolitionists of the Americas, 167, 177–79

Alexander, Michelle, 188

Alexander, Roberta, 146–47

Alien Registration Act of 1940. *See* Smith Act

Alston, Ashanti, 154, 172–73

American Indians. *See* Native Americans

American Medical Bureau (Medical Bureau to Aid Spanish Democracy), 64, 65, 68

anarchism, 155, 164–73 passim, 177

Anarchism and the Black Revolution (Ervin), 155

Anderson, Carol, 107, 122

Anderson, William C., 8, 166, 173, 202–3

antagonism, 170–76

anti-Blackness, 4–5, 9, 19, 35, 38, 43, 165, 194–203 passim; capitalism and, 135; Césaire and, 21; lynch law roots in, 32; Nazism and Fascism roots in, 8, 21

anticommunism, 56, 94, 104, 105, 106, 118, 120

"Antifa," 203, 212–13

Anti-Fascist Civil Rights Declaration for 1944, 105

anti-immigrant bills and laws, 12, 18, 105, 204

antisemitism, 13; Fascist Italy, 16, 102

apartheid, 81, 192, 193, 197

Aptheker, Bettina, 5

Aptheker, Herbert, 108

Are Prisons Obsolete? (Davis), 184, 191–92, 193

armed self-defense. *See* self-defense, armed

Asian American Political Alliance (AAPA), 125, 128, 146, 147

268   THE BLACK ANTIFASCIST TRADTION

Attica Prison rebellion, 1971, 186–87, 188

Bailey, Moya, 39
Baker, Frazier, 39, 40
Balagoon, Kuwasi, 171, 186
Baldwin, James, 156
Bandy, Robert, 83
bank robberies, 163, 166, 176
Baraka, Amiri, 193
Bardner, Benjamin, 93
Barr, William, 203
Bass, Charlotta, 110
The Beautiful Are Not Yet Born (Nkrumah), 195
Berger, Dan, 189–90
Bethune, Mary McLeod, 40–41
Bilbo, Theodore G., 15, 79, 108
BLA. *See* Black Liberation Army (BLA)
Black and Brown queer and trans organizing, 174–76, 202
Black Autonomy Federation, 168, 207
Black Codes, 14
Black Feminist Thought (Collins), 194
Black Liberation Army (BLA), 155, 163–66 passim, 170–73 passim
Black Lives Matter (BLM), 203–4, 212–14 passim
Black mayors, 160–62
Black Nationalists and Nationalism, 56, 133–34, 171–72, 173; BPP and, 140–41
Blackness, 15–16. *See also* anti-Blackness
Black newspapers, 73, 74, 77–79 passim, 84, 88, 93, 94; Bass, 110; BPP, 127–28, 151; Hughes, 66; Wells-Barnett, 32, 33
Black Panther, 127–28, 151

Black Panther Party (BPP), 125–28, 131, 137–51, 160–67 passim, 171–75 passim, 202; "fascist corporativism," 184; newspaper, 127–28, 151; Panther 21 (New York), 185–86; in prisons, 185
Black Power, 123–51 passim, 170
Black queer and trans organizing. *See* Black and Brown queer and trans organizing
Black rapist myth and allegations, 36, 37, 50, 82; Martinsville Seven, 111–12, 119; "Scottsboro Boys," 23, 57, 101–2, 104, 109; Willie McGee, 109–10, 111
"Black Scare/Red Scare" (Burden-Stelly), 99, 118
Black women's clubs, 33–34, 40–41, 42
Black Youth Project. *See* BYP100
Blood in My Eye (Jackson), 154, 155, 157
"blood quantum," 15–16
Bolsonaro, Jair, 210
boycotts, 53
BPP. *See* Black Panther Party (BPP)
Bradley, Tom, 161–62
Braz, Rose, 191
Brooks, Gwendolyn, 90
Brotherhood of Sleeping Car Porters, 58, 69
Brown, Elaine, 139, 146
Brown, Lloyd: *Stand Up to Freedom!*, 119
Brown, Michael, 45
Burden-Stelly, Charisse, 99, 118
Burnham, Louis, 109
Burroughs, Margaret, 78, 87, 88, 93
Butler, Octavia: *Parable of the Sower*, 1–2, 216
BYP100, 200
Byrne, James, 108

INDEX

269

Camp Logan Mutiny. *See* Houston Race Riot of 1917

Capitol insurrection, January 6, 2021. *See* January 6, 2021, Capitol insurrection

Carmichael, Stokely. *See* Ture, Kwame

Césaire, Aimé, 4, 23, 27, 48; *Discourse on Colonialism*, 20–22, 77

Chicago Defender, 78, 79, 88, 93, 94

Chicago Police Department (CPD), 200–201

Chicago Race Riot of 1919, 44, 51

China: Robert F. Williams, 133. *See also* Mao Zedong

Civil Rights Congress (CRC), 22, 100, 109–25, 183, 196, 200–201

Civil Rights Movement, 130; SCLC, 125, 130; SNCC, 167, 199

Cleaver, Eldridge, 143, 151; *Soul on Ice*, 145

Cleaver, Kathleen, 142

Cohen, Cathy, 174, 176, 200

COINTELPRO, 94, 126, 163, 199, 202

Collins, Patricia Hill, 194

Comintern, 51–55 passim, 86, 95, 143–44, 193

Communist Party USA (CPUSA), 23, 55–56, 70, 92, 93, 104, 110, 127; Chicago, 93; CRC and, 100, 113; criminalization, 105, 118; ILD and, 101; Popular Front, 81, 105, 110; UFAF conference, 125

concentration camps. *See* internment camps

conscientious objectors, 79, 188

CRC. *See* Civil Rights Congress (CRC)

Crenshaw, Kimberlé, 194, 211

Critical Race Theory (CRT), 117, 210–11

Critical Resistance (CR), 190–91, 202, 204, 205; Anti-Policing Group, 182–83, 191

Crockett, George, 121, 123

Crusader, 129, 133–36 passim, *135*, *136*

Cuba, 14, 133, 167

Cueria y Obrit, Basilio, 60

Dalitso, Ruwe, 38

Davenport, Charles, 38

Davis, Angela, 4, 5, 23–24, 153–60 passim, 165, 175, 182–92 passim, 197; *Are Prisons Obsolete?*, 184, 191–92, 193–94; Free Angela Davis Committee, 186, 187, 192; *If They Come in the Morning*, 155, 184, 185

Davis, Ben, 93, 123

Davis, Frank Marshall, 88–89

Davis, Mike, 184

Day, Aviah Sarah, 206

Dearborn (Mich.) Independent, 13

deportation, 18, 52, 78, 81, 105, 123

desegregation, 130, 131

determinists and determinism, 10–11

Dickerson, Earl, 119

Dies, Martin, 104, 106

Dies Committee, 70, 104, 105, 106. *See also* House Un-American Activities Committee (HUAC)

Dimitrov, Georgi: *United Front*, 143–44

Discourse on Colonialism (Césaire), 20–22, 77

Doss, Erika, 85

Double Victory campaign. *See* Double Victory campaign

Douglass, Frederick, 31–32, 214

Dower, John, 77

Dred Scott v. Sandford, 14, 186

Du Bois, W. E. B., 19–20, 41–44 passim, 49–50, 80, 95–97, 116, 121, 192; "African Roots of War," 54; Aptheker and, 108; *Black Reconstruction*, 75, 116; Germany visit, 75; on Nazism, 75–76; UN, 106–7

Durban Conference against Racism, 2001. *See* World Conference against Racism, Durban, South Africa, 2001

Dyer Bill (Leonidas Dyer), 1918, 43, 44, 45

East St. Louis Massacre, 1917, 43–44, 93

Edwards, Thyra, 58–60, 63, 67–69, 92

Einstein, Albert, 57, 111

Ellison, Ralph, 81, 87

Ervin, Lorenzo Kom'Boa, 154, 166–68, 206–7; *Anarchism and the Black Revolution*, 155, 166–68 passim

Ervin, Woods, 205–6

Esch, Betsy, 134

Ethiopia: Italian invasion, 20, 47–64 passim, 74–75, 76, 81, 86, 95, 104

Ethiopian Pacific Movement, 91–92

"Ethiopian Utopia" (Du Bois), 95–96

eugenics, 13, 15, 38, 79; Fascist Italy, 16

Fair Employment Practices Commission (FEPC), 80, 105

Fanon, Frantz, 6, 88, 127, 139

Faulkner, William, 111

FBI, 69, 126, 105; COINTELPRO, 94, 126, 163, 199, 202; founding, 103; RACON, 92, 94; Robert F. Williams and, 133

First Red Scare, 103

Flynn, Elizabeth Gurley, 110

Folsom Prisoners' Manifesto, 185

Forced Passages: Imprisoned Radical Intellectuals and the U.S. Prison Regime (Rodriguez), 190

Ford, Henry, 13

Ford, James, 53

Fourteenth Amendment, 14, 102

Franco, Francisco, 65, 67–68, 70, 76, 80. *See also* Spanish Civil War

Freire, Paulo, 253–54n58

Friends of the Abraham Lincoln Brigade (FALB), 70

Fritsch, Theodor, 13

Garland, Walter, 62, 70

Garvey, Amy Ashwood, 52–53, 54

Garvey, Marcus, 121

genocide, 33, UN convention on, 112–17 passim, 122. *See also* Jewish Holocaust; "We Charge Genocide" movement and petition

George Jackson Brigade, 176

Germany: African colonialism, 19, 49, 50, 54; Du Bois visit, 75; Patterson visit, 101; political prisoners, 101; Thyra Edwards visit, 59. *See also* Nazis and Nazism

Gilmore, Ruth Wilson, 182, 183, 190, 191, 197–98, 204–5, 206

Gitlin, Murray, 69

Gordon, Avery, 177

Great Replacement Theory, 14

Grossman, Aubrey, 109

Haiti: revolution, 48; US occupation, 52

Hall, Felix, 82

Hall, Stuart: *Policing the Crisis*, 197–98

Hampton, Fred, 143

Harlem Riot of 1943, 83, 91

Harrington, Ollie, 87, 92–94 passim

INDEX

Haywood, Harry, 44, 50–51, 56, 62, 80, 81

Herndon, Angelo, 55, 57, 62, 101

Herndon, Milton, 62–63, 68

Higginbotham, Eleanor Brooks, 41

Hilliard, David, 144

Hitler, Adolf, 15, 20, 21, 50–51, 74, 94, 101–2, 108; in fictitious news story, 78; influence on US prison guards, 164; *Lebensraum*, 49; in poetry, 83–84, 88; Robert F. Williams and, 129; unions and, 81; US influence on, 12–13, 16; *Zweites Buch*, 12–13

Hoffman, Frederick: *Race Traits and the Tendencies of the American Negro*, 10–12

Holocaust, Jewish. *See* Jewish Holocaust

"homonationalism" (Puar), 175

Hoover, Herbert, 69, 92, 126, 135, *135*

Hope, Lugenia Burns, 42, *43*

House Un-American Activities Committee (HUAC), 70, 104, 121, 127

Houston Race Riot of 1917, 44–45, 58, 79

Huggins, Ericka, 143, 145, 146, 149

Hughes, Langston, 48, 59–62 passim, 66–67, 74, 79, 89–94 passim; "Beaumont to Detroit: 1943," 83–84; on Zoot Suit Riot, 84

Hunton, Alphaeus, 104

Ibarruri, Dolores, 60

If They Come in the Morning (Davis), 155, 184, 185

immigrants and immigration, 18, 38. *See also* anti-immigrant bills and laws

Indigenous Americans. *See* Native Americans

Instead of Prisons: A Handbook for Abolitionists (Knopp), 189

Intercommunal Committees to Combat Fascism (ICCFs), 148–51

"intercommunalism" (Newton). *See* "revolutionary intercommunalism" (Newton)

intermarriage, 69, 212; anti-miscegenation laws, 16, 17

International African Friends of Ethiopia (IAFE), 53, 76

International African Service Bureau (IASB), 54, 95

International Labor Defense (ILD), 23, 101–3 passim, 109

international law, 100, 107, 117

International Trade Union Committee of Negro Workers (ITUCNW), 51–52

internment camps, 50, 84, 147–48; COs, 79

Intersectional Abolitionist Antifascism, 193–206 passim

Isaac, Gem, 201

Israel, 197

Italy: invasion of Ethiopia, 20, 47–64 passim, 74–75, 76, 81, 86, 95, 104; Fascist era, 8, 16–17, 20, 60, 102–3; Libya colonization, 75, 76

ITUCNW. *See* International Trade Union Committee of Negro Workers (ITUCNW)

Jackson, George, 153–65 passim, 184, 190, 191, 199; *Blood in My Eye*, 154, 155, 157; *Soledad Brother*, 153, 154. *See also* George Jackson Brigade

Jackson, Robert H., 112

James, C. L. R., 52–53, 54, 56, 73, 75, 139

January 6, 2021, Capitol insurrection, 212–15 passim

Japanese Americans, 70, 84, 147–48

Jewish Holocaust, 8, 9, 13, 21, 22, 129; Du Bois view, 76

Jews: expulsion from Europe, 17; Hitler and, 20, 50, 101; Italy, 16, 102–3; Russian pogroms, 33. *See also* antisemitism; Jewish Holocaust

Jim Crow laws, 8, 17, 94, 105–6; influence on Nazi Germany and Fascist Italy, 103. *See also* desegregation

Johnson, James Weldon, 103

Johnson, Marsha, 174, *174*, 175, 202

Jones, Claudia, 41, 104, 123

Jordan, Robert O., 91–92

Kaba, Mariame, 24, 150, 196, 200, 203, 204

Kea, Salaria, 60, 63–65, 68, 69

Kelley, Robin D. G., 5, 19, 21, 32, 56, 134

Kennedy, John F., 135–36, *135*

Kennedy, Robert F., 121, 135, *135*

Kenyatta, Jomo, 53, 54, 95

King, Martin Luther, Jr., 132

Knopp, Fay Honey, 188–89

Knox, Owen A., 105

Korean War, 112, 118, 119

Ku Klux Klan (KKK), 55, 106, 114, *135*, 136; Gary, Ind., 58; Monroe County, N.C., 131

labor unions. *See* unions

Landra, Guido, 16

Law, Oliver, 63

League of Nations, 50, 75

Lee, Bubbles Rose ("Bubbles Rose Marie"), 174

Lemkin, Raphael, 112

LGBTQIA+ organizing, 174–76, 202

LGBTQIA+ people, attacks on, 201–2

Libya, 75, 76

Lim, Anne B., 135–36

Livingston, Michael, 16

Logan, Rayford, 107

Look for Me in the Whirlwind, 186

Los Angeles: Zoot Suit Riots. *See* Zoot Suit Riots, 1943

lynching and lynchings, 12, 15, 27, 31–46 passim, 55, 82, 93; antilynching bills, 80, 110–11; CRC and, 110; ILD and, 101

Mackey, Virginia, 188

Makalani, Minkah, 52

Makonnen, T. Ras, 95

Malcolm X Grassroots Movement (MXGM), 45, 173, 199

male supremacy and chauvinism, 145–47

Malloy, Sean: *Out of Oakland*, 138–39

Malzac, Hugh, 81

The Man Who Lived Underground (Wright), 92

Mao Zedong, 133–34, 139

Marcantonio, Vito, 105

Marshall, George, 105, 123

Martin, Trayvon, 200

Martinique, 76–77

Martinsville Seven case, 111–12, 119

Marxists and Marxism, 6, 54, 58, 75, 109, 116; Césaire, 20, 23; Marxist-Leninist-Maoism (MLM), 127, 134

mass shootings, 14, 212

INDEX

Mathiesen, Thomas, 189; *Politics of Abolition*, 188

mayors, Black. *See* Black mayors

Mbembe, Achille, 196–97

McBean, Shanice Octavia, 206

McCarran Internal Security Act, 121

McDonald, Cece, 201–2

McGee, Willie, 109–10, 111, 119

McKay, Claude, 53, 61, 103–4

McWilliams, Carey, 105

Medical Bureau to Aid Spanish Democracy. *See* American Medical Bureau (Medical Bureau to Aid Spanish Democracy)

Medina, Harold, 120, 121

Memmi, Albert, 49, 139

merchant marines, 80, 81

miscegenation. *See* intermarriage

misogynoir, 33, 39, 41

Mitford, Jessica, 111

Morgan, Crawford, 61, 70–71

Morocco and Moroccans, 59, 65–68

Morrison, Toni, 205

Moss, Thomas, 35

MOVE, 155, 169

Mullen, Bill, 144

Murch, Donna, 137–38

Murphy, J. T., 135

Mussolini, Benito, 8, 15, 20, 32, 102; in poetry, 83; unions and, 81

Nakatsu, Penny, 146, 147–48

National Association for the Advancement of Colored People (NAACP), 32, 80, 82, 107–8; opposition to "We Charge Genocide," 122; Robert F. Williams, 130–33 passim

National Association of Colored Women (NACW), 32, 42

National Association of Colored Women's Clubs (NACWC), 40–41

National Committees to Combat Fascism (NCCFs), 148

National Council of Negro Women (NCNW), 41

National Federation for Constitutional Liberties (NFCL), 105–6, 109

National Lawyers Guild, 110

National Maritime Union (NMU), 80, 81

National Negro Congress (NNC), 56–57, 60, 86, 109

Native Americans, 13, 15–16, 50, 187

Native Son (Wright), 91

Nazis and Nazism, 8, 9, 16–22 passim, 59, 101–2, 112, 129; influence on US prison guards, 164; *Lebensraum*, 49; Nuremberg Race Laws, 8, 17, 102–3

"necropolitics" (Mbembe), 196–97

Negro Committee to Aid Spain, 64

Negroes with Guns (Williams), 133, 137

Negro National Congress (NNC), 56–57, 81, 88, 104; Edwards, 59, 60; Negro People's Front, 86

Negro Story, 88–89

Negro Worker, 51–52

Neighborhood Union, Atlanta, 42–43, 43

New Afrika Movement, 171–72, 199

Newton, Huey P., 127, 128, 137, 140–43 passim, 151, 154, 173

NFCL. *See* National Federation for Constitutional Liberties (NFCL)

Nkrumah, Kwame: *Beautiful Are Not Yet Born*, 195

NNC. *See* National Negro Congress (NNC)

Norway: prisons, 188

Nuremberg Race Laws, 8, 17, 102–3

Oakland Community School (OCS), 149–50

Omi, Michael, 15, 17

"one drop" rule, 15

O'Reilly, John Patrick, 65, 69

Ormes, Jackie, 92–93, 96

Out of Oakland: Black Panther Party Internationalism during the Cold War (Malloy), 138–39

Padmore, George, 51–54 passim, 95

Pan-African Federation, 49, 95, 96

Pan-African Movement, 48, 53, 76, 95

Parable of the Sower (Butler), 1–2, 216

Patterson, Louise, 24, 59

Patterson, William, 22, 23–24, 40, 59, 101–4 passim, 127; CRC, 109, 112; jail, 121, 123; Scottsboro case, 101, 102; "We Charge Genocide" petition, 120–21

Pelley, William Dudley, 106

Perez, Jasson, 10

Petry, Ann, 87, 91

Plessy v. Ferguson, 35, 48

police abolition, 150

"police brutality" (term), 123

police killing of African Americans, 45–46, 117

Policing the Crisis: Mugging, the State, and Law and Order (Hall), 197–98

political prisoners, 148, 154–66 passim, 175, 177, 193, 199–200; Germany, 101

The Politics of Abolition (Mathiesen), 188

politics of respectability, 41

Port Chicago Mutiny, 85

positivists and positivism, 10–11

Powell, Curtis, 186

Powell, Lewis, 157–58

prison, 183–93 passim; Norway, 188. *See also* abolitionism and abolitionism; political prisoners; prison industrial complex (PIC)

prisoner strikes and uprisings, 185–89 passim

prison industrial complex (PIC), 140, 184, 188, 190, 191, 203

Prison Research Education Action Program (PREAP), 188–89

Proud Boys, 213, 214–15

"pseudo-humanism" (Césaire), 21–22

pseudoscience, 10–12, 13

Puar, Jasbir, 175

Puerto Ricans and Puerto Rico, 13–14

queer organizing. *See* LGBTQIA+ organizing

race riots, 43–45, 51, 58, 79, 82–83

Race Traits and the Tendencies of the American Negro (Hoffman), 10–12

racialization, 15–17 passim

racial purity, 15–18, 37, 39

Randolph, A. Philip, 57, 58, 80

Rankin, John Elliott, 74, 79, 85

rape, 36–39 passim, 117, 194. *See also* Black rapist myth and allegations

Rasberry, Vaughn, 82, 90

Reco, Charles J., 82

Reconstruction, 10, 31, 32, 34, 116

Red Guard Party, 125, 139

INDEX

Red International of Labor Unions (RILU), 51

A Red Record: Tabulated Statistics and Alleged Causes of Lynching in the United States, 1892–1893–1894 (Wells), 33, 36

Red Scare, 1917–20. *See* First Red Scare

"Red Scare/Black Scare" (Burden-Stelly). *See* "Black Scare/Red Scare" (Burden-Stelly)

"Red Summer" (1991), 51, 103

Replacement Theory. *See* Great Replacement Theory

reproductive rights, 14, 211, 212; Italy, 60

Republic of New Afrika (RNA), 172

respectability politics. *See* politics of respectability

Revolutionary Action Movement (RAM), 134

"revolutionary intercommunalism" (Newton), 140–43 passim

Rivera, Sylvia, 174, *174*, 175

Roberts, Frank, 175–76

Robeson, Paul, 57–58, 67, 86, 87–88, 93, 120–21, 127; Robert F. Williams compared, 133

Robinson, Cedric, 3–4, 7, 19, 32, 160

Rockefeller, Nelson, 187, 188

Rodney, Walter, 4

Rodriguez, Dylan, 182, 183, 190, 191, 202; *White Reconstruction*, 161

Roe v. Wade, 14, 211, 212

Roosevelt, Eleanor, 41, 107

Roosevelt, Franklin, 62, 75, 80

Safe Society Committee, 189

Sampson, Edith, 122

Samudzi, Zoé, 8, 166, 202–3

scientific racism, 10–12, 13, 15

"Scottsboro Boys" case, 23, 57, 101–2, 104, 109

Seale, Bobby, 125, 140, 144, 149, 151, 160–61, 162

segregation. *See* desegregation; Jim Crow laws; "separate but equal"

self-defense, armed, 42, 129, 130, 131, 137

"separate but equal," 35, 37, 48

sexism, 37, 39, 41, 69, 145–47 passim; BPP, 145

Shakur, Assata, 154, 163–64, 171, 193

Shakur, Zayd, 163

slavery, 21; abolition, 10, 11; slave codes, 9–10

Sleeping Car Porters. *See* Brotherhood of Sleeping Car Porters

Small, Tolbert, 149

Smith, Ferdinand, 81

Smith, Howard, 119

Smith, William Thomas, 78

Smith Act, 69, 70, 81, 105, 114, 118–23 passim

SNCC. *See* Student Nonviolent Coordinating Committee (SNCC)

Soledad Brother: The Prison Letters of George Jackson, 153, 154

Soledad Brothers, 153, 186, 199

Sostre, Martin, 154, 166, 167

Soul on Ice (Cleaver), 145

South Africa, 81, 108, 192–97 passim

Southern Christian Leadership Conference (SCLC), 125, 130

Southern Horrors: Lynch Law in All Its Phases (Wells-Barnett), 31, 38, 137

Southwest Africa, 50

Soviet Union, 52, 55

Spain: Morocco colonization, 65–67 passim. *See also* Spanish Civil War

Spanish Civil War, 20, 48, 59–70 passim, 74–76 passim, 80, 86, 87. *See also* Abraham Lincoln Brigade

Stalin, Joseph, 52

Stand Up to Freedom! The Negro People vs. the Smith Act, (Brown), 119

STAR. *See* Street Transvestite Action Revolutionaries (STAR)

sterilization, forced, 15, 38

Stern, Alfred K., 105

Stockholm Petition, 121

The Street (Petry), 91

Street Transvestite Action Revolutionaries (STAR), 174–76, *174*, 202

strikes, 44, 58; prisoners', 185; students', 126, 139

Student Nonviolent Coordinating Committee (SNCC), 167, 199

Supreme Court cases. *See* US Supreme Court cases

swimming pool desegregation, 131

Third International. *See* Comintern

Third World Liberation Front (TWLF), 125, 126, 139

Third World War. *See* World War III (foreseen)

Thirteenth Amendment, 10, 102

Thompson, Heather Ann, 188

Tompkins, Grace, 89

Treaty of Versailles, 95–96

Trinidad, 52, 53

Truman, Harry, 115

Trump, Donald, 18, 201, 203, 204, 209, 210, 213–14

Ture, Kwame, 124

Tyson, Timothy, 129

unions, 134; Hitler and Mussolini and, 81; maritime workers, 56, 80, 81; sleeping car porters, 58, 69

United Front Against Fascism (UFAF) conference, Oakland, 1969, 125–28, 144–48, 162

United Nations (UN), 96–97, 106–9 passim; Commission on Human Rights, 107; Committee against Torture, 24, 183, 201; Convention against Torture, 201; genocide convention, 112–17 passim, 122; "We Charge Genocide" petition, 22, 99–124 passim

Unite the Right rally, Charlotteville, Virginia, 2017, 200, 204

Universal Negro Improvement Association, 121

US Congress: Dies Committee, 70, 104, 105, 106; HUAC, 70, 104, 121, 127; Overman Committee, 103

US Constitution: *Dred Scott* and "Three-Fifths Compromise," 14. *See also* Fourteenth Amendment; Thirteenth Amendment

USSR. *See* Soviet Union

US Supreme Court cases, 17, 212; *Brown*, 130; *Dred Scott*, 14, 186; *Plessy*, 35, 48; *Roe v. Wade*, 14, 211, 212

Veterans of the Abraham Lincoln Brigade, 70

Vials, Christopher, 144

Walker, David, 56

Washington, Booker T., 42

Watson, Morris, 105

INDEX

We Charge Genocide (group), 24, 183, 196, 200
"We Charge Genocide" movement and petition, 22, 99–124 passim, 192, 194, 196, 200
Wells-Barnett, Ida B., 23, 27, 31–46 passim; *Southern Horrors*, 31, 38, 137
West, Michael O., 41
Westbrook, Richard, 119
Wheatley, Phillis, 55–56
White, Walter, 82, 122
"white-identity fascism," 17
white male fragility, 37
white male sexual violence, 38–39
whiteness, 16, 17–18, 37–38
White Reconstruction: Domestic Warfare and the Logics of Genocide (Rodriguez), 161
white supremacy, 14, 85; Hitler, 20; Reconstruction, 34
white womanhood, 37
Why Accountability?, 201
Wilderson, Frank, III, 165, 194–98 passim
Wilkins, Roy, 131–32
Williams, Ellen, 128, 129
Williams, Mabel, 129, 132, 133
Williams, Robert F., 127–37
Williams, Sikes, 128, 129
Winant, Howard, 15, 17
women's bodies, control of, 37, 38; Italy, 60. *See also* reproductive rights; sterilization, forced
women's clubs. *See* Black women's clubs
World Conference against Racism, Durban, South Africa, 2001, 192
World War I, 49, 50, 53, 103; Africa, 95–96

World War II, 49–50, 70, 115; COs, 79; Double Victory campaign, 20, 71, 73–99 passim, 118; Fanon, 76–77; Hiroshima, 115; Nuremberg trials, 112, 116–17
World War III (foreseen), 96, 115
The Wretched of the Earth (Fanon), 76
Wright, Cleo, 93
Wright, Richard, 68, 87, 93; *Man Who Lived Underground*, 92; *Native Son*, 91
Wu, Judy Tzu-Chun, 134

Yamahtta-Taylor, Keeanga, 162
Yates, James, 54–56, 61, 70, 92
Young Lords, 125, 126, 175
Young Patriots Organization (YPO), 125, 126

Zoot Suit Riots, 1943, 84
Zweites Buch (Hitler), 12–13

ACKNOWLEDGMENTS

THIS BOOK was a true collaboration and collective effort. We are indebted to a number of scholars, archivists, comrades, mentors, friends, family, and community members who have helped make this work possible.

We are especially grateful for the support of the archivists and staff at the Schomburg Center for Research in Black Culture; Freedom Archives; the African American Museum and Library in Oakland; the Bentley Historical Library; the Atlanta University Center and Robert W. Woodruff Library; and New York's Lesbian, Gay, Bisexual & Transgender Community Center Archives. We are most appreciative of the staff who were able to digitize materials for us, as this project began in 2020 during the height of the COVID-19 pandemic. The archival materials from these various repositories are at the crux of this project and it would not have been possible to stitch together *The Black Antifascist Tradition* without engaging these institutions.

While this book highlights the dynamic lives of many Black Antifascists, there are countless others whom we simply did not have the space to include, but whose activism and work has influenced this project. Jeanelle would like to acknowledge the many Antifascist activists she has been in community with while living in California and Texas. She would also like to acknowledge the late Black activist and community organizer Nikeeta Slade, who was deeply influential in shaping her early understanding of Black Antifascism. This book is for you all. A luta continua!

Jeanelle would also like to thank Diane C. Fujino, Shane Burley, and Kirsten West Savali for their integral feedback on earlier iterations of this project. Furthermore, she is forever grateful for the support of her

ACKNOWLEDGMENTS 279

co-author, comrade, and mentor, Bill Mullen. She is deeply appreciative of Bill's guidance and willingness to support this work, and of his wisdom in helping her navigate constructing an audacious project. Furthermore, Bill has been the most generous thought-partner and writer during this process, and his earlier books have helped inform and shape this project.

Finally, Jeanelle would like to thank family and friends who have made it possible to carry out the writing of this project and who assisted her with finding much needed moments of #blackjoy to escape the very harrowing study of Fascism. *Jane and Stokely, my loves, thank you for doing life with me and always being mommy's biggest cheerleaders.* Jeanelle recognizes her most dedicated writing companions— her dogs, Afro and Carver. She would also like to thank Jasmine H. Wade, Robyn Magalit Rodriguez, Shaina Travis, Dominique Williams, Chinelo Etta, Dominique Creer, Carla Hart, and Jean Grant.

Bill would like to acknowledge his co-author Jeanelle Hope as an amazing writing partner, innovative thinker, and the originator of this book's concept and trajectory. It was Jeanelle's June 2020 *Essence* article "Black Antifa AF: The Enduring Legacies of Black Antifascism" that opened the door for a conversation about the making of this book. Jeanelle also devised the concept for this project: "The Black Antifascist Tradition." Throughout, she has been an inspiring intellectual guide, co-author, coeditor, critic, thinker, and organizer. Her activist orientation to the question of Black Antifascism, and to the fight against Fascism, is another reason this book exists as it does.

In addition, Bill would like to thank and acknowledge fellow activists, writers, and organizers who have shaped his own thinking and approach to writing this book. First and foremost are members of the Campus Antifascist Network, who, in 2017, began to build chapters on college campuses to de-platform white supremacists like Richard Spencer and Charles Murray, trying to spread their Fascist poison. Especially important in helping to build that struggle were Christopher Vials, David Palumbo-Liu, Grant Mandarino, Meleiza Figueroa, Max

280   **THE BLACK ANTIFASCIST TRADTION**

Alvarez, and Aaron Jaffe. Chris also invited Bill into collaboration on a book that feels like a prequel to this one: *The U.S. Antifascism Reader,* which included writings by a number of Black Antifascists discussed in this book: George Padmore, W. E. B. Du Bois, Kathleen Cleaver, Aimé Césaire, the Black Panther Party, and the Civil Rights Congress.

Other inspiring people and writers who have influenced the ideas behind this book (some of them discussed in its pages) are Robin D. G. Kelley, Ruth Wilson Gilmore, Angela Davis, Mariame Kaba, the We Charge Genocide movement in Chicago, Critical Resistance, Mike Davis, and Dylan Rodriguez.

Finally, Bill thanks and acknowledges friends and family who have helped make the work of writing this book easier, better, and more hopeful: Jack Mullen, Jean Mullen, Max Mullen, Shayari Shanti, Tithi Bhattacharya, Mike Mergenthaler.

ABOUT THE AUTHORS

JEANELLE K. HOPE is the director and associate professor of African American Studies at Prairie View A&M University. She is a native of Oakland, California, and a scholar-activist, having formerly been engaged in organizing with Socialist Alternative, Black Lives Matter–Sacramento, and various campus groups. Her work has been published in several academic journals and public outlets, including *The American Studies Journal*, *Amerasia Journal*, *Black Camera*, *Essence*, and *The Forum* magazine. She lives in Houston, Texas.

BILL V. MULLEN is Professor Emeritus of American Studies at Purdue. He is a long-time activist and organizer. He is a member of the editorial collective for *puntorojo*, of the United States Campaign for the Academic and Cultural Boycott of Israel collective, and is a cofounder of the Campus Antifascist Network. His other books include *James Baldwin: Living in Fire*, *Un-American: W. E. B. Du Bois and the Century of World Revolution*, *Popular Fronts: Chicago and African American Politics*, *Afro-Orientalism*, and *Against Apartheid: The Case for Boycotting Israeli Universities*. He lives in West Lafayette, Indiana.

ABOUT HAYMARKET BOOKS

Haymarket Books is a radical, independent, nonprofit book publisher based in Chicago. Our mission is to publish books that contribute to struggles for social and economic justice. We strive to make our books a vibrant and organic part of social movements and the education and development of a critical, engaged, and internationalist Left.

We take inspiration and courage from our namesakes, the Haymarket Martyrs, who gave their lives fighting for a better world. Their 1886 struggle for the eight-hour day—which gave us May Day, the international workers' holiday—reminds workers around the world that ordinary people can organize and struggle for their own liberation. These struggles—against oppression, exploitation, environmental devastation, and war—continue today across the globe.

Since our founding in 2001, Haymarket has published more than nine hundred titles. Radically independent, we seek to drive a wedge into the risk-averse world of corporate book publishing. Our authors include Angela Y. Davis, Arundhati Roy, Keeanga-Yamahtta Taylor, Eve Ewing, Aja Monet, Mariame Kaba, Naomi Klein, Rebecca Solnit, Olúfẹ́mi O. Táíwò, Mohammed El-Kurd, José Olivarez, Noam Chomsky, Winona LaDuke, Robyn Maynard, Leanne Betasamosake Simpson, Howard Zinn, Mike Davis, Marc Lamont Hill, Dave Zirin, Astra Taylor, and Amy Goodman, among many other leading writers of our time. We are also the trade publishers of the acclaimed Historical Materialism Book Series.

Haymarket also manages a vibrant community organizing and event space in Chicago, Haymarket House, the popular Haymarket Books Live event series and podcast, and the annual Socialism Conference.

www.ingramcontent.com/pod-product-compliance
Lightning Source LLC
Jackson TN
JSHW012258030125
76456JS00002B/11